Collins

Cambridge International AS & A Level Global Perspectives and Research

STUDENT'S BOOK

Series editor: Mike Gould
Authors: Mike Gould, Lucinda Misiewicz, Mike Morris, Lucy Norris and Clair Rawlingson

William Collins' dream of knowledge for all began with the publication of his first book in 1819. A self-educated mill worker, he not only enriched millions of lives, but also founded a flourishing publishing house. Today, staying true to this spirit, Collins books are packed with inspiration, innovation and practical expertise. They place you at the centre of a world of possibility and give you exactly what you need to explore it.

Collins. Freedom to teach.

Published by Collins
An imprint of HarperCollins*Publishers*
The News Building, 1 London Bridge Street, London,
SE1 9GF, UK

HarperCollins Publishers
1st Floor, Watermarque Building, Ringsend Road,
Dublin 4, Ireland

Browse the complete Collins catalogue at
www.collins.co.uk

© HarperCollins*Publishers* Limited 2021

10 9 8 7 6 5 4 3 2 1

ISBN 978-0-00-841417-7

All rights reserved. No part of this publication may be reproduced, stored in a retrieval system, or transmitted in any form by any means, electronic, mechanical, photocopying, recording or otherwise, without the prior written permission of the Publisher or a licence permitting restricted copying in the United Kingdom issued by the Copyright Licensing Agency Ltd, 5th Floor, Shackleton House, 4 Battle Bridge Lane, London SE1 2HX.

British Library Cataloguing-in-Publication Data
A catalogue record for this publication is available from the British Library.

Authors: Mike Gould, Lucinda Misiewicz, Mike Morris, Lucy Norris and Clair Rawlingson
Series editor: Mike Gould
Publisher: Elaine Higgleton
Product managers: Lucy Cooper and Sundus Pasha
Product developer: Natasha Paul
Content editor: Tina Pietron
Development editor: Judith Walters
Copyeditor: Catherine Dakin
Proofreaders: Sonya Newland and Catherine Dakin
Indexer: Jackie Butterley
Cover designer: Gordon MacGilp
Internal designer and illustrator: Jouve UK LTD
Typesetter: Jouve UK LTD
Permissions researcher: Rachel Thorne
Production controller: Lyndsey Rogers
Printed and bound by Grafica Veneta in Italy

Cambridge International copyright material in this publication is reproduced under licence and remains the intellectual property of Cambridge Assessment International Education.

Third-party websites and resources referred to in this publication have not been endorsed by Cambridge Assessment International Education.

Exam-style questions [and sample answers] have been written by the authors. In examinations, the way marks are awarded may be different. References to assessment and/ or assessment preparation are the publisher's interpretation of the syllabus requirements and may not fully reflect the approach of Cambridge Assessment International Education.

Cambridge International recommends that teachers consider using a range of teaching and learning resources in preparing learners for assessment, based on their own professional judgement of their students' needs.

MIX
Paper from responsible sources
FSC
www.fsc.org FSC™ C007454

This book is produced from independently certified FSC™ paper to ensure responsible forest management.

For more information visit:
www.harpercollins.co.uk/green

Contents

Introduction and How to use this book   v

Section A: Introduction to Collins Cambridge International AS & A Level Global Perspectives and Research

Chapter 1 Understanding the course   1
1.1 Becoming a global thinker   2
1.2 Topics, issues and themes   6
1.3 What is the Critical Path?   11
1.4 Exploring the Critical Path approach to topics, themes and issues   15

Section B: Core skills and concepts

Chapter 2 Analysing arguments and perspectives   20
2.1 Analysing arguments   21
2.2 Understanding perspectives   30
2.3 Evaluating evidence   37

Chapter 3 Researching and using sources   45
3.1 Identifying sources   46
3.2 Evaluating sources   50
3.3 Using sources   54
3.4 Academic style   58
3.5 Referencing   63

Chapter 4 Ways of working   66
4.1 Working independently   67
4.2 Working in a team   70
4.3 Developing reflection   73

Section C: Approaching the written examination

Chapter 5 Reading and responding to sources   76
5.1 Reading unseen sources   77
5.2 Identifying key points and issues   80
5.3 Writing about evidence from an unseen source   83
5.4 Evaluating arguments and perspectives from two sources   86

Section D: The Essay

Chapter 6 Planning and researching a coursework essay   94
6.1 Choosing a topic   95
6.2 Time management   103
6.3 Research for your coursework essay   106

Chapter 7 Structuring and writing a coursework essay — 110
7.1 Organising your ideas — 111
7.2 Structuring and preparing to write — 114
7.3 Writing, editing and referencing — 121

Section E: The Team Project

Chapter 8 Preparing and presenting the Team Project — 126
8.1 What is the Team Project? — 127
8.2 Selecting suitable problems to research — 131
8.3 Preparing for your presentation — 133
8.4 Organising your argument — 138
8.5 Using language to present effectively — 142
8.6 Supporting your presentation visually — 146
8.7 Practice and evaluation — 149

Chapter 9 Reflecting on the Team Project: the Reflective Paper — 151
9.1 Reflection and reflective models — 152
9.2 Reflecting on collaboration — 155
9.3 Writing the Reflective Paper — 159

Section F: The Cambridge Research Report

Chapter 10 The Cambridge Research Report — 166
10.1 Understanding the task — 167
10.2 Writing the proposal — 170
10.3 Research log — 174
10.4 Identifying a topic — 180
10.5 Primary research and the research process — 186

Chapter 11 Writing the report — 193
11.1 Planning for the Cambridge Research Report — 194
11.2 Structuring the report — 199
11.3 Writing the report — 207

Glossary — 215

Index — 217

Acknowledgements — 222

Introduction

Introduction to Collins Cambridge International AS & A Level Global Perspectives and Research

About the syllabus

Unlike other syllabuses, Cambridge International AS & A Level Global Perspectives and Research (9239) is predominantly skills-based. It allows you to explore your own interests, whether in the future of artificial intelligence, in global inequalities, or in the causes and management of global pandemics.

Cambridge Global Perspectives™ encourages the development of high-order skills such as analysis, problem-solving and critical thinking, as well as research, collaboration, communication and reflection. These skills are relevant and highly transferable to other subjects of study and to the world beyond.

The Student's Book

This Student's Book is designed to equip you with all the skills and understanding you need for success in your study of Cambridge Global Perspectives.

As you follow the course you will:
- learn how to carry out effective research by identifying, evaluating and using source documents
- research a topic and write an essay on a global issue
- take part in a collaborative team project and presentation on a local issue
- produce an extensive research report on an issue of your own choice
- develop and demonstrate reflective understanding of your own learning.

The material in this Student's Book is designed to be clear, well demonstrated and supportive.

As you work through the chapters, you will be introduced to a range of knowledge and skills. You will see how to apply them through worked demonstrations and case studies. You will also be given a supportive framework that will allow you to apply your skills and understanding to each aspect of the qualification.

How the book is structured

Chapters 1–4 introduce concepts, skills and ways of working that underpin the Cambridge International AS & A Level Global Perspectives and Research syllabus. These chapters provide a foundation that you will be able to draw on later in the course.

> *Information in chapters 5–11 in this book is based on Cambridge International AS & A Level Global Perspectives and Research (9239) syllabus. However, all the advice and guidance is written by the authors of this book. References to assessment and assessment preparation are the publisher's interpretation of the syllabus requirements and may not fully reflect the approach of Cambridge Assessment International Education. You should always refer to the appropriate syllabus document for the year of your examination to confirm the details and for more information. The syllabus document is available on the Cambridge International website at www.cambridgeinternational.org.*

Chapter 5 focuses on the written examination and introduces you to the skills of responding to texts and structuring responses. It ends with a practice section of sources and responses at different levels.

Chapters 6 and 7 focus on the essay. You will work through the process of choosing a topic, managing your time, carrying out research, organising your ideas and structuring your essay. You will also learn how to write in an appropriate style and edit effectively.

Chapters 8 and 9 focus on the Team Project. Chapter 8 focuses on working as a team and effective presentation skills, while Chapter 9 focuses on using reflective models to develop understanding and on writing the Reflective Paper that brings together learning from the Team Project.

Chapters 10 and 11 focus on the Cambridge Research Report. This looks at the higher-level thinking skills involved in this aspect of your study, as well as how to research, plan, develop and write the research report and its accompanying research log.

Registered Cambridge International Schools benefit from high-quality programmes, assessments and a wide range of support so that teachers can effectively deliver Cambridge qualifications.

Visit https://schoolsupporthub.cambridgeinternational.org to find out more.

HOW TO USE THIS BOOK

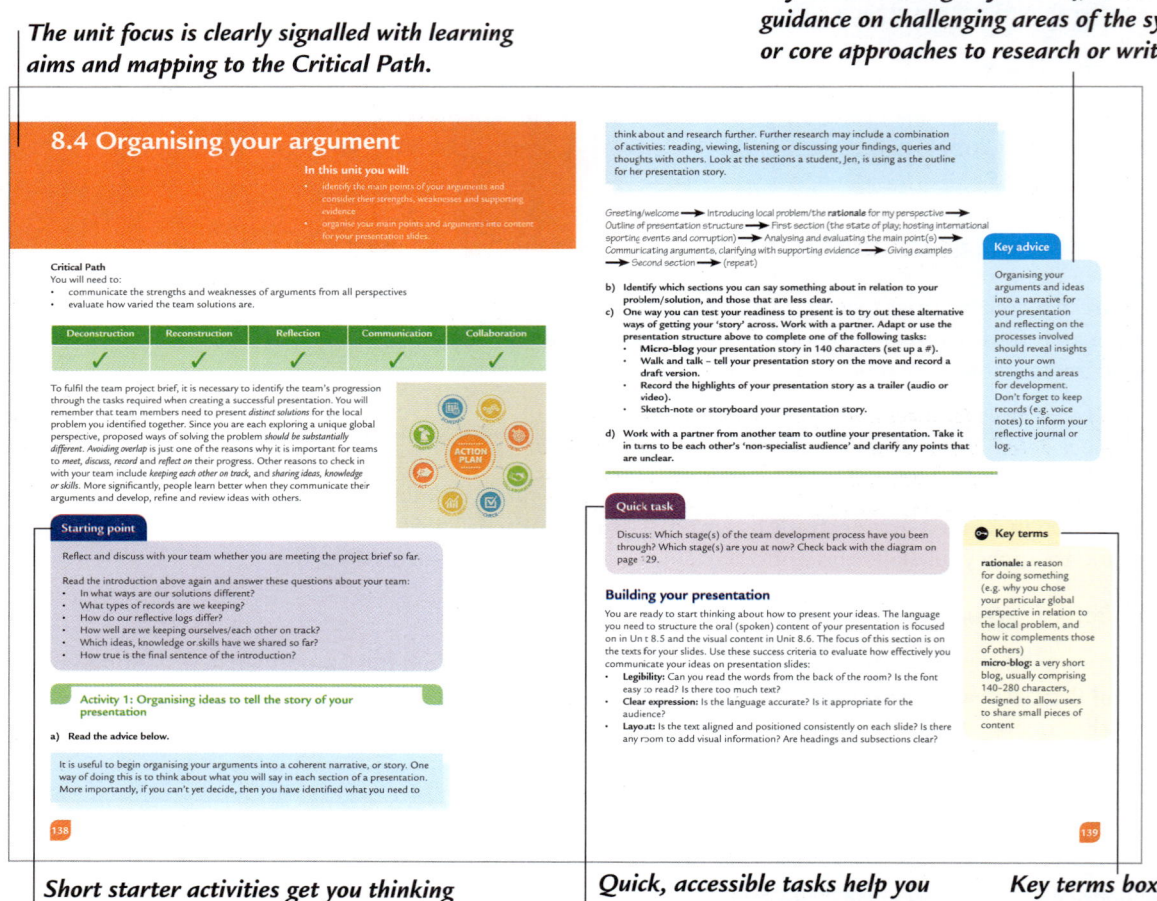

The unit focus is clearly signalled with learning aims and mapping to the Critical Path.

Key advice boxes give you brief, concise guidance on challenging areas of the syllabus or core approaches to research or writing.

Short starter activities get you thinking about what you will learn.

Quick, accessible tasks help you check your knowledge instantly and keep you thinking.

Key terms boxes highlight key terms and definitions.

Activity boxes appear throughout each unit so that you can check and consolidate your learning across a range of topics, issues and perspectives. This may be written work or discussion.

Final tasks appear at the end of each unit, giving you a chance to pull everything together and apply your learning.

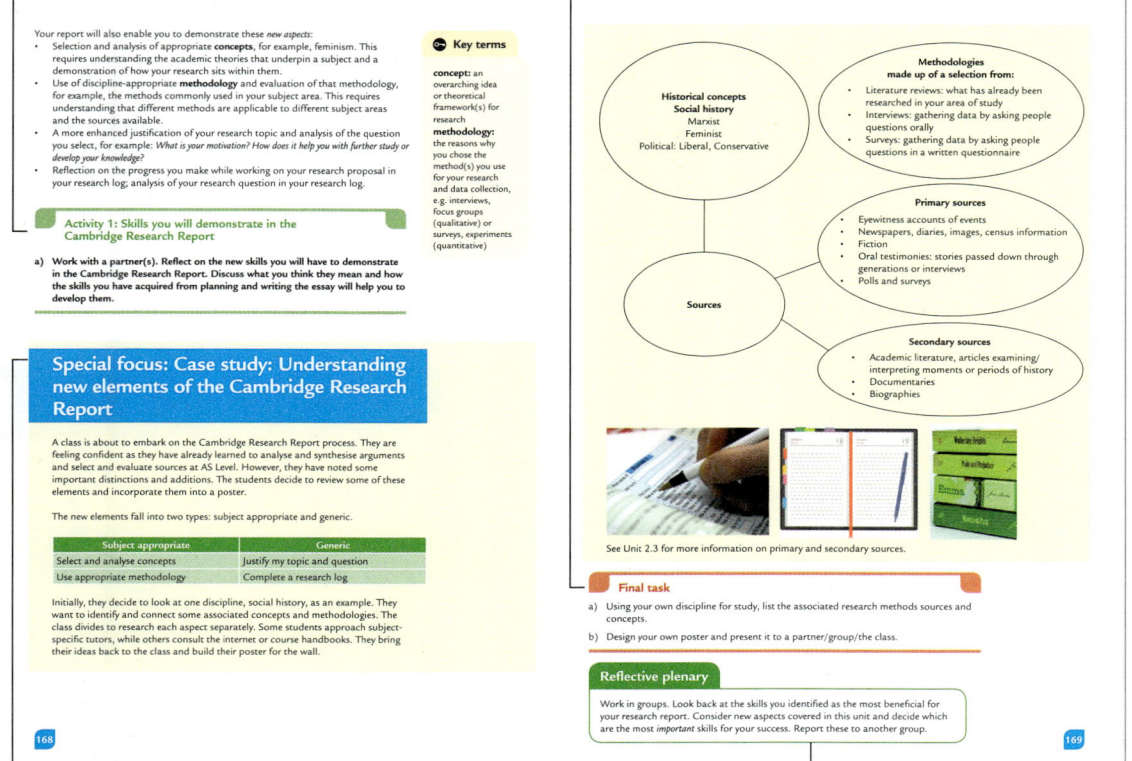

Special focus features allow you to focus on a topic in more detail. Often these involve extended exploration of a particular idea or approach, and in some cases they deal with case studies looking at another student's work.

Reflective plenaries give you a chance to pause and reflect on your learning.

Chapter 1
Understanding the course

This opening chapter will introduce you to some key ideas that underpin your study of Cambridge International AS & A Level Global Perspectives and Research. You will have a chance to broaden your understanding of global topics with examples taken from sustainable tourism and migration, and you will begin to identify topics and develop issues that are of particular interest to you.

Central to this course of study is the concept of the Critical Path, which is designed to help you develop your research, reasoning and communication skills in a systematic way. This chapter introduces the Critical Path and demonstrates it in action for the first time.

1.1 Becoming a global thinker
1.2 Topics, issues and themes
1.3 What is the Critical Path?
1.4 Exploring the Critical Path approach to topics, themes and issues

1.1 Becoming a global thinker

In this unit you will:
- explore the thinking that underpins the Cambridge International AS & A Level Global Perspectives and Research syllabus
- reflect on your skill-set and new skills you may need as you progress.

The Cambridge International AS & A Level Global Perspectives and Research syllabus is unique in its focus on the development of a set of *skills* over and beyond a particular content or body of knowledge. This is not to say that content is unimportant, simply that it is how you apply skills to content that really matters. Through following the syllabus and this Student's Book, you will develop skills that you can use beyond school and exam requirements, which will enable you to engage with ideas similar and different to yours, and which will help you navigate your way through further study and life.

Starting point

Why did you choose this course? What do you hope to get out of it? Share your thoughts with other members of your group. Consider how similar your reasons are to theirs.

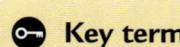 Key term

audit: a dispassionate review of your strengths and weaknesses

Being a reflective learner

As you will see in the subsequent units in this chapter, the ability to be reflective is at the heart of the Cambridge International AS & A Level Global Perspectives and Research syllabus. So, it is a good idea to begin with a sort of **audit** of what *type* of learner you are. This may not be something you have thought about, but you will probably be aware of situations when you learn most easily, and others when you find it more difficult.

 Activity 1: Types of learner

a) Which type of learner from the table below best describes *you*? (You may feel that one, more than one or all of them correspond to your view of yourself.)

*Visual	You prefer or respond well to visual learning – with perhaps a particularly enhanced spatial awareness. A good observer, you respond well to explanations or knowledge presented graphically, whether in pictures, diagrams or charts.
Auditory	You learn best when there is a spoken element to the learning, for example, when written explanations are reinforced with sound. You may be a confident or fluent speaker, and prefer to explain things verbally.
Reading/Writing	You are drawn to learning through reading and writing text, and while there may be cross-over with visual learning, you are perfectly comfortable with the written word without graphical support. This is sometimes claimed to be the conventional model of school-based study, although it may vary according to subject area.

| Kinaesthetic | You learn best in a physical way – by doing things. This may manifest itself through enjoyment of making or creating things, or through performance or other forms of movement. You may find it difficult to spend prolonged time in class without moving around, and may be drawn to subjects, such as Performing Arts or Physical Education. |

*from a 1992 study by Neil D. Fleming and Coleen E. Mills)

Why does any of this matter?

In a way, it doesn't: the four categories are not fixed and there have been other studies which have extended the groupings further. However, the key message is that it is important to understand your own capabilities, both what you can do well and what you struggle with – for example, what methods of enquiry work for you, and which don't. A learner who struggles with deconstructing print texts may find that listening to an audio version of the same material is beneficial.

Reviewing your own skills

It is equally, if not more important to have an understanding of the skills you possess. At this point in your school or college life, there is a very good chance you already have a wide range of skills – whatever type of learner you are.

Here, a student called Turgut assesses his own strengths and weaknesses:

"Well, I think I'm pretty independent and determined. If I'm given a task, I like to make my own judgements, and I'm not easily swayed. I can usually back up what I say confidently, but I also know that I sometimes cut corners and tend to look for the easiest route to get the information I need. This can be a strength, when a job needs doing, but it means I'm not always the best person to work with as I get impatient and don't take advice well. In a recent Economics class, our group worked on a statistical analysis of some finances from a business to assess how profitable the company was; I **jumped to conclusions*** rather than following a careful, logical process.

*Glossary
jump to conclusions: to make a judgement without considering all the evidence

Activity 2

a) How would you sum up Turgut's skills? How similar or different are you to him?

b) Now audit your own skills, using the pointers below (as you will see, there are some links to learning styles). Use a scale of 1 to 5 to assess your skills on each point.

Ability to:
- work independently
- work collaboratively/in teams
- analyse carefully
- be curious and enquiring
- follow and apply processes or methods
- be logical and use reasoned judgements
- critique and evaluate opinions and information
- communicate verbally
- communicate in writing

The skills of others in your class are almost as important as your own, especially as you will be working in groups or teams at many stages during the course.

Activity 3: Sharing your audit

a) Once you have completed your self-audit, share your reflections with a small group.
   - What do others say about themselves? Are your skill-sets similar or different?
   - Do you/they agree with the assessments you all made? If their perspective is different, how does that make you feel?
   - Is there anything you would like to change or improve in your skill-set? How could you do this?

Being a global thinker

It is not often that we have time to stop and consider what is happening around us. The day-to-day pressures of life, and the schedules we follow, can sometimes mean we are very 'locked in' to the local and immediate. There is nothing wrong with this – local issues and the relationships that affect us on a regular basis are often the most pressing. However, this course is designed to get you to look at what is happening around you in a more informed and reflective way, and also to become more rounded in the way you tackle issues that affect you or the world more widely.

Becoming a global thinker is about recognising *what* you think about something and *why* you think it. It is also about recognising that there will be different (sometimes opposing) views, influenced by a variety of factors such as age, class, culture, gender and ethnicity. As a critical, global thinker, you will learn to analyse and evaluate the views, assumptions and arguments around an issue, and come to your own *independent* way of thinking.

Tackling 'big' issues

Consider a pressing issue of the day, such as the Black Lives Matter movement. Take a few minutes to think about it without writing anything down. Try to gather in your mind the images you associate with the phrase or movement, and any knowledge you have about it.

Activity 4: Understanding the provenance of ideas

a) It is important to identify where your perspectives and ideas come from – their **provenance** – and how accurate those perspectives are. Now, make a few notes about Black Lives Matter, just jotting down what comes to mind. You could ask yourself:
   - 'What do I know about this? Is this all there is to know, or is there more?'
   - 'What are my opinions and knowledge based on? Where did I get my information or these views? Was it from something I experienced directly – or read or heard about? What other opinions might there be on this issue?'

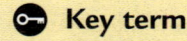 **Key term**

provenance: the place of origin or history of something

Why group or team perspectives are important

You may have very strong views on this issue, and that is fine. However, part of being a global thinker is to ensure that the views you hold are based on the best possible evidence, so an important part of your development is to hold these ideas up to **scrutiny**.

Activity 5: Allowing scrutiny

a) Now share your ideas and assumptions about Black Lives Matter with a small group of 4–5 classmates or friends. Think of the group as a sort of **crucible** in which your ideas and those of the other students can be merged so that a better sort of understanding emerges.

b) Once you have shared your views, ask yourself these final questions:
- What would I need to do if I wanted to know more about this issue?
- Where would I look for information?
- What questions would I need to ask?

*Glossary

scrutiny: detailed, critical analysis

crucible: a container in which metals are melted together at high temperature

Moving towards the Critical Path

Essentially, what you have done in this very short exercise is to complete much of the process we refer to as the Critical Path, which you will find out more about in the following units. Here, the *content* you have been taking apart and putting back together with new understanding has been yourself. But the process is the same whatever the topic. And you have also collaborated, communicated and reflected on this process.

Finally, the key thing to remember is that throughout this Student's Book, the skills that you apply – whether in direct preparation for assessment or for less tangible outcomes – are ones that will benefit you as a learner and person more widely. Much of the work you do will involve working independently on the topics and issues that interest you, even if they are regularly subjected to the scrutiny of others.

Reflective plenary

Write a personal review of yourself in the third person, outlining your attributes and weaknesses as a learner – both in terms of how you tackle things, and the skills you do and don't possess. This might help you to express yourself in an objective way. You could begin:

He/she has a number of strengths as a learner. For example, he/she is able to...

Keep this review in mind as you work through Units 1.2 to 1.4, and consider to what extent these initial observations prove to be correct.

1.2 Topics, issues and themes

In this unit you will:
- understand what topics, issues and themes are
- identify the links between topics, issues and themes.

As a 21st-century student learning in a globalised world, studying this course will allow you to broaden your understanding of a range of contemporary topics, engage with new ways of looking at the world and find issues of your own to explore. You will develop your knowledge and understanding through the application of new research skills specially designed for the digital age. The Cambridge International AS & A Level Global Perspectives and Research syllabus is designed to develop your research, reasoning and communication skills systematically, using an approach called the Critical Path. This approach helps you to interrogate information, explore different perspectives and develop reflective learning practices through the study of global topics.

What are topics?

Topics are broad categories or areas of interest. The syllabus provides a set list of diverse global topics that offer fascinating areas of interest to explore. You will have the opportunity to select topics that appeal to you, and use them as a starting point from which to dig deeper to find issues that engage your curiosity as a global citizen.

Key term

topics: broad areas of interest that have global significance; they provide the context for more defined research from which issues will arise

Starting point

Choose three topics from the list below that look most interesting to you. Work with a partner to compare and discuss your choices. Why do these topics appeal to you?

Global topics

Animal rights	Urbanisation	Climate change
Arts in an international context	Changing identities	Demographic changes
Crime	Cultural heritage	Endangered cultures
Distribution of wealth	Economics of food	Ethical foreign policies
Energy	Environmental priorities	Global inequality
Ethics of food	Globalisation	Impact of technology
Health issues	Human rights	International law
Industrial pollution	International aid	Migration and work
Media and communication	Medical ethics and priorities	Scientific innovation
Political power and resistance	Quality of life	Sport in an international context
Social change and development	Social inequality	Transport
Sustainable futures	Tourism	

You will see from the list that there is potential for overlap between global topics. For example, it is easy to see how the topics of *Industrial pollution* and *Energy* feed into each other. The same could be said for *Migration and work* and *Demographic changes*.

Activity 1: Making links

a) Which other subjects are you studying? The diagram below shows an example of how the subject of History links to global topics from the list opposite.

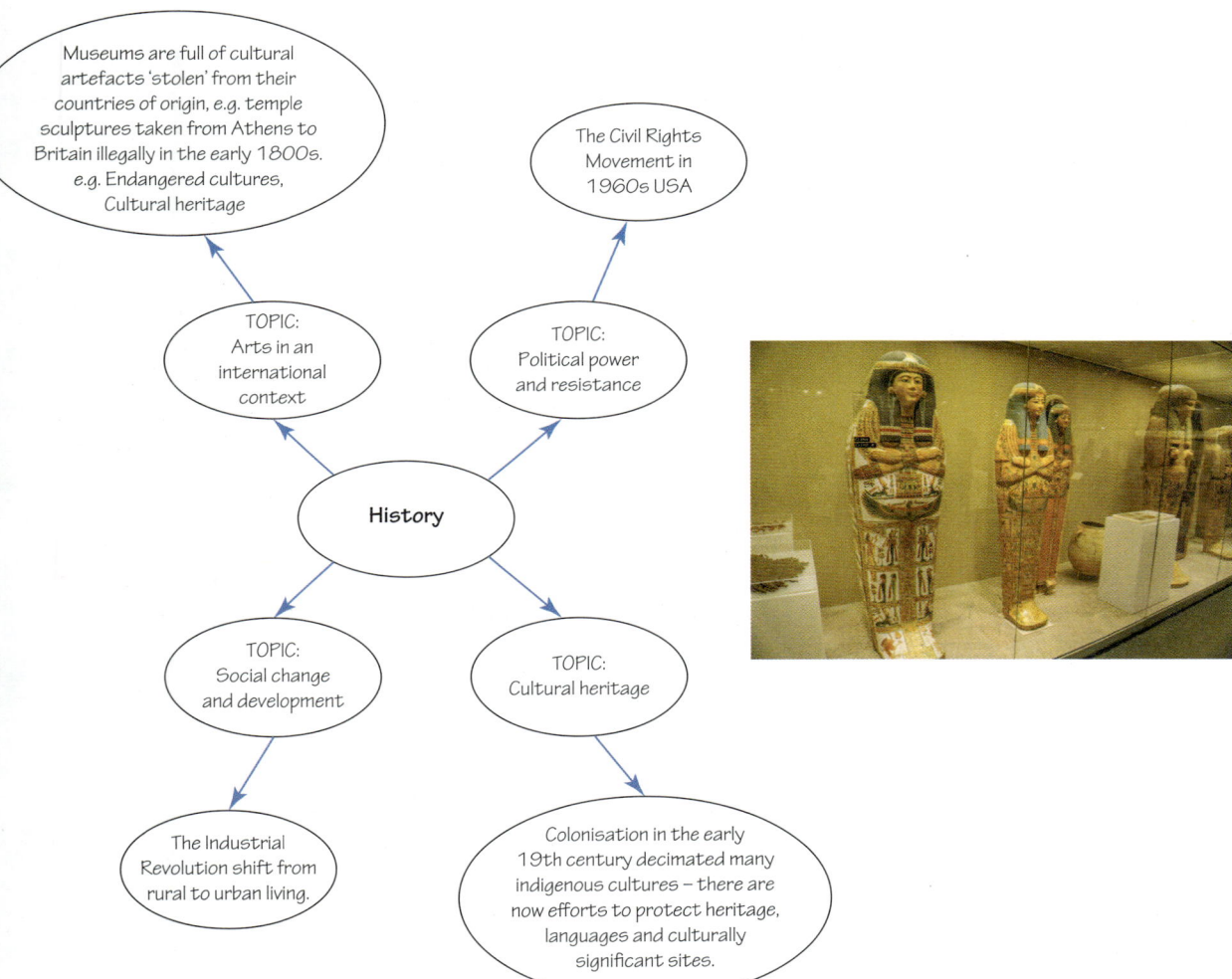

a) Create a spider diagram for two of the subjects you study. What links can you make between these and the global topics in the list? Present these to a partner or group. If you chose the same subject, discuss whether you came up with the same topics or different ones. Are there others you could add?

What is an issue?

So what exactly do we mean by the term **issue**? Issues are specific, more precisely defined aspects within a topic that can provide opportunities for further focused research. Issues are likely to be contested. That means that for each issue, different people will hold contrasting points of view. The following diagram shows some possible issues arising

7

from the globally significant topic of *Urbanisation*. Let's consider the issue of air pollution and environmental degradation for this topic. What **points of view** could exist around the issue? Contrasting points of view are those which are not only different, but may also be in direct opposition to one another. For instance, we know that air pollution and environmental degradation are linked with industrial processes, such as making cars or plastics. You could take the view that because such industry provides employment and boosts the local economy, there is potential for urbanisation to lift people from poverty and provide a steady income. On the other hand, you could say that urban living has the potential to threaten people's lives, because industrial air pollution causes ill-health and disease.

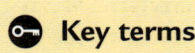

Key terms

issue: a specific, defined area within a topic, often with global relevance, that is suitable as a subject for deeper research; people may hold different points of view about an issue

point of view: the opinion you have about something – the way you consider or see an issue

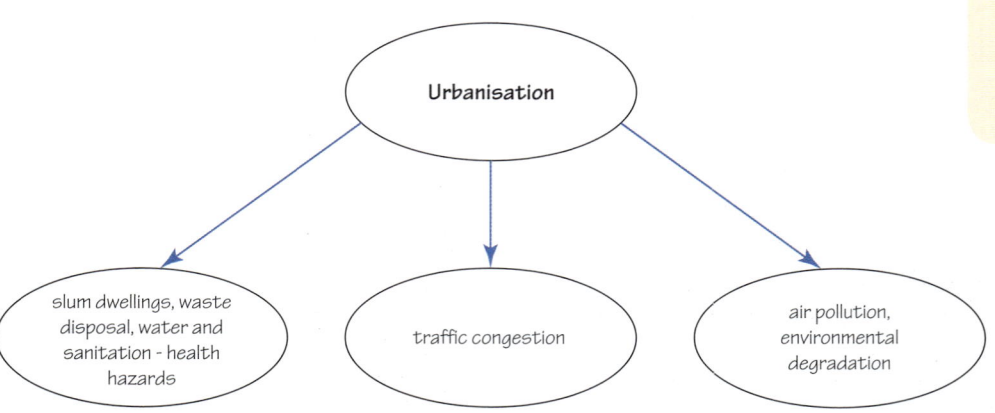

Activity 2: Topics and issues

a) Work with a partner or group. Take three of the global topics from the list on page 6 and identify two issues for each one.

Activity 3: Contrasting viewpoints

Consider the process for identifying issues and contrasting points of view that you have explored.

a) Choose one of the issues you identified in Activity 2. Carry out some initial research about the issue and identify two contrasting points of view.

b) Briefly summarise the two points of view to a small group in your class. What discussions do the contrasting points of view provoke?

What are themes?

Once you have understood the terms, global topics and issues, you next need to understand what **themes** are and how they are useful. Themes offer a way of approaching a topic or issue that will help you to understand more about it; they provide a way of seeing an issue or topic that will help you identify and frame specific routes of enquiry.

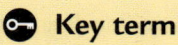

Key term

theme: an approach to a topic or issue – for example, technology or ethics; a thematic approach can help you to identify a perspective and focus your research

There are seven different themes in the syllabus:

Ethics
Politics
Environment
Global topic
Science
Economics
Technology
Culture

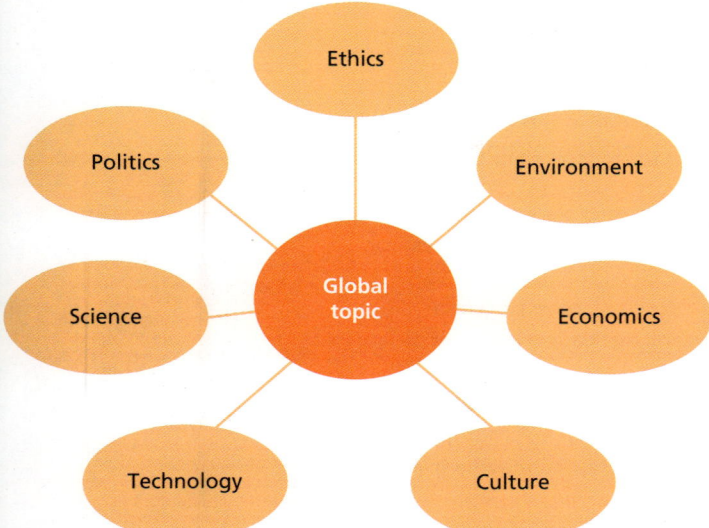

If you consider the topic of *Migration and work*, you might be able to identify a few relevant issues straight away – for example, how poverty and low pay might cause the movement of people from one country to another. To deepen your understanding and generate different lines of enquiry, you will need to look at the topic or issue through one or more themes.

The diagram below shows the relationship between themes, issues and topics, and illustrates how themes can be applied to a topic to generate issues for further research and discussion. The questions are designed to provoke debate and encourage you to explore contrasting points of view.

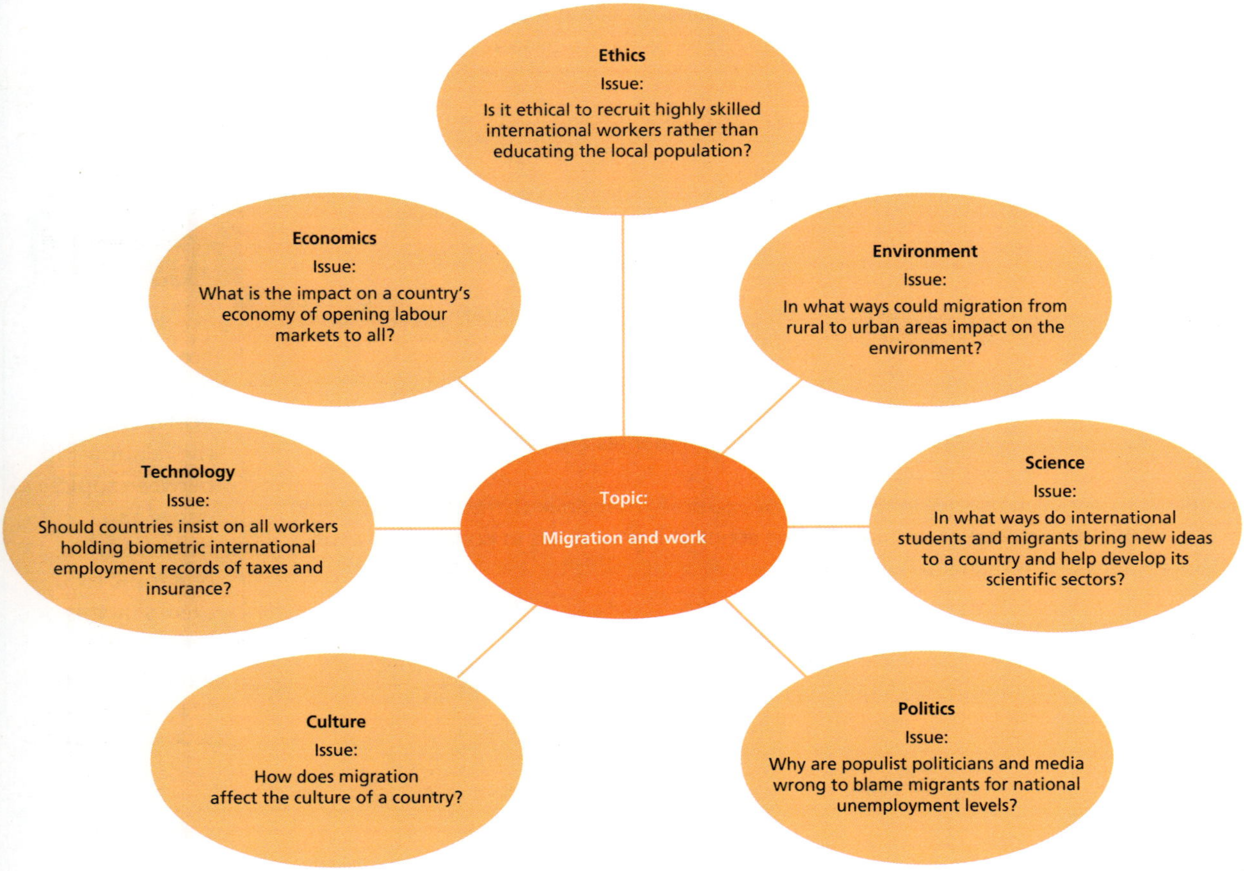
Ethics
Issue:
Is it ethical to recruit highly skilled international workers rather than educating the local population?
Economics
Issue:
What is the impact on a country's economy of opening labour markets to all?
Environment
Issue:
In what ways could migration from rural to urban areas impact on the environment?
Technology
Issue:
Should countries insist on all workers holding biometric international employment records of taxes and insurance?
Topic:
Migration and work
Science
Issue:
In what ways do international students and migrants bring new ideas to a country and help develop its scientific sectors?
Culture
Issue:
How does migration affect the culture of a country?
Politics
Issue:
Why are populist politicians and media wrong to blame migrants for national unemployment levels?

Themes provide broad ways of looking at an issue or topic. Some themes may overlap – for example, science and technology or economics and politics – whereas others may be more distinct.

Culture – Culture is a very broad term but in essence, cultural questions will ask whether an issue has consequences for the way communities of people live and interact.

Economics – The issues you explore may have macro or micro economic implications. Does the issue impact on global trading patterns or local employment rates, for example?

Environment – Many issues and topics that you explore will have potential environmental impacts, which could be global (e.g. rising sea levels) or local (e.g. river pollution).

Ethics – This theme is more conceptual and refers to matters of right and wrong, depending on your culture, education or personal standpoint. For example, is it right to spend money on space programmes when millions of citizens may be living in poverty?

Science – By approaching topics or issues scientifically, you may ask questions about the nature of **empirical** evidence used to support particular points of view.

Politics – This refers to power relations and decision-making processes. Most global issues will have a political dimension. How and why do governments react to specific global issues?

Technology – This theme refers to practical application and use of scientific knowledge.

Before we explore in more detail the example topic of *Migration and work* set out in the diagram on page 9, it should be noted that it isn't always possible to apply every theme to a topic or issue. In order to successfully develop perspectives, you should try and find an issue that has at least three thematic links. This will give you the opportunity to have a broad-based discussion in your assignments.

 Key term

empirical: derived from or relating to experiment and observation rather than theory

Final task

Work in a small group. Decide together how you will divide the work to be done to complete this task effectively.

a) Carry out an internet search using the term 'issues related to migration and work'. Try at least two different search engines.
b) Complete a quick analysis of the first 100 results. Break down the results and classify them into the seven themes. (Breaking down and analysing the information is an example of deconstruction – see Unit 1.3.) Which themes are the most dominant, i.e. which have the most results?
c) Make links between themes and issues. For example, economic themes may raise the issue of the importance of immigration to economic growth or, in contrast, that of falling wages and reduced labour costs.

Reflective plenary

Work with a group to make a mind-map poster showing the relationship between topics, issues and themes. Choose one topic to exemplify this. Present this to another group/the class.

Analysing different content to make links is an example of reconstruction (see Unit 1.3). By answering the questions above, you have begun to use skills that will focus your research and narrow down the topic into something manageable for an assignment.

1.3 What is the Critical Path?

In this unit you will:
- become familiar with the different aspects of the Critical Path
- begin to understand the Critical Path approach to research and reasoning.

A central concept in all the investigation and learning on this course is that of the Critical Path.

What is the Critical Path approach?

The Critical Path is designed to help you develop research, reasoning and communication skills in a systematic way. *Deconstruction*, *reconstruction* and *reflection* are stages of the Critical Path, with each stage progressing from the previous one. Each stage develops thinking and learning skills. The three progressive stages are underpinned by the skills of *communication and collaboration*. You will develop the skills embedded in the Critical Path through the exploration of global issues.

In the following chapters, you will always see a grid that will help you to locate your learning on the Critical Path.

Starting point

The terms used to refer to the stages of the Critical Path are *deconstruction*, *reconstruction* and *reflection*. Before you learn more about each stage, write a sentence describing what each term means to you.

What are the different stages of the Critical Path?

Deconstruction

This initial stage of research and reasoning involves asking yourself a series of questions:
- What is the global issue you are investigating?
- Are there different points of view relating to this global issue?
- What is supporting the reasoning behind each point of view?
- What evidence is being used?
- Where is this information coming from – which person or institution is 'speaking'?

When you completed the starter activity, it is likely that you summarised the term 'deconstruction' as taking things apart, or something similar. The initial part of the deconstruction process is therefore related to **analysis**. Analysis means breaking down something complex into its essential features. When you begin the process of deconstruction, you are in effect closely examining something by breaking it down into smaller parts. This is particularly important when trying to make judgements about source material you have researched.

 **Key term**

analysis: a way of examining something complex in close detail, by breaking down the whole into smaller parts so it can be more clearly understood

Deconstruction does not end with analysis – you are also going to undertake some **evaluation**. When evaluating, you are making a judgement about the quality of something. Here you might apply the following questions:
- Are the arguments supporting different points of view coherent and logical?
- Is the evidence strong or weak?
- Is the person making the argument qualified to do so?

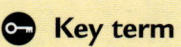

evaluation: identifying strengths and weaknesses in order to make a judgement

Quick task

Work with a partner/group. What differences do you notice between the questions applied for analysis under the heading 'Deconstruction' and those applied for evaluation?

Reconstruction

When you completed the starter activity, you probably defined 'reconstruction' as rebuilding something that has been damaged. The process of reconstruction in the Critical Path is not simply to rebuild what you have taken apart through deconstruction. In essence, the reconstruction stage requires you to make links between evidence, arguments and points of view, and to synthesise these elements into overarching perspectives. For now, it is useful to think of a perspective as a point of view; its more specific definition is explored in Chapter 2.

In the same way that deconstruction is linked to analysis, reconstruction can be said to link to **synthesis**. Synthesis is the combination of elements to form a larger coherent and connected whole.

When moving from deconstruction to reconstruction, you might ask yourself the following questions:
- What are the similarities and differences between arguments that are used to support a particular point of view?
- Are there connections between evidence from different contexts?
- Who are the people or institutions that are supporting this point of view?
- Do arguments and evidence **corroborate** or contradict each other?

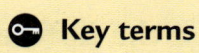

synthesis: the combination of multiple sources and ideas from research to create perspectives

corroborate: to support a statement with evidence (e.g. evidence provided by the World Economic Forum in relation to inequality is corroborated by the arguments put forward by the International Monetary Fund)

These initial questions form the first part of the reconstruction process. Their purpose is to make links, spot similarities and differences, and group elements together. Having made links between your research materials, you will be in a position to evaluate evidence and sources for and against competing points of view.

As you move to the evaluation aspect of reconstruction, you might ask the following type of questions:
- Does the body of evidence lead to a single conclusion?
- Does the global context of source material impact the arguments being made?
- Why do these people or institutions hold this point of view?
- Which point of view seems stronger and why?

> **Quick task**
>
> Why do you think it is best to form opinions and make conclusions based on a wide range of source material?

Reflection

The third stage of the Critical Path approach to research and reasoning is reflection. Reflection is a thinking skill designed to develop self-awareness; it is a form of self-questioning to better understand ourselves, our motivations and our experiences. You will learn more about reflection in Chapter 4.

You will come across a number of reflective questions on this course:
- What are your thoughts about a global issue before embarking on research?
- How does your initial viewpoint relate to other viewpoints you encounter through research?
- How do research findings impact your thinking?
- What are the limitations of your findings and conclusions?

Communication and collaboration

Communication is a core skill on the Critical Path and is fundamental to how you express and explain your deconstruction, reconstruction and reflection. In your academic and future professional life, as well as your personal life, the ability to communicate is a vital skill.

Academic essays need to be logical, coherent and well structured. You will be required to communicate complex global issues in a style that is accessible by non-subject specialists. You will research global issues of particular interest to you and develop expert knowledge in these areas. It is important to bear in mind that those you communicate with may not have the same specialist knowledge, so you will need to learn to adjust your styles and forms of communication accordingly.

> **Activity 1: Successful communication**
>
> a) Work with a partner to find an example of a complex issue that is communicated clearly in a newspaper, book or lecture (e.g. a TED talk). What features make the communication clear and meaningful?
>
> b) Now think of a time when you tried to communicate an idea or thought to somebody, but they didn't understand. Why do you think your idea was not successfully communicated?

You will also have the opportunity give a presentation on a global issue. This form of communication is particularly important professionally; many workplaces value presentation skills highly.

In addition to verbal and written communication skills, you will also need to consider non-verbal communication when giving a presentation. This refers to using appropriate visual material to support the argument and making clear eye contact with the audience or camera. Chapter 8 offers more guidance on presentation skills.

Collaboration refers to teamwork – working with other people towards a common goal. Of course, communication skills are essential here too. For example, active listening is required for successful collaborative work. This goes beyond simply hearing the words of a teammate; it also requires you to listen without judgement and ensure that you understand the meaning behind the words spoken.

Collaboration skills, often referred to as 'soft skills', are highly desired by employers. These include things like emotional intelligence and respect for your teammates. Collaboration skills are explored further in Chapters 4 and 8.

Final task

How would you summarise *deconstruction*, *reconstruction* and *reflection*? Write your own short definitions of each with a brief example of how you think it might be used.

Reflective plenary

The deconstruction, reconstruction and reflection stages of the Critical Path are underpinned by the skills of communication and collaboration. Why do you think communication and collaboration skills are so important to the research and reasoning process?

1.4 Exploring the Critical Path approach to topics, themes and issues

In this unit you will:
- explore how key aspects of the Critical Path can be applied in practice.

Critical Path

You will need to:
- deconstruct source material and identify themes, issues and topics
- make links and connections between source materials through reconstruction.

Deconstruction	Reconstruction	Reflection	Communication	Collaboration
✓	✓			

In this unit, you are going to look at a very specific topic. This forms a case study which you can use as a useful model for understanding the Critical Path in your own interest area. Such case studies appear throughout the book.

Starting point

Work with a partner to remind yourselves of the differences between 'topics', 'themes' and 'issues'. This will be important for your understanding in this unit, so look back to Unit 1.2 if you are not sure.

Special focus: Case study: Deconstruction and reconstruction

Bethany, an Australian student with a keen interest in conservation, found two texts while undertaking some research. Extracts from the texts appear on the following pages.

Activity 1: Summarising extracts

a) Read Text 1 and write a short summary.

You can draw upon skills from Cambridge IGCSE™ English or other English syllabuses, but here are some general guidelines:
- Read the whole text to understand the overall point the writer is making.
- Check any vocabulary you don't know or isn't clear.
- Decide on the key point made in each paragraph (for example, by looking at the topic sentence).
- Reduce these points to a short paragraph of no more than 40–50 words summing up what the text is about.

Text 1

Singapore eco-tourism plan sparks squawks of protest

Singapore is creating a vast ecotourism zone in a bid to bring in more visitors, but environmentalists fear the development will damage natural habitats and are already blaming it for a series of animal deaths.

While it may be best known as a financial hub with scores of high-rise buildings, tropical Singapore is still home to patches of rainforest and an array of wildlife, from monkeys to pangolins – also known as scaly anteaters.

In one green corner of the city sits a zoo and two sister attractions – a night safari and river safari – that have long been big draws for foreign and local visitors.

Now jungle is being cleared in the same area to make way for a bird park, a rainforest park and a 400-room resort, to create a green tourism hub it is hoped will eventually attract millions of visitors a year.

But the project in the Mandai district has ruffled the feathers of environmentalists.

They believe that rather than promote biodiversity, it is too imposing for the area, will destroy forest habitats and they say insufficient safeguards were put in place before work began – leading to animals being killed on roads.

The row has highlighted concerns about rapid development in space-starved Singapore, and worries that some of the country's more wild and green corners are being lost only to be replaced with something more artificial.

'I think you are getting your priorities wrong if you are replacing natural heritage with captive breeding,' Subaraj Rajathurai, a veteran wildlife consultant, told AFP.

With the new development, it appears that 'making money was more of a priority than finding the balance and preserving biodiversity', he added.

From Agence France-Presse / 02:07 PM January 09, 2019

Now read and summarise Text 2.

Text 2

Below the Surface: The Impacts of Ecotourism in Costa Rica

To be sure, the promotion of ecotourism in Costa Rica has led to several desirable outcomes. For example, the continued expansion of ecotourism has created opportunities for income generation and employment, at both the national and local levels. Additionally, ecotourism has provided greater incentives for natural resource conservation in the form of state-protected areas and private lands. As a result, natural resource conservation is on the rise.

> With nearly ½ million acres of land designated as protected areas, tourism to that country has surged, with scientific and nature tourists from around the world converging on this naturally endowed, tourist's paradise. Finally, heightened emphasis has been placed on environmental education.
>
> While the Costa Rican government has successfully stimulated economic growth and environmental preservation by marketing the country's ecotourism destinations, recent studies suggest that it has not invested adequate attention or resources for the management of the natural assets which attract tourists or in the infrastructure required to support ecotourism. As a result, fragile sites of ecological or cultural significance have been exposed to the threat of degradation by unregulated tourism development and over-visitation. In short, while the tourist explosion has attracted world attention and new funds to Costa Rica, it has also put a strain on the country's environment and population.
>
> Clearly ecotourism is a multi-dimensional, complex practice that has resulted in tradeoffs, in costs and benefits for Costa Rica. All the same, it is a practice that is being promoted with increasing fervor by the Costa Rican government and the tourism industry. But how long can this practice sustain itself? Is ecotourism sustainable?
>
> From lifestyle.inquirer.net by Sujata Narayan

Activity 2

a) Based on your initial readings and your summary, how would you compare and contrast the two articles? Consider how similar or different the following features are:
- the perspective
- the content used to support these perspectives.

b) Once you have done this, share your findings within a small group, seeing if you can work towards a consensus of what each text is saying. (You are going to look in a more focused way at the content next – so this consensus view may change.)

Deconstruction

Next, Bethany's teacher asked her to begin the process of *deconstruction* to understand what topics the texts were related to.

Activity 3: Deconstruction: Linking texts to global issues

a) In pairs, discuss and note down which of the global topics from page 6 each text is related to.

Reconstruction

Having deconstructed each article, Bethany then began the process of *reconstruction* to see if there were *topical* connections between the articles. She formulated her initial thoughts in a grid.

Topic	Text 1	Text 2	Initial thoughts
Animal rights	Yes	No	Animals will be killed through construction work (Text 1) but the link feels tenuous.
Environmental priorities	Yes	Yes	Both articles discuss the balance between environmental protection and development.
Quality of life	Possibly	Yes	Quality of life is implicit in the articles, but not a main feature.
Sustainable futures	No	Yes	Text 2 ends with the question 'Is ecotourism sustainable?' but the topic lacks relevance to Text 1.
Tourism	Yes	Yes	Both articles have tourism as the central theme, although there seems to be different priorities and points of view in each text.

This process was a useful way for Bethany to collate her thinking and decide upon a topic. Both *Environmental priorities* and *Tourism* have a strong presence in each article. Bethany decided that *Tourism* would provide a tighter focus when considering her interest in conservation.

Quick task

Has Bethany missed any topics from the texts in her grid? Do you agree with her initial thoughts?

Next, Bethany's teacher asked her to continue her analysis or deconstruction and see what *themes* were embedded in each of the articles.

Activity 4: Deconstruction: Identifying themes

a) **Work in pairs to identify themes related to the topics in the article. You may need to refer back to the themes shown in the diagram on page 9.**

The themes are broad and may overlap. Bethany found that she could spot five different themes when analysing the articles: *Ethics, Economics, Politics, Science* and *Environment*.

Bethany's teacher suggested basing her research on three different themes. This would provide sufficient focus and prevent the assignment from becoming too broad, while still offering a good opportunity to develop contrasting perspectives. (You will read more about perspectives in Chapter 2.)

Bethany continued to make links between these two texts as part of the reconstruction process. She found that the strongest and most easily defined thematic links were *Environment, Politics* and *Economics*.

Having settled on the topic of *Tourism*, Bethany began to apply her chosen themes to it in order to see what issues might arise. Her approach can be seen in the chart opposite.

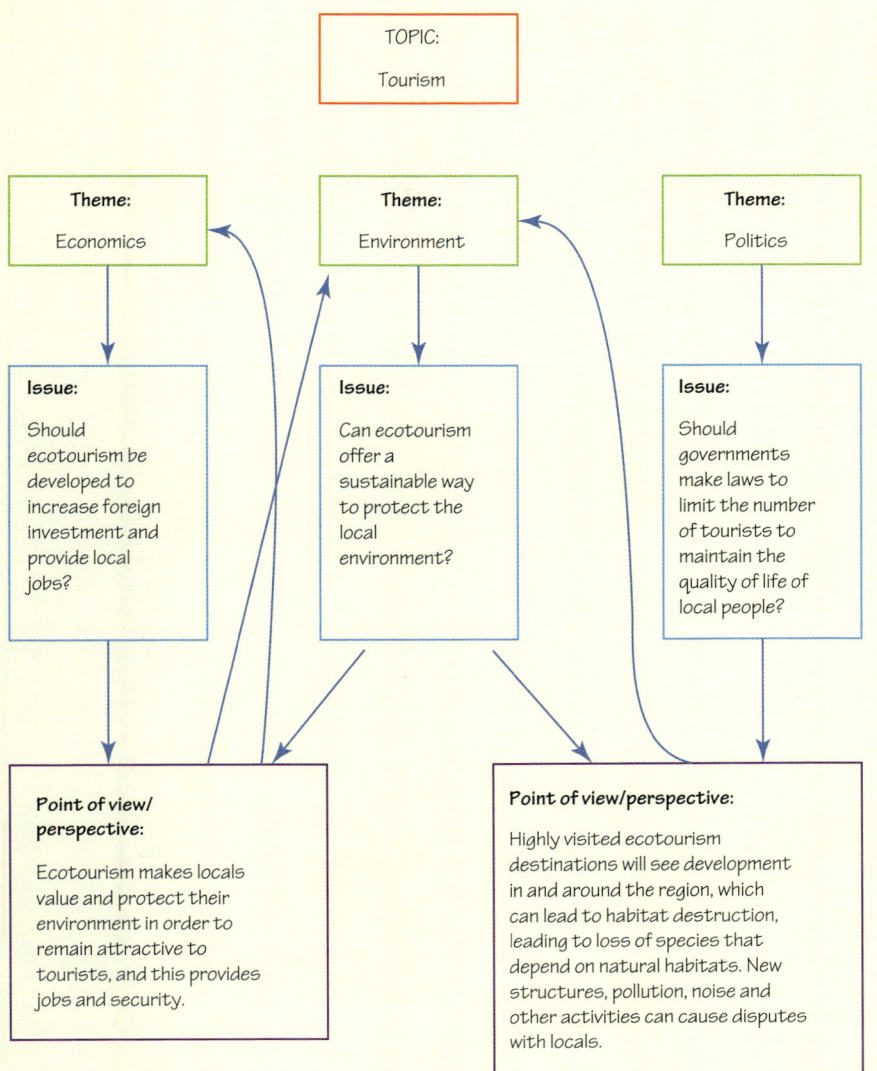

You can see from Bethany's chart that her early research into conservation has helped her to make links between themes and topics, which has in turn brought particular issues to the fore.

After her initial research, Bethany deconstructed the articles she found, making a note of topics and themes. She then moved to reconstruction by making links across her research findings. This process enabled her to become more focused and begin to identify particular issues for further research.

The issues Bethany found have been worded as problems or questions that lead to different points of view or perspectives.

Reflective plenary

In a log or journal, reflect on the particular skills Cambridge International AS & A Level Global Perspectives and Research will help you develop. What benefits in particular do you hope it will bring you in terms of:
- you as a person
- you as a learner?

Final task

Take a moment now to look back at Bethany's chart visualising the links between issues, themes and the topic of *Tourism*. Choose a different topic from the list on page 6 and make a similar chart to the one above, drawing links between themes and issues in relation to the topic you have chosen.

Chapter 2
Analysing arguments and perspectives

This chapter is central to your understanding of some of the core skills you will need in your studies. You will learn how to analyse an argument, learn what a perspective is and how perspectives are more complex than points of view. You will also learn how to evaluate evidence when carrying out research.

The most important aspects of the Critical Path for this chapter will be deconstruction and communication. Through analysis, you will learn to deconstruct perspectives and arguments. By analysing real examples, you will develop your knowledge and understanding of the different ways arguments can be communicated.

2.1 Analysing arguments
2.2 Understanding perspectives
2.3 Evaluating evidence

2.1 Analysing arguments

In this unit you will:
- learn to recognise and evaluate an argument.

Critical Path

You will need to:
- deconstruct arguments through analysis
- understand the importance of communication styles in making arguments persuasive.

Deconstruction	Reconstruction	Reflection	Communication	Collaboration
✓			✓	

What is an argument?

Arguments are part of our everyday lives. They take different forms and are encountered in, for example, television documentaries, newspaper articles, social media and classroom discussions. This unit will show you how to deconstruct an argument, identify its key elements and assess how strong or weak the argument is.

For the purposes of this coursebook, the term 'argument' refers to expressing a point of view (or standpoint) and putting forward reasons, often supported with evidence, that lead to a conclusion. Arguments can be spoken or written, and are designed to convince an audience to accept the point of view expressed and concur with the argument's **conclusion**.

This type of argument, found in academic or political debate, is not to be confused with the angry exchange of views in disagreements with friends, or between a parent and a teenager, for example, about what time to come home after a night out with friends.

Key terms

argument: one or more reasons given to persuade readers or listeners to support or oppose an idea or viewpoint, and lead to a conclusion

conclusion: a judgement reached by reasoning, based on preceding argument and evidence

Starting point

Work with a partner. List arguments in favour of and against the idea that students should learn to drive at school from the age of 16. Present these to another pair/group.
Idea: Students should learn to drive at school from the age of 16.
For example:

For	Against
Road accidents would decrease.	Traffic congestion would increase.

An argument is essentially a **claim** followed by one or more **reasons**, leading to a conclusion. Look at the following diagram, which represents this process as a series of steps.

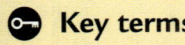
Key terms

claim: a statement that may or may not be true – it is debatable (e.g. during a democratic election campaign, a candidate will claim they are the best person to lead the country)
reason: an explanation of why something is true or happens (e.g. a reason why Earth is getting warmer is because human activity creates greenhouse gases)

CLAIM: Capturing and posting selfies leads to narcissism.

REASONS:
People who take lots of selfies see themselves as the most important thing in any environment.

People posting selfies need to be admired by others.

Posting selfies can be addictive.

CONCLUSION: Those people repeatedly posting selfies can cause an increase in narcissism.

Activity 1: Finding arguments to support a conclusion

a) **Here are three conclusions. With a partner, work backwards to complete a flow chart for each conclusion.**

conclusion → reason(s) → claim

- **So, pets have legal rights.**
- **So, mobile phones should not be allowed in teenagers' bedrooms.**
- **It is important to eat fresh fruit and vegetables.**

If a claim is made without any support or reasoning, this is known as an **assertion**. Assertions are deemed to be a weakness in arguments, despite being very common.

What makes an argument convincing?

Throughout this course, you will need to consider what makes one argument more convincing or stronger than another. You probably already judge arguments on a daily basis, and you may have a process for deciding which arguments you think are strong and which are weak. The problem with this is that your process might be **subjective**. For example, you might be inclined to think that arguments you agree with are stronger than those you do not agree with. By following the Critical Path you will become a more **objective** learner, considering arguments on their merits rather than on preconceived ideas.

 Key terms

subjective: describes judgements that are influenced by or based on personal beliefs or feelings
objective: describes judgements that are made without personal beliefs or preconceived ideas influencing the process

 Key term

assertion: an unsupported claim; the purpose of research is to find evidence and reasons to substantiate a claim

Key advice

It is vital that you engage with a number of different arguments and a diversity of opinion. It is a good idea to visit the websites of a variety of news outlets from around the world, as the geographical origin of arguments will provide a diversity of perspective, style and opinion. Some good news sites to explore are *South China Morning Post*, *The Jakarta Post*, Al Jazeera, The Conversation, AP News and Reuters, to name just a few.

How to assess the strength of an argument

A number of elements affect whether or not an argument is effective.

Who is making the argument?
- What authority or expertise does the person making the argument possess? It would be perfectly reasonable to consider a doctor's argument about how to treat an illness as more reliable than that of a taxi driver.
- Where was the argument published or broadcast? Some publications or broadcasters have a clear political stance. For example, *The National Review* and Fox News both support the Republican Party in the USA, so their arguments are likely to contain **bias**.
- Why is the argument being made? Many arguments in the media exist to attract readers so that advertising revenue can be earned. If so, the argument may contain exaggerations in order to spark interest among a wider audience.

What evidence is used to support the argument?
- Is any evidence given or is the argument an assertion without evidence?
- What is the quality of the evidence?
- Does the evidence come from a reliable and appropriate source? An argument that claims cycle lanes are dangerous in city centres that is supported by a source of road traffic data will be stronger than an argument that uses personal anecdotes or stories.

Does the argument make logical sense?
- At a simple level, clearly an argument has to make sense. The reasoning needs to be logical. There needs to be an understandable flow as an argument moves from its claim to its reason(s) and then its conclusion.

> **Key term**
>
> **bias:** an inclination or prejudice for or against an argument, opinion, person or group

In Activity 1, you worked backwards from a conclusion to construct a claim and a reason that would lead to the conclusion given. In so doing, you created a logical argument.

In the example about selfies, the claim – which may or may not be true – makes perfect sense. The reasoning is explicitly linked to the claim: capturing and posting selfies leads to narcissism. The conclusion follows on logically from the claim and the reasoning. Now look at the example below. Does it make sense? Why, or why not?

> **CLAIM:** The ant hills on pavements are getting bigger.

> **CONCLUSION:** So you should bring an umbrella.

This argument lacks logic. There is no obvious relationship between the claim and the conclusion. The argument is therefore weakened because it doesn't appear to make sense. The reason the argument doesn't make sense is because it makes assumptions, or relies on unstated reasons. We often make assumptions because there are certain things we assume everybody knows so it isn't necessary to state them explicitly. For example, a simple statement such as 'the days are getting shorter and winter will be here soon' would make perfect sense to most people. We don't need the reasoning regarding Earth's orbit of the Sun.

However, the argument about the ant hills needs reasoning to make sense. The assumptions require explaining.

> **CLAIM:** The ant hills on the pavement are getting bigger.

> **REASON:** Ants can sense air pressure and humidity changes that indicate rain; they respond by changing their nest structure.

> **CONCLUSION:** So you should bring an umbrella.

The argument now makes sense. It should be noted that certain people, entomologists (those who study insects) for example, would have understood the first argument that appears illogical to most people. They would have made the inferences which non-specialists would have missed. For non-specialists, there is an **inferential gap**.

> **Key term**
>
> **inferential gap:** the gap between the knowledge of a person trying to explain an idea and the knowledge of the person trying to understand it

Common problems with arguments: generalisation and questions of correlation or causation

As you've seen, some arguments do not progress logically, and sometimes the links between the claim and the reasoning or between the reasoning and the conclusion do not make sense. Some other common problems are outlined below.

Generalisations
Generalisations are sometimes called 'sweeping statements' and involve an author making a broad statement based on limited evidence or reasoning. For example, if you wander through a couple of streets in a town and the few people you meet say hello and appear pleasant, it would be a generalisation to say the people of that town are friendly. When you encounter generalisations, however, they will not always be quite so obvious.

It is worth considering that generalisations may be seen as a weakness in an argument but, depending on how those generalisations are conveyed, they may still be very convincing. A strong argument isn't necessarily convincing and a convincing argument isn't necessarily strong.

Causation or correlation?
To understand the difference between **causation** and **correlation**, let's look at this old saying: 'An apple a day keeps the doctor away.'

If you eat an apple each day then it is clear you are somebody who has access to healthy food and is happy to eat it. There is clearly a correlation between a good diet and physical well-being. However, stating that not needing to see doctor is *caused* by eating an apple a day is clearly untrue.

How is the correlation misleading in the diagram opposite?

24

Identifying strengths and weaknesses in arguments

Read the following extract about an infrastructure project in Mozambique. As you do so, consider what the argument is and the evidence supporting it.

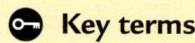 **Key terms**

generalisation: a broad universal statement based on only one or a few facts

causation: the act of causing or producing an effect or a result (e.g. photosynthesis produces oxygen)

correlation: the relationship or connection that exists between two or more things

> **Rebuilding a bridge over Mozambique's troubled waters**
>
> Since the bridge was rebuilt, it takes only 15 minutes again to get from the village's agricultural and residential area to the district headquarters.
>
> As the Derre District Administrator, Mr Santiago Marques, put it, the Lua Lua river bridge represents a lifeline between the rural communities on both sides of the river. Restoring the bridge didn't just help Derre. It also benefited communities some distance away by allowing Derre-area farmers to get their products to them. These included the city of Mocuba north of Derre, the village of Morrumbala in the south, and the strategic village of Zero along National Road number 1 (N1).
>
> For families, the difference was immediate. Corn, which cost residents such as Júlio Maque 25 Mozambican meticais during the bridge's impassibility, now costs 10.
>
> Restoring the bridge has practically demonstrated that nothing works without a robust road network. Access to health care, agriculture, education, and every aspect of reconstruction requires a functional and adequate road system.
>
> From blogs.worldbank.org

Activity 2: Strengths and weaknesses in arguments

a) In the extract, find at least one example of:
- a reason or evidence supporting the claim that the bridge has improved life for locals
- correlation presented as causation (paragraph 3)
- a generalisation (final paragraph).

b) Compare your responses with a partner.

Using counter-argument

 Key term

counter-argument: an argument made to challenge another argument

A **counter-argument** is used by an author to anticipate an opposite point of view in order to 'knock it down' or oppose it.

An example for the extract above might be:

Some might say that building a bridge has increased traffic congestion in and around Derre; while others could argue that it is a vital lifeline that allows traffic to flow in and out of the surrounding areas.

At first glance, it may appear strange for an author to include counter-arguments when trying to convince an audience of something. However, offering a counter-argument is generally seen as a strength.
- Firstly, it shows that the author of the argument recognises that there is an alternative point of view. The author demonstrates a level of objectivity by acknowledging that not everybody shares their point of view. Then, offering a compelling rebuttal, the author makes their argument more persuasive.

- Secondly, a counter-argument may be used as a **rhetorical device** to make an argument more convincing. If an author offers a counter-argument, this gives voice to the likely doubts and questions an audience might have. By acknowledging the opposing views in advance and then offering a compelling **rebuttal**, an argument will be more persuasive.

Activity 3: Using counter-arguments

Sometimes, you will find that counter-arguments are far from obvious.
a) Read the extract below, then summarise the author's main argument about UN peacekeeping missions.
b) Identify the **rhetorical question** in paragraph 3, and then identify the counter-argument and rebuttal that follow.
c) What is the impact of using a counter-argument?

 Key terms

rhetorical device: language deliberately designed to convey a specific message or meaning, to persuade an audience and evoke particular emotions

rebuttal: a statement that contradicts what has been said, pointing out the ways it is not true

rhetorical question: a question asked for the purpose of making a statement; a question that does not expect an answer

> **Most people think peacekeeping doesn't work. They're wrong.**
>
> […] Numerous statistical studies have explored the role of third-party peacekeeping in reducing violence around the world. They all come to the same conclusion: Peacekeeping works better than almost anything else we know.
>
> […]
>
> Not only that, but every study that looked at diverse types of peacekeeping missions found that the UN was more effective in preventing and reducing violence than non-UN missions.
>
> […]
>
> Why, then, does the public believe just the opposite? Part of the problem has to do with media coverage that emphasizes failed missions over successful ones. […] Everyone has heard about the UN's failure to stop the genocide in Rwanda, but no one has heard of how the UN averted war in Macedonia. Add to this the fact that newspaper accounts don't distinguish between feeble missions and robust ones, and you have a recipe for believing that all missions are inherently bad.
>
> […]
>
> If people continue to believe that peacekeeping doesn't work, the entire system could be mistakenly dismantled. It took the world years to figure out that peacekeeping was critical to reducing violence, and more years to figure out how to do it right. What we now have is 'very good' and could be even better.
>
> From blogs.worldbank.org

Special focus: Audience and rhetoric

The convincing aspect of an argument may not be what is said but *how* it is said, or the **mode of address**. An argument can be made to seem convincing by the language and communication tools used. These include choice of vocabulary, use of rhetorical devices and patterns of speech.

- The mode of address may vary according to who the intended audience is, the medium by which the argument is presented and the context of the argument's presentation. The vocabulary must suit the audience. For example, very technical language may alienate a general audience of non-specialists.
- Rhetorical devices include analogy, rhetorical questions, and repetition of words or phrases at the beginning of statements to increase their power. The 'rule of three' is another rhetorical device, which presents ideas in a sequence of three to make them striking and memorable.

 Key term

mode of address: the way an author communicates with the audience

Read this extract from a speech made by Jacinda Ardern, the Prime Minister of New Zealand, following a terrorist attack in Christchurch in 2019.

> **'Let us be the nation we believe ourselves to be'**
>
> What words adequately express the pain and suffering of 50 men, women and children lost, and so many injured? What words capture the anguish of our Muslim community being the target of hatred and violence? What words express the grief of a city that has already known so much pain?
>
> I thought there were none. And then I came here and was met with this simple greeting. As-salaam Alaikum. Peace be upon you. They were simple words, repeated by community leaders who witnessed the loss of their friends and loved ones. Simple words, whispered by the injured from their hospital beds. Simple words, spoken by the bereaved and everyone I met who has been affected by this attack.
>
> From a speech by Jacinda Ardern, Christchurch, 2019

Rhetorical questions engage the audience and get people thinking.

Use of repetition and rule of three.

Ardern engages the audience with emotive language, expressing anguish and pain throughout the speech. This gives her argument a personal quality that will affect the emotions of listeners.

Ardern's mode of address is emotional, direct and unwavering. Skilfully, she is able to speak to the audience in front of her and the wider television audience at the same time, conveying the heartfelt argument to 'let us be the nation we believe ourselves to be'. Given Ardern's ability to communicate, coupled with the context and theme of the speech, it was clearly convincing to many.

Activity 4: Rhetorical features and language

a) Compare the rhetorical features used in the short extract from Jacinda Ardern's speech with the extract about peacekeeping on page 26. Does the peacekeeping extract use any of the same emotive language or direct appeal as Ardern's? If not, how does the writer stress their ideas?

b) Now look up the full Christchurch speech from Jacinda Ardern, 'Let us be the nation we believe ourselves to be'. Work independently to identify further powerful rhetorical features and language in the rest of the speech. How effective do you think the speech is?

Key advice

There are many historical examples of great orators delivering convincing and rousing speeches to huge audiences. Often these speeches are emotive and represent a call to action.

Famous examples include: Mahatma Gandhi's 'Quit India' speech; Queen Elizabeth I's speech to the troops at Tilbury; Abraham Lincoln's Gettysburg Address; Martin Luther King's 'I Have a Dream' speech; Nelson Mandela's 'I am Prepared to Die' speech. There are, of course, more contemporary examples too.

You might find it useful to look at two or three of these speeches for their use of rhetorical devices.

Final task: Analysing an argument

a) Read the extract and answer the questions that follow.

A fair deal for all

Around the world people in less industrialised countries are continually exploited. Particularly vulnerable are those children working in food production. Some of the poorest children in the world are denied an education and are forced to work harvesting crops. Children are working in dangerous situations for tiny wages so people in more industrialised countries can buy reasonably priced produce all year round. Whether it be cocoa, coffee or bananas, the workers on these plantations are paid poorly and treated badly.

Is there a solution to this problem? Is there a way to prevent exploitation in food production? Is it possible to be ethical when shopping for food? The answer to these questions is a resounding yes. Yes, we can all buy good quality food that has been produced in a way that doesn't exploit the workers. How? The answer is simple: just look for the Fairtrade logo when you shop.

Fairtrade has its critics. Some say it perpetuates the production of primary products in less industrialised countries while those in more industrialised countries make huge profits through added value. Others say Fairtrade just inflates the price without addressing the root cause of exploitation.

Is the Fairtrade system perfect? The answer is no. Fairtrade was founded in the UK in 1992 and since then, the dedicated staff continue to change and adapt to criticisms, and are constantly improving their organisation to benefit farmers in less industrialised countries.

Firstly, the Premium Fund. Fairtrade helps local committees to open bank accounts that manage the Premium Fund, which is used to support community projects that will help everyone in the area.

Secondly, to guarantee the credibility of the Fairtrade Certification Mark, they use an independent auditing company called FLOCERT, which ensures local farmers always receive the best prices.

Finally Fairtrade continues to expand its global reach. In so doing, they are committed to improving the life chances of the poorest workers across the world.

So, in the words of the Fairtrade themselves: 'You have the power to change the world every day. With simple shopping choices you can get farmers a better deal. And that means they can make their own decisions, control their future and lead the dignified life everyone deserves.'

1. How would you sum up the author's argument?
2. Which key elements of the argument can you identify?
3. What are the strengths of the argument?
4. Think of two different ways you could improve the argument.
   Work with a partner or small group. Present and refine your answers.

b) Compare your answers in small groups. Use this task to think critically about your own responses and to reflect on how to improve them.

Reflective plenary

In pairs, create a spider diagram with 'argument' at the centre. Add associated terms and ideas with examples to clarify what the differences mean.

2.2 Understanding perspectives

In this unit you will:
- understand what makes up a 'perspective'
- identify different perspectives.

Critical Path
You will need to:
- deconstruct perspectives through analysis.

Deconstruction	Reconstruction	Reflection	Communication	Collaboration
✓				

The idea of 'perspectives' is something that runs through all your work during the course. Understanding how to recognise perspectives, what these perspectives are or represent, and their key parts are all central to your exploration of themes and issues.

Starting point: What is a perspective?

[Cartoon panel 1: A person on a small island with a palm tree points at the sea and exclaims "BOAT!"]

[Cartoon panel 2: A person in a boat points at an island with a palm tree and exclaims "LAND!"]

1. Discuss in pairs.
   a) What does the cartoon tell you about the idea of different perspectives?
   b) Can more than one perspective be right?

The word 'perspective' is commonly used in everyday conversation and is often taken to mean 'a point of view'. Though this definition is useful, it does not quite convey the breadth and depth of the term as it is used in the syllabus.

According to the syllabus:

> A perspective is a coherent world view [1] which is a response to an issue. A perspective is made up of **argument**, **evidence** and **assumptions** and may be influenced by a particular **context**.

[1] This signifies that a perspective is more complex than a single point of view, and is made up of a set of interconnecting ideas that have been considered carefully.

(Definition taken from the Cambridge International AS & A Level Global Perspectives and Research syllabus)

Quick task

In pairs, discuss what you understand by the term 'issue' and list three examples. You may need to look back at Unit 2.1.

How is a perspective constructed?

The word 'coherent' is important. Let us use an analogy here. Imagine a perspective is a piece of rope. From a distance, it appears to be a single unified object. However, a rope is in fact a group of strands that are twisted together into a stronger form. The strands are all working together to form a coherent whole. These strands represent the different elements of a perspective: argument, evidence, **assumptions** and the influence of a particular **context**. When they are synthesised, they form a coherent world view: a perspective.

Here you will see an example of how a particular perspective is arrived at in relation to the issue of *Rising sea levels*. The table shows just one argument, one example of evidence, and some aspects of context, but there could be more in each case.

Key terms

assumption: an unstated reason that is accepted to be true without proof

context: the things that influence an issue or event, including geographical location and environment (where), the people cultures and languages involved (who) and timing (when)

Issue	Rising sea levels
Assumption	A rise in sea level could be beneficial for coral reefs.
Argument	Water temperature is one of the major stresses coral reefs face; therefore, if rising water levels lead to cooler seas, then coral reefs might be less threatened.
Evidence	Professor Ryan Lowe is an expert whose research seeks to understand and predict coastal processes. He states that a modest rise in sea level could help lower the water temperature of the reef and may also partially reduce reef heat extremes in the world's warming oceans.
Context	Professor Ryan Lowe works at the University of Western Australia. Australia's coral reefs are currently suffering from bleaching caused by the rising sea temperature.
Summary of perspective	This perspective responds to the issue of rising sea levels by acknowledging the possible benefits higher water levels might have for coral reefs.

Activity 1: Alternative perspectives

Take five minutes to complete an internet search for 'island communities affected by rising sea levels'.
a) Identify a different perspective on rising sea levels that is informed by assumptions, arguments and evidence that arise from a *different geographical context,* such as that of the island of Micronesia or the Marshall Islands. People living in large coastal cities like Edinburgh or Los Angeles face different issues.
b) Copy and complete the diagram below by adding the perspective you researched.

You could think about:
- those living in communities only accessible by air or water
- those living in heavily populated cities in large land masses.

Perspective 1: Rising sea levels benefit coral reefs.

Perspective 2:

Issue Rising sea levels

You should now be able to identify different perspectives on the issue of *Rising sea levels* by considering different contexts.

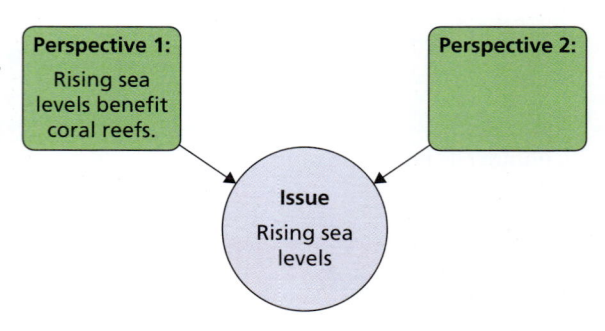

Read the following extract from a document on the issue of gender equality.

> It is undeniable that gender equality is a benefit to all societies. By raising female employment levels to be equal with men, evidence suggests that GDP (Gross Domestic Product) would be dramatically increased. The Borgen project claims GDP could rise by 34% in Egypt and 10% in South Africa.
>
> Increasing women's rights has a profound effect on family planning decisions, allowing women to decide when and how many children they will have. This improves the lives of mothers and children alike.
>
> Across the world we are seeing more female leaders. Diverse countries such as Finland, Germany, New Zealand, South Korea and Ethiopia have female leaders. According to the *Leadership Quarterly Journal*, women are more likely than men to lead in a style that is effective. It is, however, recognised that balancing gender power relationships will involve deep cultural changes in some countries.
>
> The male-dominated areas of science and technology are slowly starting to change. School programmes to encourage girls to study science and technology have been successful, and now more women are entering associated professions.

Activity 2: Identifying elements of a perspective

a) Copy and complete the grid below to identify elements of the text's perspective on gender equality.

Issue	
Assumption	Gender equality benefits everyone.
Argument	
Evidence	
Context	
Summary of perspective	

Why is it important to explore a range of perspectives?

Looking back to the example of coral reefs benefiting from rising sea levels, you can see that it was quite a limited perspective. Although there will be benefits for a few, the most dominant response to rising sea levels is one of concern for communities and ecosystems. However, as you move through the course it is important to engage with perspectives that challenge the consensus view. For this, you need to examine a range of sources with different arguments and evidence – something researchers do when trying to get a broader picture of an issue.

How does considering themes help broaden perspectives?

Using different themes to approach an issue adds another element to a perspective. On page 9, you looked at seven themes: Culture, Economics, Environment, Ethics, Politics, Science and Technology.

The perspective that suggests that rising sea levels could protect coral reefs comes from only one theme: that of the environment. It is likely that when you completed your internet research in Activity 1, the environment was not the only theme you noticed. However, the impact of rising sea levels on island communities can be approached through the themes of culture and economics, as well as the environment.

- Looking at the issue through the theme of culture could enable you to explore how society has represented concerns through art or literature, or the impact on language. For example, in the Pacific Islands, indigenous people are at risk from rising sea levels – important cultural sites such as ancient graveyards are at risk of being 'washed out'.
- Looking at the issue through the theme of economics could enable you to explore impacts on standards of living, employment statistics, rates of birth or mortality, and so on. For example, agriculture and fishing are important economic activities for island communities, and these industries are at risk from salt contamination caused by rising sea levels.

Activity 3: Identifying sources of evidence and themes

Look again at the article on gender equality on page 32.

a) How many sources of evidence can you identify in the article?
b) How many of the seven themes are evident?
c) Note down at least three more themes linked to the perspective that gender equality is of benefit to all societies.
d) How does the inclusion of multiple themes affect the strength of a perspective?

Special focus: A framework for comparing texts: different or contrasting perspectives?

Although perspectives may be different from one another, it doesn't necessarily follow that they will be contrasting perspectives.

Activity 4: Identifying contrasting perspectives

The two extracts below are from articles that deal with the broad topic of global inequality and the specific issue of global education and how it can be achieved.

Extract 1

According to the United Nations, education is a right to which all human beings are entitled. Since 2000, the UN has been promoting the Millennium Development Goal to achieve free universal primary education for all. It is argued that if children receive basic primary education, they will be able to read, write and do arithmetic. This in turn will give children the basic social and life skills necessary to join the workforce, be an active member of society and to lead a meaningful life.

Free education for all is important across the globe. In less industrialised countries, free education for all will increase the skills of the people and reduce poverty. In more industrialised countries free education is crucial for reducing social inequality by giving everyone a chance to succeed.

> **Extract 2**
>
> As the price of technology falls around the world, now more than ever the benefits of **e-learning** should be recognised. Around the world, education systems should seek to develop e-learning and be prepared to adapt to the global digital revolution.
>
> In more industrialised countries, e-learning is said to increase collaboration, improve knowledge retention and encourage student engagement. Furthermore, e-learning gives students skills for life and allows teachers to continually improve their teaching.
>
> E-learning is beneficial for less industrialised countries too. The e-Learning Africa conference is held every year. Recent conferences have recognised how e-learning has enabled millions of Africans to broaden their horizons and grasp the many opportunities it offers.

If you want to understand and compare the perspectives of two connected texts like these, you first need to work through the following process.

a) Read each text, then copy and complete the grid, identifying the elements of each perspective. One of these has been completed for you.

Elements	Extract 1	Extract 2
Issue		
Assumption		E-learning provides benefits to learners.
Argument		
Evidence		
Context		
Summary of perspective		

b) What is similar and what is different in their perspectives on an issue? Are these perspectives *different* or *contrasting*?

c) Now compare your answers in pairs. Use this activity to think critically about your own responses and to reflect on how to improve them.

In completing Activity 4 above, you will have been able to recognise two distinct perspectives on global education. Both perspectives are focused on education across the world, but their individual emphasis is different. The first extract builds on the assumption that free education is a human right and benefits everybody. The second extract makes the claim that all education systems should develop e-learning capability because of its multiple benefits.

Clearly then, the two perspectives are different – but are they contrasting? The short answer is no. There is no effective contrast between each perspective. The perspective laid out in Extract 1 does not directly oppose the perspective put forward in Extract 2.

> **Key term**
>
> **e-learning:** learning that occurs via electronic media, typically on the internet, digitally delivering all or part of a course of study

Engaging with challenging perspectives

The burning of fossil fuels for energy has become a mainstream issue over the last few years, with activists such as Greta Thunberg gaining worldwide recognition. Given such coverage, it is likely that you have already formed an opinion on the matter. Regardless of your initial point of view, it is important that you approach issues in a balanced way and engage with perspectives that might challenge your initial thinking.

> **Fossil fuels are the food of food**
>
> In providing the fuel that makes modern, industrialized, globalized, fertilized agriculture possible, the oil-and-gas industry has sustained and improved billions of lives. Surely this must rank as one of the great achievements of our time. When we consider the problems that the industry creates, we should take into account that it fed and feeds the world. And how often does the industry get credit for it? Bono and other celebrity activists get more credit for caring than the oil and energy industries get for doing.
>
> Not to give the industry its due credit is a dangerous injustice. When activists clamor to 'keep fossil fuels in the ground,' they do not know, or perhaps don't care, that if their advice were heeded, people would starve.
>
> Without the broader energy industry, the world could not support a population of 7 billion — or 3.6 billion, or perhaps not even 1 billion. To starve our machines of energy would be to starve ourselves.
>
> As the industry that powers all others, energy can be considered the master industry. Computers, electronics, health care, pharmaceuticals — every industry uses machines and resources that are manufactured thanks to the energy industry, which makes our society more productive and saves time. The more productive industry is, the more resources and machinery we have, and the more time we have to enjoy our lives. As we debate energy policy during the 2020 election campaigns, the fundamental role that low-cost energy plays in our lives, and the unique ability of the fossil-fuel industry to produce it, needs to be part of every conversation.
>
> From 'Energy Means Food and Time' by Alex Epstein, nationalreview.com, 2019

Final task: Engaging with a challenging perspective

a) Use the framework below as a basis for engaging with the perspectives raised in this challenging text.

Issue	
Assumption	
Argument	
Evidence	
Context	
Summary of perspective	

b) In what way does the text challenge your existing understanding of this issue?

c) Identify the themes that make up this perspective, and comment on how broad it is. How convincing do you find it? Why?

Reflective plenary

With a partner, look back over last week's news (local, national or global). What are the key issues that are being reported? Using the knowledge gained in this lesson, try to identify then summarise the perspectives presented in response to the issues you have chosen.

2.3 Evaluating evidence

In this unit you will:
- learn to identify and evaluate evidence.

Critical Path
You will need to:
- deconstruct arguments by identifying evidence
- identify whether evidence gives strong or weak support to the argument.

Deconstruction	Reconstruction	Reflection	Communication	Collaboration
✓				

Having learned that evidence is important for supporting arguments and perspectives, the question remains: what counts as evidence? In this unit, you will take an in-depth look at the characteristics of evidence.

Starting point

Work with a partner or small group. Imagine you are prosecuting someone for criminal damage. List types of evidence needed to support your case. Discuss and justify your choices with another group. Decide on the best ones and present these to the class.

What is evidence?

Evidence refers to facts or other information used to support an argument or perspective. While it is possible to construct an argument without evidence, a lack of evidence is considered to be a weakness. A perspective always requires evidence because without it, the perspective would not give 'a coherent world view' in response to an issue. Evidence is one of the core elements that develops a point of view on an issue into a perspective, together with argument, assumptions and understanding of the context.

What types of evidence are there?

It is important to recognise that there are different types of evidence. Here are four types:
- **Primary:** evidence that is based on original thinking or in original form, such as a birth certificate, interview or speech; 'first-hand' information reporting new research findings. If you undertook a survey into attitudes towards school canteen food, the resulting data would be primary evidence. Both original historical documents, such as Anne Frank's diary from the Second World War, and raw mobile film footage could be primary evidence.
- **Secondary:** evidence that has been analysed or interpreted from its primary source. Sources of secondary evidence can be found in newspapers, journals, documentaries, books and websites. For example, an academic thesis or dissertation could present primary evidence, but a journalist might use this primary evidence to produce a newspaper article that would be secondary evidence.

> **Key term**
>
> **evidence:** facts, research, data or testimony that is used to support reasoning, arguments or perspectives

- **Quantitative:** evidence that comes in the form of numbers, such as crime statistics or birth rates, often presented in charts or graphs. It can be useful for comparisons, such as the change in crime rates over a given period of time. This is usually considered to be objective evidence.
- **Qualitative:** evidence used to refer to information that cannot be expressed in numbers, graphs or charts. Examples of qualitative evidence include personal testimony, interviews or minutes of a meeting. These can be seen as subjective evidence.

Some types of evidence are more appropriate than others, depending on the context in which they are used. Different academic fields or subjects often rely on particular types of evidence. For example, the evidence required to support a scientific argument might come from a laboratory where variables are very tightly controlled, whereas evidence used to support political theory might not be so objective.

Fact or opinion?

When identifying evidence, you should ask yourself whether the evidence is fact or opinion. Both are important sources of evidence. A fact is something that is known to be true or can be proved, for example, it is a fact that oil floats on water. An opinion is something that can be contested and challenged by others – for example, the biggest threat to marine wildlife comes from oil tanker spillages.

Activity 1: Identifying suitable supporting evidence

a) What is the best film you have ever seen? Work with a partner who chose a different film, and make a list of the evidence you can use to support your choice of film.

b) Imagine someone in your class decided that *Avengers: Endgame* was the best film. Which of the sources below could provide the best evidence to support this claim?

1. Box-office data
2. Number of awards and nominations
3. Critical reviews
4. Personal reaction to the special effects used
5. The cast and director
6. Where the film was watched

There may be other pieces of evidence, but using the sources listed in Activity 1 you can begin to categorise different types of evidence, such as in the table opposite.

Evidence	Type	Comment
Box-office data	Quantitative/ secondary	Box-office data refers to the amount of money a film generates from ticket sales. As long as all sales are recorded in the same way, then this evidence can be seen to be *objective*. The evidence will be in the form of a number, which means it is *quantitative* evidence.
Number of awards and nominations	Qualitative/secondary	This evidence is not necessarily *objective*. What influences the process of nominations for awards? Is a Golden Globe worth as much as an Oscar? Nominations and awards are decided subjectively; that said, the number of awards each film receives will be a statement of *fact*.
Critical reviews	Qualitative/secondary	Critical reviews are generally published in the media in written form, though they may be broadcast as podcasts, radio, television or video content. These documents and content are descriptive and opinion-based, so categorised as *qualitative evidence*. It should be noted that a critical review is likely to be written by a film expert and therefore is an **informed opinion**. Opinion is not fact and generally cannot be proved or disproved yet it can be challenged.
Personal reaction to the special effects used	Qualitative/primary	Any documented reaction to the special effects is evidence (e.g. a diary entry or personal correspondence such as a text chat). In essence, this is **personal opinion** and is *primary evidence*.
The cast and director	Qualitative/secondary	Making reference to the abilities of the cast and director is likely to rely on *secondary evidence*. For example, to support the opinion that Scarlett Johansson is one of the greatest actors, you might make reference to her body of work represented in publications from the field of film studies or acting, filmography, or critical reviews.
Where the film was watched	Irrelevant evidence	Personal evidence about where you watched the film and who with is essentially *irrelevant evidence*. Irrelevant evidence may be used to deflect attention away from the issue or be used to cover for a lack of relevant evidence.

🔑 Key terms

informed opinion: the opinion of someone who is an acknowledged expert in their field, seen as creditable evidence to support a claim or argument (however, all opinions can be contested, and other experts may disagree with the informed opinion presented as evidence)

personal opinion: an individual's own thoughts or feelings about an issue; often used in journalism, it can be useful for gauging public opinion, but it is likely to be subjective

Activity 2: Identifying and categorising evidence

a) Read the extract below. Identify all the pieces of evidence and then categorise them using these terms:

primary   secondary   expert opinion   qualitative   quantitative   irrelevant

Note: Any single piece evidence may fit more than one category.

Addiction to painkillers

Over the last few years, more and more reporting about the epidemic of painkiller addiction has been seen in the USA. These painkilling tablets, which are clinically used for treating mild to severe pain in patients, are referred to as 'opioid painkillers'. Although the opioids relieve the pain, they have other effects too. According to the Mayo Clinic: 'Opioids trigger the release of endorphins, your brain's feel-good neurotransmitters. Endorphins muffle your perception of pain and boost feelings of pleasure, creating a temporary but powerful sense of well-being.'

Not everyone who uses opioids becomes addicted, but it can happen quickly without the victim realising. Susan, a self-confessed opioid addict, told me that she suffered back pain and was prescribed opioids for it. Susan says, 'It happened before I even knew it. I couldn't stop, I couldn't turn back. I didn't know what I was going to do. I'd lost my family, my career, my home, everything.'

According to the National Institute on Drug Abuse (NIDA), in 2018 an estimated 1.7 million people in the United States suffered from substance-use disorders related to prescription opioid painkillers. There are both personal and wider economic costs. NIDA also report that 21–29 per cent of patients prescribed opioids for chronic pain misuse them. The Centers for Disease Control and Prevention (CDC) estimates that the total cost of prescription opioid misuse in the United States is $78.5 billion a year.

Are there any solutions to this problem? Jim Jennings, a local firefighter, told me that yoga was the answer. 'If more people turn to yoga and learn to connect mind, body and spirit,' he said, 'then I'm sure this problem can be cured.'

How do you evaluate evidence?

When you identify different types of evidence, you are already beginning to make a judgement of how valid it is. But there are several other aspects you must consider.

Credibility

One of the first things you should consider is where the evidence came from. Can you trust the source of the evidence? Is it credible?

Activity 3: Is the evidence credible?

a) Look at the three examples of evidence below and rank them in order of the credibility of the source.
b) Having ranked the evidence, take a moment to reflect upon how you made your judgement. Discuss your thinking process with a partner.

A
The sugar tax is an example of governments interfering in the lives of ordinary people, according to Stephen Wood. He adds: 'it should be scrapped, people should be free to buy the drinks they like.'
Stephen Wood is head of public relations for the Soft Drink Producers Alliance (SDPA).

B
'The sugar tax won't reduce the consumption of high-sugar soft drinks for young people. The survey I carried out found that 70 per cent of students said they didn't think about the price when buying soft drinks.'
This evidence comes from a Humanities student who carried out a survey for a school assignment.

C
Mila Schneider, professor of nutrition, states that 'just adding 10 per cent to the price of sugary soft drinks would prevent 120 000 cases of obesity over the next five years.'
Professor Schneider works at Heidelberg University and is currently leading a research project assessing the effectiveness of levies on unhealthy foods.

You probably ranked statement C as the highest. The evidence was offered by a professor of nutrition. The status of a professor is high and they are unlikely to put forward evidence that might bring them or their university into disrepute. Not only that, but the professor's specialism is closely linked to the subject to which the evidence relates. This is often referred to as 'the **ability to see**'. Not only does the professor have status or reputation but their expertise is highly relevant too.

It is also likely that you ranked statement B as the lowest. A college student clearly lacks academic status and is probably not qualified enough to carry out an effective survey on such a complex subject. However, the credibility of the source is only one criterion by which to judge the quality of the evidence. Remember, it is possible for somebody with high credibility to give false evidence and for somebody with lower credibility to give accurate evidence. For example, a politician may have credibility and status, but they may present weak evidence to suit a political cause.

Statement A is more difficult to judge without doing further research into the SDPA. It is possible to assume that the SDPA may well have a **vested interest** in the issue of taxing soft drinks, so the group may use selective evidence to support the case they are pursuing.

> **Key terms**
>
> **ability to see:** how close the source is to the evidence, and whether the author has first-hand knowledge or relevant expertise
>
> **vested interest:** a personal reason for getting involved in an issue, usually because it offers financial or some other type of gain
>
> **uncited:** describes information or evidence an author uses without stating where it comes from

What if a source isn't provided?

When you are checking sources, you might come across instances when evidence is given without a source. This is known as **uncited** or unsourced evidence. When evidence lacks a source, this is always deemed a weakness. However, the weakness of unsourced evidence may be partially offset by the provenance of the published article that uses the evidence.

Activity 4: Looking into provenance

a) Carry out some research to see which news sources your classmates and teachers rate as:
- the most/least credible (and why)
- the most/least biased (with reasons).

b) How can you find out more to evaluate the credibility and bias of news sources?

Those writers and journalists that work for news agencies rated as being unbiased, such as Associated Press, are likely to have a level of professionalism that ensures they check evidence before publishing. Articles published by Associated Press could therefore be said to have a strong provenance.

Selective evidence and bias

Another factor to bear in mind is that evidence presented by those who are biased or have a vested interest may be selective. Selective evidence is chosen not because it is necessarily the best evidence, but because it fits best with someone's argument or perspective. When you conduct your own research, using evidence from a wide range of competing sources will prevent you from offering selective evidence.

How meaningful is the evidence?

Another criterion by which to evaluate evidence is how *meaningful* it is. Look at this statement from the article on page 40.

> **Key advice**
>
> When evaluating the bias and provenance of evidence, these are the questions you should be asking:
> - Is it clear where the information has come from?
> - Can you identify the authors or organisations responsible?
> - Where was it published?
> - Who finances the publication, what are the aims/political stance of the organisation/publisher?

> The Centers for Disease Control and Prevention (CDC) estimates that the total cost of prescription opioid misuse in the United States is $78.5 billion a year.

Clearly $78.5 billion is a large sum of money but what does it mean in this context? We do not know how it was calculated, nor do we have anything to compare it to. The figure may be accurate, but with no other information to compare it with in a similar context, it is hard to gauge the significance of this amount.

Activity 5: Is the evidence meaningful?

In Activity 3 you looked at some evidence from a school assignment: 'The survey I carried out found that 70 per cent of students said they didn't think about the price when buying soft drinks.'

Initially you evaluated this evidence in terms of the credibility of the author. For now, put the author's credibility to one side and consider the meaningfulness of the evidence presented.

a) How meaningful is the evidence presented?

b) Does the 70 per cent figure hold more meaning here than the $78.5 billion quoted above?

Share your thoughts with a partner.

By offering a percentage, there is at least some context and therefore a percentage may carry more meaning than just a raw number. However, to be sure of quantitative evidence, we either need to know how it was calculated or have faith in the source that provided the evidence. If you look more deeply at the student's study carried out in college, you would see issues with the *representativeness* of the evidence – how well it applies to the wider population. The student's evidence will only relate to a small group of people who are of similar age and who live in the same part of one country. If the evidence is not representative, then it cannot be used to draw wider conclusions. To do so would be making a generalisation.

Why is corroborated evidence important?

The topics and issues you will explore on this course are global. If evidence from one country or cultural context supports evidence from a different country or cultural context, it may be safer to draw conclusions. The relative strength or weakness of evidence may depend upon its relationship to other evidence used. During the evaluation process, it is worth considering how different pieces of evidence corroborate each other (see page 12). A strong perspective is built on relevant evidence from various contexts. For example, evidence showing that ice caps in Antarctica are melting could be corroborated with evidence of coastal erosion in the Maldives. From this, generalisations may be made with some justification.

The diagram below explores some of the questions to consider when evaluating evidence.

Questions to ask when evaluating evidence

- Is the evidence provided by a person with the 'ability to see'?
- Does the source have a vested interest?
- What's the provenance?
- Is the evidence corroborated?
- Evidence
- Is the evidence relevant?
- Is the evidence representative?
- How credible is the source of evidence?
- Is the evidence meaningful – does it have context?

In this unit, you have learned how to identify and categorise evidence into different types. Once you are able to identify evidence, then you can begin to evaluate it against the criteria outlined in the diagram above. You are now going to apply these questions to the evidence in another article.

As you read the article, jot down the evidence as you find it and then complete the task that follows.

> **Nuclear is the way to go**
>
> Like all energy sources, nuclear power has both advantages and disadvantages. Many environmentalists worry about accidents and the problems associated with radioactive waste. At first glance, such concerns seem plausible but Jenny Jones, who works as a lobbyist for the nuclear industry claims that, 'There have only ever been three large-scale accidents at nuclear power plants and in each case, the worst initial fears about contamination were never realised.' Her confidence in the industry is supported by Zhang Wei who is a professor of aeronautics. He argues that nuclear waste is stored safely and securely in impenetrable concrete and steel casks deep in the ground.
>
> In 2018, nuclear plants supplied 2563 TWh of electricity around the world and this is set to increase. In France, 71% of the nation's electricity comes from nuclear power which is one of the largest percentages for any country in the world. Across the border in Spain, 21% of their electricity comes from nuclear. One of the surprising benefits is the number of jobs the sector provides for local economies. According to the Nuclear Energy Institute, 'A single nuclear power plant creates more jobs than any other type of energy generation facility.' When old reactors are shut down, the loss of jobs can be devastating. Chuck Johnson who lives in Zion, Illinois saw the impact of a shutdown at first-hand, 'Zion has never recovered. This used to be a thriving town when the reactor was operational but today it's like a ghost town.'
>
> It is perhaps most important that nuclear power plants produce no greenhouse gas emissions during their operation. Professor Gupta, a climate change expert, argues that meeting the Paris Agreement means keeping the global temperature rise to below two degrees Celsius, which in his opinion can only happen by increasing our use of nuclear energy.
>
> From an article by Dahlia Larsen, published on her personal blog

Final task

a) Using the questions in the diagram on page 43, evaluate each piece of evidence. (Remember that any one piece of evidence may have both strengths and weaknesses.) When you have done that, come to an overall judgement as to whether you think the evidence supporting the blog post is strong or weak.

b) Now work in a small group to compare your thought process and your final judgements. Make sure you all have an equal chance to speak and listen carefully to each other. When you have finished, think about how effectively the group worked and reflect on how you might improve your responses.

Reflective plenary

In what ways has your understanding of the texts and sources you read or use as part of your study, or in your life in general, changed as a result of the work in this unit? Note down in a log or journal two key messages you can take away from the work you have done.

Chapter 3
Researching and using sources

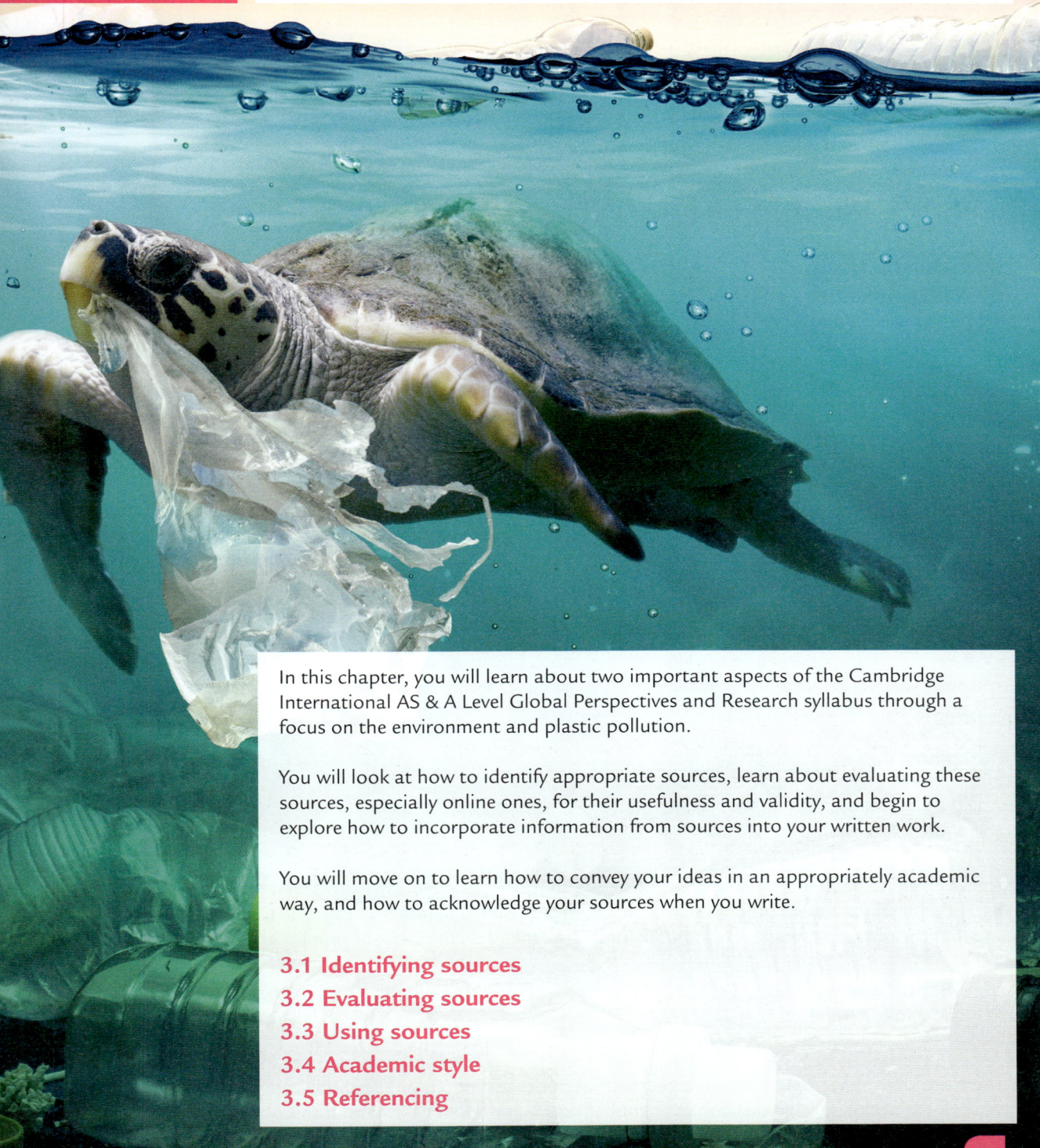

In this chapter, you will learn about two important aspects of the Cambridge International AS & A Level Global Perspectives and Research syllabus through a focus on the environment and plastic pollution.

You will look at how to identify appropriate sources, learn about evaluating these sources, especially online ones, for their usefulness and validity, and begin to explore how to incorporate information from sources into your written work.

You will move on to learn how to convey your ideas in an appropriately academic way, and how to acknowledge your sources when you write.

3.1 Identifying sources
3.2 Evaluating sources
3.3 Using sources
3.4 Academic style
3.5 Referencing

3.1 Identifying sources

In this unit you will:
- learn how to identify different types of sources.

Critical Path
You will need to:
- collaborate to identify appropriate content
- weigh up the validity of material.

Deconstruction	Reconstruction	Reflection	Communication	Collaboration
✓				✓

In the previous chapter, you looked at how certain evidence can support an argument, but where does this evidence come from? The answer is that it comes from sources – a variety of types of text and other material in printed, digital, visual and oral forms.

Starting point

Work with a partner. Where could you find information about the effect of plastic pollution? Discuss and list potential sources and then compare these to another pair's or group's list. Did you come up with the same answers? Which sources might be the most difficult to access?

The relevant information might be from published sources such as books, journal articles, reports and news stories, or other media broadcasts such as talks, lectures and interviews. Traditionally, print was the primary (or main) way of accessing reference material, but the internet opened up global access to information sources published digitally.

You will have identified some of the following sources of evidence in the starter activity:
- books, textbooks, reference works
- television/radio news outlets (CNN, BBC, Al Jazeera, Russia Today, etc.)
- newspapers and magazines (*The Economist*, *The New York Times*, *The Guardian*, etc.)
- brochures, leaflets, company documentation
- academic journals
- reports, theses
- podcasts and TED Talks
- websites (government/public health/United Nations/environment/energy)
- interviews with experts in your topic.

You will need to be aware that each type of source comes with its own challenges. You might find both digital and print-based resources in your library and a librarian will be able to help you, but the relevance and how up-to-date these are depend on the stock of your library.

Academic journals and reports can be strong sources of information, but these are lengthy and written in specialist language for an academic audience, so they can be a challenge to access. Such sources will require careful note-making skills.

There are also many useful audio sources, such as podcasts and TED Talks, and these can be useful to access specific viewpoints or lines of reasoning. You may need to transcribe sections of these sources as you take notes. Similarly, multimedia sources such as television, film and video (available on YouTube or similar streaming platforms) provide audiovisual information. Here, the challenge is to be able to record and summarise information precisely and to maintain an unbiased view of what you are seeing.

Perhaps the most obvious place to start searching for sources is online. This can be an overwhelming experience, and we will look at how best to search for sources online and how to evaluate them in the following units.

Activity 1: Identifying sources

a) Work with a partner. Identify which type of source the following extracts come from. Discuss how you came to your conclusion with another pair.

Extract 1
'I want to talk about how it feels to be a sea or river animal living with plastic. [Indicates to a screen.] Imagine you are swimming in a pool filled with empty plastic bottles, discarded coffee cups and plastic cutlery...'

Comment section of a national newspaper. It suggests a link for more detailed research through the university mentioned. Newspapers provide current information, but often in a brief form which may need further research to confirm reliability of the information.

Extract 2
'Many plastic items originate in school and university cafeterias. A toolkit has been developed to help reduce levels of plastic waste in these areas.'

National Geographic-style monthly magazine. It provides global reach on the topic. These types of magazines are keen to explore global issues and are aimed at a global audience.

Extract 3
'Galapagos Grief
The Galapagos Islands, once known only as a remote, environmental haven, is about to drown in a flotsam of plastic waste...'

TED Talk. This would focus on one perspective. TED Talks tend to be given by experts in a field with a keen interest in exploring or exposing a specific aspect.

Extract 4
'When is an iceberg not made of ice? When it is made of plastic. Recent research by a team from the University of [...] has shown that the visible plastic on the surface of the Atlantic Ocean is only the tip of the disaster that is overwhelming the planet.'

Government environmental protection website. It confirms what constitutes waste. Government sites tend to be factual but can have a bias depending on the government.

Key advice

How do I find the sources I need?
- Go to your school or local library. Ask librarians for help with search terms and how to use the library record system.
- Ask your teacher to guide you.
- Use broad internet word searches (discussed below).
- Discuss your ideas with peers and others in your teaching and learning community.
- Start to engage with the news, especially on your topic of interest.

Recording sources

When you find a potential information source, it is important to record it. You could record sources digitally, using a reference management tool or spreadsheet, or you can record them manually in a notebook.

Plastic pollution: record of sources

Source	Title	Date of text and date of access	Audience
TED Talk: A B Cook URL: https://…	Plastic is becoming my food	20 April 2020 Accessed 25 July 2020	US focus Middle-class educated perspective

- Based on USA, so limited.
- Dates important to ensure information is still relevant.
- Title suggests environmental and negative perspective.
- Note URL so you can revisit site.

How can I use internet search engines effectively?

Online research can be overwhelming: a search for the word 'encyclopaedia', for example, produces over 35 million results in a split second. So, while search engines are an important starting point to help you find relevant information, it is how you narrow down and use the information that is crucial to the success of your research. It is helpful to start with a keyword or phrase related to your topic, and to try a variety of search engines.

One way to narrow down your search results is to check the domain names. Domain suffixes help to define the type of website and might even give you a clue as to possible vested interest, bias or general **reliability**.

> - **.com** – originally intended for a **commercial** website, now the most recognised domain suffix used by many individuals as well as businesses and organisations
> - **.org** – for organisations, generally non-profit but again free to use by anyone
> - **.net** – internet administrative site
> - **.gov** – government site
> - **.ac** – UK academic site
> - **.edu** – US education site
> - **.co/.ac/.gov etc. + country code** – every country has a unique suffix code to be used for sites within a particular country; these can also be used to specify different versions of an international website
> - **.nhs/.mod/.store/.biz/.pro etc.** – domain suffixes for job areas or specific groups.

Key term

reliability: how trustworthy or reliable something is

Other important considerations when identifying sources from an internet search are the date and publication. Always check the date of the original creation and also the date you accessed the publication to ensure the information is current, and that you can reference it accurately when you come to use the evidence.

Quick task

Try searching for a video called 'Did You Know?' Look at the range of dates in your results and try to work out which is the original and which are updated versions.

Final task

a) Imagine you are going to carry out a search for information on an issue that interests you or that is relevant to the subjects you study.
   - Which online or print sources could you go to? If you can, carry out an online search.
   - What challenges do you think you might face?
   - How will you record your search?

b) Work in a small group to share your ideas about how to search for information on each topic. Do you draw any conclusions?

Reflective plenary

Make a bullet-point list of what you have learned about identifying sources in this unit. Work with a partner to compare and expand your lists.

3.2 Evaluating sources

In this unit you will:
- learn how to evaluate research information.

Critical Path

You will need to:
- understand how to deconstruct sources
- be able to reconstruct information for your purposes.

Deconstruction	Reconstruction	Reflection	Communication	Collaboration
✓	✓			

This unit focuses on how to distinguish *useful* information from the vast range of potential sources available. Following the Critical Path, you will begin to deconstruct sources and evaluate their reliability and **credibility**. Research is as much about discarding irrelevant, invalid or untrustworthy information as it is about finding evidence.

> **Key term**
>
> **credibility:** how believable a claim is

Starting point

Work with a partner. Discuss which of the following sources you think might be more useful for conducting research on plastic pollution. Keep in mind words like 'credible' and 'reliable', which you will explore in more detail in this unit.

Source A: A social media story, posted with a photograph showing someone finding and saving a bird trapped by a plastic ring top.

Source B: A WBSJ (Wild Bird Society of Japan) article about the dangers of plastic ring tops.

For a source to be useful to you, it should be relevant, credible, authoritative and, sometimes, reveal a particular perspective.

Source A is relevant in that it details the dangers of plastic pollution, but as an anecdote, it lacks corroboration and therefore credibility. There is no indication of who the person is, which calls their **authority** into question. Source B is also relevant to the topic, but the provenance – the WBSJ – lends it authority. It might be possible to use Source A as additional evidence in an argument, adding detail to Source B, but not on its own.

> **Key term**
>
> **authority:** the right someone has to influence an issue based on their level of understanding and expertise

How can I evaluate sources?

You looked at the status of experts, vested interest, provenance and uncited sources in Chapter 2. You will see how these concepts can also be used here to evaluate source material through careful deconstruction.

Two common approaches to evaluating sources are represented by the acronyms RAVEN and CRAAP. They are useful memory aids for testing out a source's validity.

Using RAVEN and CRAAP tests

The RAVEN Test	
Reputation/reliability	Who wrote the source? Where?
Ability to see	Is the source giving first-hand information – was the writer/producer there?
Vested interest	Might the source or writer benefit?
Expertise	Is the writer knowledgeable about this topic?
Neutrality/bias	How objective/subjective is the source?

The CRAAP Test	
Currency	Is the source recent enough to be useful?
Relevance	Does the source contribute to the topic?
Authority	Does the source carry weight – is it serious?
Accuracy	Is the information supported by verifiable evidence? Does the source have any glaring spelling/grammar errors?
Purpose	What is the purpose of the source? Does it have any bias or agenda?

> **Key term**
>
> **currency:** how recent information is and whether it is still relevant

You will notice that the two tests are not mutually exclusive, and you can use either. A simple comment about the vested interest of an organisation behind a source, or the date it was produced, can add weight to your argument.

What is meant by reliability?

When asking if something is reliable, the aim is to find out how much trust can be put in the information. Photographic evidence is generally seen as reliable – a picture cannot lie, right? But even pictures need to be assessed; you have probably seen pictures of an event being 'reused' on social media months or even years later for a different purpose. Similarly, photographs and videos can be edited to add completely false information.

> **Quick task**
>
> Try applying one of the tests to Sources A and B above. How does it help with your evaluation?

Be very wary about any information sourced on social media, where sharing and forwarding make it almost impossible to trace the original source. Be aware also that reliability and expertise do not necessarily work in tandem. Your teacher is a reliable source but is unlikely to be an expert in oceanic science.

What clues might suggest that an online text is unreliable?
- **Poor website design:** Does it look professional?
- **Use of hyperbole and emotive language:** Too much exaggeration, sweeping statements and overly dramatic language can suggest subjectivity or a lack of real argument. However, such sites might also add to a particular viewpoint if carefully evaluated.
- **Grammar and spelling:** Could you take a website seriously where it says: 'write or wrong' when clearly meaning 'right or wrong'?
- **Poor use of capitalisation and bad punctuation.**

Activity 1: Evaluating sources

a) **Take a look at the sources below and assess them using either RAVEN or CRAAP.**
b) **Discuss your assessment in pairs and suggest whether and how each source could be used.**

A   Information from an acknowledged expert, a medical practitioner, published in a leading medical journal with a recent date.

> The trial was co-ordinated from the Medical Research Council Laboratories in Seoul. The field work was carried out by five local health authorities Busan, Incheon, Daegu, Daejeon and Ulsan… The aim was to trial influenza vaccines produced in South Korea and Russia for effectiveness in controlling the spread of new influenza related virus borne diseases.

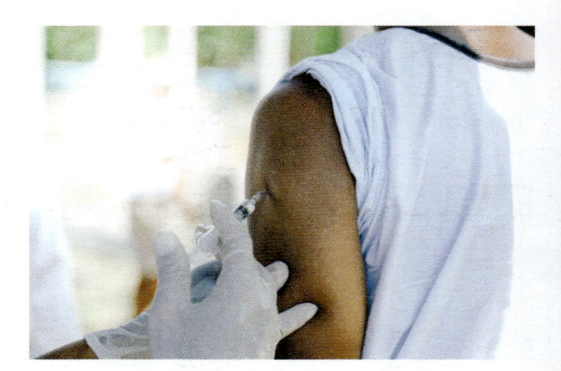

B   A news report in a national newspaper today, written by the journalist responsible for breaking medical news.

> **Vaccine Head to Head**
> The Medical Research Council announced today that it would be trialling new flu vaccines in major South Korean hospitals. Two batches of vaccine, one from South Korean research and a cheaper one from Russia are to be pitted against each other as the government tries to find a new way to control the spread of the virus this winter.

C   A social media post.

> Muthernosbest Fri 06-July 2021 08:52:24
> What. South Korea versus Russia in vaccines. No way I am allowing my children to be the football here. I know it would be good to be protected against the flu but not this way.

Special focus: Using Wikipedia

Wikipedia is a widely used source of information, so it is worth focusing on how best to use it and what to be wary of.

The following extract is from Wikipedia's article on plastic pollution. It was started some time before July 2013 and has been edited multiple times by multiple contributors since.

Quick task

What do you know about how Wikipedia is authored and edited? How do you think this affects the ways in which you might use it as a source?

Effects of plastic on oceans

> ⚠️ **This section has multiple issues.** Please help **improve it** or discuss these issues on the **talk page**. (*Learn how and when to remove these template messages*)
>
> This section's **factual accuracy** is **disputed**. (*January 2018*)

See also: Marine pollution § Plastic debris, and North Atlantic garbage patch [2]

As of 2016 it was estimated that there was approximately 150 million tonnes of plastic pollution in the world's oceans, estimated to grow to 250 million tonnes in 2025.[50] [3] Another study estimated that in 2012, it was approximately 165 million tonnes.[21] The Ocean Conservancy reported that China, Indonesia, Philippines, Thailand, and Vietnam dump more plastic in the sea than all other countries combined [3].[18]

One study estimated that there are more than 5 trillion plastic pieces (defined into the four classes of small microplastics, large microplastics, meso- and macroplastics) [4] afloat at sea [3].[49]

The litter that is being delivered into the oceans is toxic to marine life, and humans. The toxins that are components of plastic include diethylhexyl phthalate, which is a toxic carcinogen, as well as lead, cadmium, and mercury. [5]

Plankton, fish, and ultimately the human race, through the food chain, [6] ingest these highly toxic carcinogens and chemicals. Consuming the fish that contain these toxins can cause an increase in cancer, immune disorders, and birth defects.[51] *[failed verification]* [7]

The majority of the litter near and in the ocean is made up of plastics and is a persistent pervasive source of marine pollution.[52] According to Dr. Marcus Eriksen [8] of The 5 Gyres Institute, there are 5.25 trillion particles of plastic pollution that weigh as much as 270 000 tonnes (2016). [9] This plastic is taken by the ocean currents and accumulates in large vortexes known as ocean gyres. The majority of the gyres become pollution dumps filled with plastic.

https://en.wikipedia.org/wiki/Plastic_pollution

Annotations:

- [1] Notice the warning! Note that the section has issues of reliability.
- [2] Links to further pages on the site.
- [3] Look up some of the references for more accurate information.
- [4] Define different types of plastic to help focus essay.
- [5] You might decide to research how plastic creates toxins.
- [6] This could provide you with a possible line of enquiry through how plastic pollution re-enters the food chain.
- [7] Note that this data needs a proven source.
- [8] A name that could lead to interesting research.
- [9] Information is dated here – what has happened since then?

Final task

Apply RAVEN or CRAAP to this Wikipedia source. Discuss in pairs how you think this source could be useful for research on plastic pollution.

Key advice

Wikipedia is a secondary information site where anyone can access the information and edit or amend it. This makes it potentially unreliable, so direct reference should not be used to provide evidence. Facts contained within entries should be corroborated. However, it can be useful for establishing ideas and lines of enquiry. It can also provide leads to other research through the references and sources given.

Reflective plenary

Think about what you have learned about gauging the usefulness of sources. Work with a small group. Discuss any challenges you have found when searching for material. How did you overcome these?

3.3 Using sources

In this unit you will:
- learn how to use research material to support arguments
- learn how to take notes on your research material.

Critical Path
You will need to:
- be able to reflect on what you read
- reconstruct the information to use in your arguments.

Deconstruction	Reconstruction	Reflection	Communication	Collaboration
	✓	✓		

The focus in this unit is on incorporating your research to add supporting detail and evidence to your arguments and to show how you have considered themes, perspectives and the global reach of your topic.

Effective use of evidence is supported by effective note-taking from sources, and this is a second focus in the unit.

Starting point

Work with a partner to create a spider diagram to show what you know currently about plastic pollution in oceans.
- Why do you think it is one of the biggest problems for the environment?
- What evidence do you need to support a detailed discussion?

Special focus: Case study: Using sources

Yendo is a student who is interested in how pollution is affecting the planet. He wants to consider whether plastic waste has become the globe's most damaging pollutant. He wants to know who holds this view and what support there is for it.

Stage 1: Finding evidence

Yendo realises that he first needs to find evidence about plastic waste. What constitutes plastic waste? What happens to this waste? How is this waste polluting the environment? He also realises that he needs to explore other forms of environmental pollution, such as chemical waste and sewage.

He uses the guidelines given in Unit 3.1 to find information, and discovers a source from *The Guardian* newspaper. The article is about sewage pollution and how it has caused an outbreak of cholera in Zimbabwe. He selects the extracts below from the article as being particularly useful. He also begins to make some basic notes to help him deconstruct the text.

> [...] Harare, the capital, has been worst hit in the latest outbreak. It is centred on the poor neighbourhood of Glen View on the outskirts of the city of 2 million people, where drinking water from boreholes has been contaminated by sewage leaking from broken pipes.
>
> *Evidence of cholera caused by sewage leak – different form of pollution than plastic.*
>
> 'Water has been a problem in this area for years. In the 10 years we have been here nothing has been done. Our lives are in danger,' said Mavis Matayi, a Glen View resident whose husband was in hospital with the disease.
>
> *Eyewitness, first-hand account.*
>
> [...] Obadiah Moyo, the newly appointed health minister, said rubbish dumps would be removed from high-risk areas of Harare and sewer pipes repaired. Riot police used water cannon to disperse vendors accused of spreading cholera by selling contaminated food in the centre of Harare.
>
> [...] 'It is alarming and quite unusual for such a medieval and preventable disease to continue to claim such valuable lives in this day and age,' said the Civil Society Health Emergency Response Coordinating Committee, a coalition of NGOs, in a statement.
>
> From *The Guardian*, 20 September 2018, '"Medieval" cholera outbreak exposes huge challenges in Zimbabwe'

Stage 2: Evaluating the evidence

Now, as discussed in Unit 3.2, using the RAVEN or CRAAP tests, he checks the source type, authorship, date and context to ensure the information he uses is relevant and valid in supporting his argument.

He notes down the following as a start:
- The Guardian article: reputable global newspaper, whole source contains first-hand photographs, giving it authority.
- Useful and relevant – provides evidence of effect of a different form of pollution and its consequences: sewage polluting the drinking supply.
- Source introduces perspective of someone living with pollution, which could be used to contrast with plastic pollution.

Clearly, there is more for Yendo to do here, but this is a useful start.

Stage 3: Synthesising information

Note-making is an active process, often using highlighters and annotations as Yendo did. However, while his notes and annotations are useful, he also needs to keep a clear and concise record of his findings. Note-making is a vital skill that has to be learned. It is not about trying to write down everything from a source in a shortened way, but about synthesising information, often paraphrasing it to avoid plagiarism. Effective notes will help with your understanding, your thought processes and your recall – as well as making sure that you have the detail you need for referencing.

To take effective notes you need to:
- take down the basic information on source, title, date, date accessed, author and URL
- identify conclusions, support, global reach, perspective
- summarise the article
- highlight useful facts
- note your judgement of the material.

The following is an extract from Yendo's notes on the source fragments from *The Guardian*. You will need to develop a style of note-taking that suits you best.

Online URL	*The Guardian* newspaper	20/09/2018 accessed 2/8/2020	Foreign affairs journalist

Conclusion: Water contamination from sewage/rubbish causing disease.
Evidence: Personal accounts.
Reach: One slum area in Africa.
Perspective: International news – looking at a viewpoint of poverty.
Summary: Reasons for cholera and methods of dealing with it.
Highlights problem of sewage: Hints at need to access clean water – could link to use of plastic containers. Govt handling not really useful but need to consider other types of rubbish.*
*this section probably needs to be filled in *after Stage 3*

> **Key advice**
>
> From the moment you start researching, you should establish a place to take notes on your material. This can be in a file, in your Workbook, or digitally in a spreadsheet or document.

Stage 4: Using sources in your research and thinking process

Yendo next sees that a source can give him ideas about how to develop his thinking and research. He realises that his sources can give factual information and that he can use statistics to provide evidence about plastic waste and where it is more polluting than other forms of waste.

His sources can also provide angles for his argument. The article on the sewage situation in a Harare suburb suggests that for those residents, raw sewage is more of a problem than plastic. The article also talks about rubbish as a whole, reminding Yendo to explore other types of waste.

While he started out thinking that plastic waste was entirely negative, Yendo now begins to consider an alternative perspective: waste plastic bottles could store precious clean drinking and washing water in poor communities.

Stage 5: Writing up ideas

Yendo now has a framework for writing up his ideas. Here are two paragraphs from a draft using *The Guardian* source. Note how Yendo has referenced the article.

Water contaminated by sewage in Harare has led to several cholera outbreaks in the recent past[3]. [1] Sewage is a bigger pollutant in many areas of the world than plastic. [2]

While plastic clearly damages the oceans, it can be argued that raw sewage is a more damaging pollutant. Evidence from Harare's recent cholera outbreak shows that water contaminated from broken sewage pipes brought the deadly disease to the slum areas[3]. This was a huge concern to local inhabitants[3] and would suggest that they perceived sewage as a primary source of pollution. [3]

[3]https://www.theguardian.com/global-development/2018/sep/20/medieval-cholera-outbreak-exposes-zimbabwe-problems] [4]

[1] Here, Yendo introduces evidence of sewage causing cholera.

[2] Yendo introduces the argument that it is therefore a major pollutant.

[3] He develops the argument with further details and reference to first-hand witness accounts.

[4] Reference from *The Guardian* cited.

How can I incorporate evidence into my writing?

Supporting evidence from your research can be used in your work in three ways. It is important that you understand the impact and pitfalls of each method. It is also vital that you remember to cite any information used.

1. **Direct quotation:** Only to be used when the words are worth repeating and the idea cannot be improved on. For example, you really might want to describe religion as 'the opiate of the masses' (Karl Marx) rather than paraphrasing to 'religion is a drug that appeals to the general public'.
2. **Paraphrase:** When you paraphrase, you express the meaning of a source/portion of a source in *your own words*. This still has to be referenced, as the paraphrased material is not your own idea.
3. **Summary:** This follows the path of deconstruction to reconstruction and is probably the most efficient way of capturing ideas. Summarising gives the outline of a page or so of a source while avoiding irrelevant detail. Again, you still have to reference anything summarised from someone else's work.

Key advice

It helps if you introduce supporting evidence into your work with a signal phrase to distinguish your ideas from those of others. Using signal words helps you to check that you have referenced correctly at the proofreading stage. Useful signal words include:

acknowledge, admit, advise, agree, argue, assert, believe, charge, claim comment, conclude, concur, confirm, contend, declare, deny, disagree, dispute, emphasise, grant, illustrate, imply, insist, note, observe, point out, reason, reject, report, respond, suggest, think.

Final task

Imagine you are continuing with Yendo's research project and considering the effect of plastic pollution. You discover the source below. Evaluate the source and annotate a copy of it to indicate how it might add to and develop Yendo's ideas. Use the teaching points on note-taking to create a useful set of notes. Compare your notes with a partner.

The True Cost of Plastic

Britta Denise Hardesty, Commonwealth Scientific and Industrial Research Organization

Plastic is here. To stay. We all use plastic in our daily lives, in myriad forms, for sundry purposes. The many polymers that compose 'plastic' and the characteristics we require from 'it' mean that managing plastic waste after end of life is challenging, even for those of us privileged to live in areas where waste-management systems exist.

Plastic is also cheap. Very cheap. Exceptionally cheap. So cheap that we readily make, use, and discard plastic things that are then lost into the environment, where they remain. We do not find the same for aluminium, copper, or other valued items. Those items, when lost or littered, are scavenged, recovered, and sold. They are valuable.

From sciencedirect.com, 24 January 2020

Reflective plenary

Work with a partner. Summarise what you have learned about why and how you are going to use sources. What challenges do you anticipate as you continue to search for information?

3.4 Academic style

In this unit you will:
- learn how to communicate your ideas in an appropriate manner
- review basic conventions of academic writing.

Critical Path

You will need to:
- practise clear, coherent communication that develops your argument.

Deconstruction	Reconstruction	Reflection	Communication	Collaboration
			✓	

The focus in this unit is to learn about and practise the conventions used in academic writing; you are expected to develop a formal style that is appropriate for your intended audience and is clearly expressed and accurate.

Starting point

In pairs, copy and complete the grid to show four different forms of writing you use regularly.

Writing form	Audience	Purpose	Style	Register
Text message	One friend	Share information/ issue invitation	Casual – abbreviated	Informal

What should I consider when using an academic register?

In academic writing, your communication needs to be formal, with your audience and purpose your central considerations.

Use the four key areas outlined below to pick out problems in Example A. The highlighted comments and questions will help you.

Example A

> **Should animal testing be used in cosmetic research?**
>
> Animal testing *is being considered* by some people as very important *testing test* for advances in cosmetics, which may range from unnecessary to *horrendously cruel*. Research conducted on *animals is being* an ongoing issue, it is one of the *most and worst unethical* ways of cosmetic production. Cosmetics have used animal testing for many years, to protect the human body or skin from irritation. Although it is no longer popular, some scientists argue that animal testing is the most accurate way of research because animal bodies are very like the human body. As a result, it continues to be used.
>
> Comment: This paragraph seems to be a series of comments on animal testing rather than an idea that is developed.

- verbs/tenses
- vocabulary
- redundancy

> The protection of customers, the environment and the workers may cause animals to be violated and force fed with harmful substances furthermore exposing them to high levels of radiation, in turn has caused a domino effect of people globally ignoring the horrors of experiments carried out on animals merely to make people more beautiful, animals such as rats and mice are affected by this. In 2011, almost 11.5 million animals were used in experiments across Europe.
>
> Comment: The last sentence provides some evidence but are we sure that it is contributing to the argument? The main sentence is 64 words long. How clear is it?

— paragraph and sentence structure

> This means that all the data that was collected was taken and used for medical research, experiments or other similar things. Alternatively, because of corporate social responsibilities, companies such as The Body Shop have found that abuse of animals has caused business profits to plunge. As a result, they are using an animal-friendly method of testing products through computer-based testing. This helps cosmetic researchers find out what materials are suitable through extrapolation. Animal testing is helping formulate very many life-saving cures and treatments such as Herceptin breast cancer cure. But animals feel pain, this makes research really cruel and it should be stopped.

— Imprecise vocabulary.
— Wrong transition word.
— Again support (good) but needs a reference.
— Interesting word.
— Continuous tense – more efficiently phrased as 'helps'.
— What is the link between evidence of Herceptin and animals' pain? And who says 'it' should be stopped – what is the perspective here?

> Some religions allow animal testing as mankind has dominion over animals but I still think it is unhuman to carry out animal testing despite the benefits to cure diseases. So, no, animal testing should not be used in cosmetic research.
>
> Comment: The student has answered the question but only by expressing a personal opinion.

— Wrong word – check confusion between 'unhuman' and 'inhumane'.

This is an extreme example of some typical problems. It could be improved in four key areas.

Key area 1: Vocabulary

Choose your words carefully (using a thesaurus if necessary) and ensure they add value.
- Consider the use of the word 'test' in the opening of Example A and the word 'unhuman' in the fourth paragraph.
- Be sure that the use of emotive words does not try to obscure lack of research. Consider the effect of 'horrendously cruel'.
- 'Hedging', or cautious language, is used to distinguish between claims and established facts. Useful verbs include: assume, seem, tend to, believe, suggest, appear to be, indicate that.
- Be clear when using pronouns to replace a noun. Look at how paragraph 3 begins – what is 'This' referring to? There is no previous idea in the paragraph.

Key area 2: Paragraph and sentence structure

Paragraphs and sentences are the means by which we can order ideas. Paragraphs can consolidate an idea in an argument. See if you can identify one main idea or point in the first paragraph of Example A. Count how many **topic sentences** there are in the example essay. Points in the topic sentences should be supported by evidence and then it should be explained how this supports the point or argument. This is a PEE (point, evidence, explanation) paragraph structure.

Key terms

paragraph: a block of text used to explore one idea, usually containing a topic sentence and supporting sentences, concluding with a transition to the next idea/paragraph

topic sentence: the sentence that contains the key idea in a paragraph, usually (but not always) the first sentence

Over-long sentences can make it very hard for a reader to follow your train of thought. Look at paragraph 2 as an example.

The essay contains very few examples of **transition words**, such as 'firstly', 'because', 'therefore', which signpost an argument and make it easier to follow. (See Unit 8.4 for more information on organising your argument.)

Key area 3: Use of verbs

Use of active verbs in the correct tense can drive ideas in an argument. Though the passive voice can be appropriate at times, be careful not to use a continuous passive incorrectly. For example, the opening sentence of Example A is passive and uses the present continuous tense. It would be more accurate and authoritative to write: 'Scientists consider that animal testing is important for cosmetic development.' Look carefully at the present continuous 'is helping' in paragraph 3. This is not correct as the present simple is used to express facts or claims: 'animal testing *helps* formulate…'.

Key area 4: Redundancy

It is important not to use too many words or vague language (known as **redundancy**) when explaining your ideas. For example, the phrase 'the most and worst' in paragraph 1 does not add any value to the argument. Also consider how uninformative 'very many life-saving cures' is (paragraph 3). It suggests that the writer has not found any concrete examples to provide evidence.

Now look at Example B below. How do the language and style give a stronger sense of an argument and possible perspectives?

> **Key terms**
>
> **transition words:** words that act as signposts, clarifying the direction of a debate; transition words can be additive, sequential, contrasting/shifting direction or causal/explanatory
>
> **redundancy:** using too many words to express a simple idea, such as 'it is often the case that' rather than 'often'

Example B

> Should animal testing be used in cosmetic research?
>
> The use of animals in research on new cosmetics is widespread, but it is a controversial issue, with claims from animal rights groups that it is inhumane. Recent surveys carried out in the local press also suggest that cosmetics users feel it is unnecessary.
>
> The argument put forward by cosmetics producers is that their customers need to be protected from adverse reactions to the chemicals in their products. Such reactions can only be gauged when tested on tissue that can be closely linked to humans. Therefore, animal testing continues to be necessary to cosmetic development.
>
> Animals also provide a cheap source of testing material. Customer research carried out in the United States in 2018 shows that 85 per cent of cosmetics users are influenced by affordability rather than ethical concerns about 'beautiful, sentient animals being tortured' (blog from animal rights activist).
>
> On the other hand, large cosmetics companies such as The Body Shop are beginning to change their attitude. A 2019 report shows that The Body Shop's profits went down by 20 per cent in 2017, only to recover after the company shifted to promoting products that had only been tested either on humans or via computer programs.
>
> Away from cosmetics, however, there is an argument for the use of animals in medical research. Life-saving cancer drugs such as Herceptin have only been authorised by the FDA and BMA as a result of extensive safety checks provided by animal-based research before human trials.

> So, whilst there is possibly a case for the use of animals in medical research, The Body Shop's experience suggests that we do not need to use them in cosmetics research, despite the arguments around profit. Therefore, animal testing should not be used in this specific area of scientific research.

Final task

Annotate the following essay, focusing on its logic and structure. Use the PEE process in each paragraph: Point (identify the topic sentence); Evidence (note examples of research); Explanation/assessment (highlight the argument). Look also for transition words that link paragraphs and ideas. Follow the steps below.

a) Read the opening paragraph and identify PEE.
   (For example, the first sentence – the topic sentence – would be a 'point'.)
b) Then continue through the essay, highlighting these features. Identify any linking and signposting devices.
c) Then read through the essay again and pick out features of academic style.
d) Work with a partner to discuss the features you identified in a)–c). How effective and appropriate is the style? Use the four key areas as a guide.

> **Should Shakespeare be taught in schools around the world?**
>
> Shakespeare is generally acknowledged to be one of the world's greatest dramatists. A quick search online shows that schoolchildren from Azerbaijan to Zimbabwe study his plays in class to this day. Another quick search reveals how words and phrases from his plays have passed into everyday English speech. We often read paraphrases of 'to be or not to be' or hear someone talk about being 'faint-hearted' or waiting with 'bated breath' or being 'eaten out of house and home'.
>
> From a child's perspective Shakespeare's language seems hard, if not impossible, to understand, with no relevance to today's world. What was Hamlet talking about when he told Ophelia to 'get thee to a nunnery'?
>
> However, whilst the language is challenging, the stories seem to have a universal appeal. Romeo keeps meeting his 'unsuitable' Juliet in the modern world. Families the world over continue to bear 'ancient grudges' which divide them. This play (*Romeo and Juliet*) about love across a seemingly insurmountable divide can be translated to many conflicted parts of the world.
>
> From a modern inclusive perspective, Shakespeare is a 'dead White male' from the West. Many 20th-century learners from around the globe are no longer willing to be lectured at by perceived colonial icons.

Yet, Shakespeare was a natural storyteller whose tales inspire, warn and transcend space and time. Modern-day Julius Caesars, taking on more power than originally granted them, can be found throughout the world. While we are familiar with the story of treachery ('Et tu, Brute?'), Shakespeare's play reworked for modern audiences encourages us to learn the lessons of history.

Upon reflection, it would seem that there are strong reasons for not studying Shakespeare globally. His writing is dated and difficult. On the other hand, his stories are contemporary and can teach us life lessons and show us what to avoid when making choices.

So, in answer to the question, it may be that we no longer need to teach the original words in schools but the ideas that Shakespeare breathed life into in his plays should continue to be taught around the world.

References: *Hamlet* (1599–1601), *Romeo and Juliet* (1595), *Julius Caesar* (1599), *Henry VI Part I* (1591–2), *Merchant of Venice* (1596–7), *Henry IV Part II* (1597–8) by William Shakespeare.

Reflective plenary

Work with a small group. Write your own checklist of dos and don'ts for academic writing style. Keep it somewhere you can easily refer to.

3.5 Referencing

In this unit you will:
- consider what constitutes plagiarism
- learn methods of referencing and how to create a bibliography.

Critical Path
You will need to:
- deconstruct your work to distinguish between your argument and researched evidence
- communicate where you have used the words or ideas of others.

Deconstruction	Reconstruction	Reflection	Communication	Collaboration
✓			✓	

Much of the work on this course concerns sourcing information. You may be interested in and excited by your chosen topic areas, but you are not expected to know everything about them. On the other hand, you cannot simply take work done by other people and claim it as your own. You have to give credit to the originator of ideas. This is done through clear **citation** and **referencing** in **footnotes** and a **bibliography**.

Plagiarism, or the copying of others' work without acknowledgement, is an academic theft that carries serious consequences.

Key terms

citation: the method used within a text to indicate the use of someone else's work; it can either be numerical or alphabetical

referencing: an overall term referring to the acknowledgement of others' work in an essay or other research assignment

footnotes: brief details of sources collated in numerical order at the bottom of a page

bibliography: a list at the end of a piece of work detailing all the sources used; it allows a reader to check resources and explore further if they wish

plagiarism: passing off the words, work or ideas of others as if they are your own – i.e. without acknowledgement

Starting point

In small groups, consider the following case studies.

1. Ken has a deadline on Monday for his final piece of A Level coursework but has been out partying over the weekend. He has found an essay close to his topic on a model answer website. He has done a lot of research, but he just does not have time to synthesise the information from his notes. He decides to cut and paste some paragraphs into his work so that it is finished in time. Even though the written expression is radically different to the style of the rest of his work, no one will notice, right?

2. Maria has to give a valedictory speech. She is struggling with ideas, then she finds a wonderful talk given by Michelle Obama that says what she would like to say about the power of education and the determination of women. She lightly reworks it, changing the school name and expanding the stories with relevant details. She is pleased with the reaction but then notices several people on their phones searching her words on the internet…

Discuss your reactions to these stories. Is there a way that either Ken or Maria could avoid charges of plagiarism?

Any form of copying information without synthesis and referencing is considered dishonest. It is vital, therefore, that you reference and cite carefully to show you have created your argument using support from credible sources that can be consulted by your readers.

Also, overuse of quotations, even if referenced, shows a reliance on the work of others and a lack of reflection on your part.

Look at the following examples. The argument is about using animals for testing cosmetics. In the first example, the writer has simply copied some facts from the internet to set up an argument that animal testing happens, but it is cruel. Even with referencing, there is no sense of the writer presenting their own ideas by careful reading and synthesis from a range of sources.

> **Example 1**
>
> 'Animal testing on cosmetics is arguably one of the most controversial areas of animal testing'.[1] Scientists say that using animals 'is easier'[2] and 'give[s] confidence'[2] to the consumer that products will not harm them. Others say that 'animals experience discomfort and suffering in the name of aesthetics'.[1]
>
> [1] http://www.aboutanimaltesting.co.uk/animal-testing-cosmetics.html
> [2] https://www.crueltyfreeinternational.org/why-we-do-it/alternatives-animal-testing

In this second version, the writer uses research to set up a line of argument that will allow them to explore in detail two contrasting perspectives on the topic. They have 'synthesised' their reading by paraphrasing and presenting ideas from both sources.

> **Example 2**
>
> The use of animals in research on new cosmetics is a widespread but controversial issue. On one hand, a scientific perspective suggests that using animals in research is easier[1] (and therefore possibly cheaper) than other alternatives. On the other hand, animal lovers say it is cruel and unnecessary.[2]
>
> [1] http://www.aboutanimaltesting.co.uk/animal-testing-cosmetics.html
> [2] https://www.crueltyfreeinternational.org/why-we-do-it/alternatives-animal-testing

How to record sources

It does not matter where you keep the information (Workbook, notebook, digitally in Excel, Word or in Notes). What is important is that you keep a running note of certain key details. These include:
- **Source** (where you found the information – in *The Economist*/*The Straits Times* or online on a government website).
- **Author(s)** (who wrote/presented the information).
- **Date of 'publication'** (if a television story – date and time aired).
- **Title of the source** (useful to help you find the source again – or to find linking information).
- Any specifically helpful details such as **publisher**, **volume** (if in a monthly magazine or journal that can be sorted by phrases like Volume V or Spring Edition), pages, format or even key words of your search.
- If an online source, the **URL** and **date accessed**. The only time you should cut and paste is for URLs so that you can be sure to take it down accurately.

The following table gives a suggestion of how to log a source.

Source	Author(s)	Date of publication	Title	URL	Any other useful data	Date accessed
OECD/NAEC Seminar Project Zero	Veronica Boix Mansilla	February 2017	Educating for Global Competence	https://www.oecd.org/naec/Education_for_Global_Competence_BOIX_MANSILLA.pdf	Project Zero part of Harvard Graduate school. VBS is senior research associate and inspiring speaker	5 June 2020

For more information on recording sources, see Unit 7.3.

Activity 1: How to log your sources

a) Create a table like the one above. Look back at the sources you explored in Unit 3.2 and practise logging the information. Make a note of any difficulties you have.

How to do citation and write a bibliography

When you cite something, you refer to it in your work. The list or log of source information that you have kept becomes the basis of your citation. There are many different ways of citing (referencing) information and you are free to choose the method you find most accessible. Your teacher can guide you on the different methods, but here are some examples.

Footnotes
With footnotes the reference will be noted and numbered at the bottom of the relevant page of the essay. Full details would then show in the bibliography at end of the essay.

Numeric reference
With numeric reference, a reference number would be noted in the essay text:

> Global warming is commonly defined as the phenomenon of increasing average air temperatures near the surface of the earth. [5]

then followed with full details in the bibliography at the end of the essay:

[5] 'Global Warming', https://www.britannica.com/science/global-warming, 2020

Author reference
Using author reference, the author's name and the year of publication would be noted in the essay text:

> Global warming is commonly considered to be one of the major contributing factors to changes that will affect the future of global security (Canning, 1985).

then followed with full details in the bibliography at the end of the essay:

> Canning, L.J., 1985. *Global Warming*, Sydney, Green Notes.

Final task

a) In pairs, find two useful sources on a topic of plastic waste.
b) Log the details in a table.
c) Make notes on the two sources and identify how they contribute to the debate on an issue.
d) Write a paragraph that compares the perspectives of the two sources, synthesising them into your argument.
e) Decide which form of referencing to use and add it to your paragraph.

Reflective plenary

Make some careful notes to confirm what you have learned in this unit. Be sure to include your understanding of why it is important to reference your work.

Chapter 4

Ways of working

In this chapter, you will explore the skills that you need for effective independent work and determine potential benefits to your learning. By conducting a skills audit, you will identify areas for development. You will also consider what teamwork involves, analyse potential obstacles, and consider the implications of working towards shared goals and solving problems. Through critical discussion and group reflection, you will create a checklist for future use. To understand the role you play during teamwork, you will analyse a sample recording of your own contributions to working practices. You will also evaluate the ways in which failure can be productive in prompting metacognition. You will distinguish between the elements of a reflective log and use a model to complete a log entry.

The most important aspects of the Critical Path for this chapter are communication, collaboration and reflection.

4.1 Working independently
4.2 Working in a team
4.3 Developing reflection

4.1 Working independently

In this unit you will:
- identify the benefits of independent learning
- understand the skills required for effective independent working.

Critical Path

You will need to:
- communicate your reflective analysis of independent learning skills.

Deconstruction	Reconstruction	Reflection	Communication	Collaboration
		✓	✓	

Introducing independent ways of working

'Independent' work is required throughout the course, in addition to working in teams. Understanding what autonomy involves, and how it supports productive work and successful learning, will be key to your success. 'To find yourself, think for yourself.' (Socrates, 470–399 BCE)

Starting point

Work with a partner. Discuss: what does the cartoon opposite say about the potential challenges of working independently? Based on your own experiences, what advice would you give to help this student?

Independent learning and research skills are valued highly by both universities and employers. Working independently means that you are in charge of your own learning, so you make informed decisions *about* and take responsibility *for* what you do *in* and *out* of class to achieve the objectives of the syllabus. It does not always imply working alone. In fact, sharing and discussing your research and learning activities, or findings and solutions to problems, with your classmates and teachers will help you to feel more confident, organised and in control.

Quick task

Read the quotation opposite and consider your own gifts, skills and choices. Discuss how 'independently' you usually work, giving examples as evidence.

' The capacity to learn is a *gift*; the ability to learn it is a *skill*; the willingness to learn it is a *choice*. '
Brian Herbert

What are the benefits of 'independent' learning?

Independent learning and research skills are transferable to other courses of study and are of lifelong value. Being aware of effective and ineffective **learning strategies** (for example, *time saving* versus *time wasting* activities and practices) will make your life easier and help you to build independence. Discussing, evaluating and reflecting on the effectiveness and weaknesses of your own, and others', study habits will enable you to organise your time productively and work more confidently. Here are some examples to help you reflect on and improve your own study habits.

Key term

learning strategies: the techniques used to maximise your ability to learn, understand and use information, and to develop new skills and competences

Ineffective practices
- only beginning study tasks at the 'last minute'
- spending hours of time, but achieving nothing
- having no plan.

Effective practices
- working out a timetable, marking the key deadlines and tasks needed to complete on a calendar
- deciding on your most productive hours – when will you achieve most, earlier or later in the day?
- create a short goal plan with measurable tasks and times.

These independent learning skills will impact positively on your current academic studies and future professional employment opportunities. At this level, a sign of success is that you start to become the 'boss' of your own learning. Your willingness to explore different ways of working, make your own choices and take responsibility for the results are all signs of successful, powerful independent working practices.

Activity 1: Developing successful independent working practices

As Spider-Man's uncle (amongst others) told him: 'With great power, comes great responsibility.' Is the opposite true? How do individual responsibilities on this course matter? Well, you are responsible to your class when preparing to participate in a debate for instance, or otherwise the discussion will be meaningless. You are also responsible to yourself, because it's very difficult to engage in a **debate** if you are unprepared and your contributions uninformed. How does taking responsibility for your own learning 'empower' you?

a) Two of the questions in the paragraph above remain unanswered. Discuss your answers with a partner/group.
b) Work with a partner to identify your responsibilities in this course of study so far. Make a list. For example:
  - Find examples of different perspectives to prepare for class debate. individual (I)/joint (J)
  - Research and find sources for possible arguments (for and against) for an essay. I
c) Compare, expand and discuss your list with another pair. How aware is this group of the individual and joint responsibilities that you have now/for the rest of the term/course? Mark these responsibilities as I or J. Present your findings to another group.

> **Key term**
>
> **debate:** a discussion or reasoned argument that reflects different, usually contrasting perspectives on an issue

What skills are required for working independently?

The **graphic organiser** in the Final task is a type of T-Chart. It shows some of the skills that enable students to be efficient and productive both in class and while studying at home or elsewhere.

> **Key term**
>
> **graphic organiser:** a knowledge map, chart or diagram showing relationships between concepts, facts or ideas that can help you to organise your thinking and make it visual

Final task

a) The chart below outlines key independent study skills, with examples of how each one contributes to successful study on this course. Work with a partner; what examples can you add to the first two columns?

Skills for working independently	Why it's important	Do I need to improve in this area? How?
Understanding why you are doing a task or assignment, how it fits the other parts of the syllabus, e.g. knowing the success criteria (ask about a successful example?).	So I/we know what we need to do, why it matters and how to start working effectively.	
Organisational, planning and time-management skills, e.g. meeting deadlines, scheduling and planning time/tasks.	So I/we can complete tasks, plan and schedule time efficiently.	
Effective note-making, such as the use of graphic organisers, sketch-noting techniques), e.g. paraphrasing, summarising main points as I read.	'To kill two birds with one stone' – effective note-making saves time and doubles research efficiency.	
Referencing skills, e.g. include sources in notes.	So I can find information again when I need, and no time is wasted.	
The ability to evaluate how successfully you have achieved something before consulting others and being able to re-evaluate this after feedback, e.g. the ability to reflect on learning and successful achievement of tasks.	So that I am able to fine-tune and edit my work before I ask my teachers/classmates for their input – better to identify areas for improvement and fix them myself first!	
Using effective learning strategies, e.g. being proactive and using your time efficiently.	So that my studies in all subjects are easier (and helps me for future study/work!)	

b) Conduct a **skills audit** similar to the one you did in Unit 1.1, using the third column to find out the skills you need to develop. Can you help each other to identify useful strategies? (For example, use your phone's calendar to set audio/text alerts before research assignments are due.)

Reflective plenary

Work in a group. Debate this question: How does independent learning empower you for a future academic and professional life?

Key term

skills audit: an assessment of your own skills (e.g. research, knowledge management, organisation) to help you identify your competences, and areas in need of development

4.2 Working in a team

In this unit you will:
- identify the characteristics of effective communication and behaviours for teamwork
- analyse the benefits and obstacles to collaborative teamworking practices.

Critical Path
You will need to:
- communicate and collaborate with others and reflect on working in teams.

Deconstruction	Reconstruction	Reflection	Communication	Collaboration
		✓	✓	✓

Working in a team

'Teamwork' work plays a vital role in ensuring your study runs smoothly, and is key to the success of your Team Project (see Chapter 8). Working in a team implies a shared purpose, with less focus on individual opinions and ideas, and more on achieving common objectives collaboratively. Successful collaboration means that members of the team must negotiate disagreements, misunderstandings and resolve problems jointly. 'Team players' are highly sought after by employers in all sectors.

Starting point: What is 'teamwork'?

Work with a partner. Look at the picture. What do the coach's words reveal about teamwork? In your experience, how can working in a team go wrong?

How many times do I have to say it? There is no 'I' in team! Less 'me' and more 'we' please…

Activity 1: Analysis of the potential benefits and pitfalls of teamwork

a) Use a T-chart like the one below to analyse the potential benefits and pitfalls of teamwork in your own experience, when compared with working individually.

Benefits	Pitfalls
You learn from other people.	Making decisions together could be more difficult (and more time-consuming?).

None of us is as smart as all of us is.

Ken Blanchard, training and leadership author

b) Work with another group to present your ideas. Listen and share your ideas, then refine and add to these after discussion and feedback.

What does teamwork involve?

Read the following statements from teachers and students reflecting on the successes and problems they have experienced during teamwork.

A

The students in one team were neither used to working with others nor taking responsibility for their own learning. Therefore, at the start they were in competition with each other. The team were brutally honest when identifying the weaknesses of individual members, though eventually they understood how different members contributed by 'playing to their strengths'. Eventually, through discussion and observation of other teams at work, the students communicated more openly to achieve the joint goal.

Ms Sula

B

In the beginning, it was so difficult for me to have the confidence to speak up and make suggestions. Three of our team are in the same friendship group, so I felt like an outsider. Also, I don't share the same language and sometimes everyone forgets that the working language is English. Our teacher rotates the roles we have in the team each lesson. To my surprise, when I was the team leader people listened to my suggestions for improving our teamwork. We agreed to pay more attention to non-verbal communication, encourage everyone to speak and stop any tension by asking questions to clarify processes, feelings and ideas.

Latika

C

Our team meet in my house to organise ourselves. In the beginning, we spent so long disagreeing and organising ourselves to complete the team's goal that we didn't make our first deadline! This was actually a huge help because we realised that we had to communicate more openly, listen more and manage our time more strictly. We decided to use online tools to help. Our team's motto is 'all for one, and one for all, united we stand, divided we fall'!

William

D

I like working in teams because we are constantly learning from each other. I learned how to make better notes and which websites were valid for the research we need to do. I enjoy helping the team to use technology more efficiently – my best skill! Teammates have helped me improve my spoken English and taught me more formal ways of speaking. We vote and make democratic decisions because there are five of us, although I am not sure that we always choose the best option.

Nkozi

Activity 2: Identifying communication and collaborative skills needed for teamwork

a) Identify the setbacks and successes of the teamwork skills referred to in statements A–D. For example, in the first statement, look at the highlighted text:
   - setback = *students did not take responsibility for their own learning*
   - success = *students communicated more openly, understood how to 'play to different strengths', achieved the joint goal*

b) Work with a partner. Discuss how the behaviours and strategies mentioned to resolve issues are helpful (H) or unhelpful (U). For example, in the first statement, look at the highlighted text again:
   - behaviour = *students were in competition with each other* (U)
   - strategy = *students were honest when identifying the weaknesses of others* (?)
   - *discussion and observation of others* (H)

Key advice

When working on a task with others, ask permission to capture (i.e. video or audio record) a short, 3–5-minute section. In what ways did you contribute? Listen after class and analyse your input.

Final task

Work in groups. What differences can you identify between ways of working in teams and working individually? You may need to check back to Unit 4.1.

Reflective plenary

Work with a partner. Think about your work with others in this unit and prepare a list of dos and don'ts for effective collaboration. Present this to the class. Make notes of useful strategies in your reflective log or journal (see pages 73–75).

For example: DO Listen mindfully, DON'T dominate or speak over others

4.3 Developing reflection

In this unit you will:
- learn what reflection is and how it supports learning and skills development
- analyse a reflective framework (model) to develop reflective skills and write a log post.

Critical Path
You will need to:
- communicate and collaborate with others to develop and explore reflective practices.

Deconstruction	Reconstruction	Reflection	Communication	Collaboration
		✓	✓	✓

Reflection

This syllabus encourages students to be 'reflective' and describes this as being able to develop a critical awareness of your own personal viewpoints and the way in which your viewpoints influence your responses to other opinions and ways of thinking. In terms of developing effective learning skills, reflection involves thinking deeply about lesson content, reading and assignments to make links between new and previous learning. Equally important to academic success is the ability to reflect on which strategies and behaviours are helpful for learning, communication and collaboration. This implies identifying those that are *un*helpful, and exploring alternatives, expressed in the syllabus as being able to reflect on what you have learned, on your judgements, and on how you work with others.

Starting point

Analyse the quotations opposite with a partner. What, if any, lessons about failure do they suggest?

> Failure is a part of that whole process, you just learn to pick yourself up. And the quicker and more resilient you become, the better you are.

Michelle Obama

How can a reflective log help develop reflection skills?

Reflective writing in a journal or log allows you to keep track of, analyse, process and reflect on your learning experiences. The aim of keeping a reflective log is to improve and fine-tune your academic skills in all areas (i.e. communication, collaboration, thinking). When you complete the Team Project, you will also write a reflective paper which demonstrates your ability to reflect on your own learning, and the effectiveness of team collaboration. The framework that follows will help you to structure and write your log entries.

> Ever tried. Ever failed. No matter. Try Again. Fail again. Fail better.

Samuel Beckett (1983, Grove Press)

A — Experiencing events – what happened? Why?

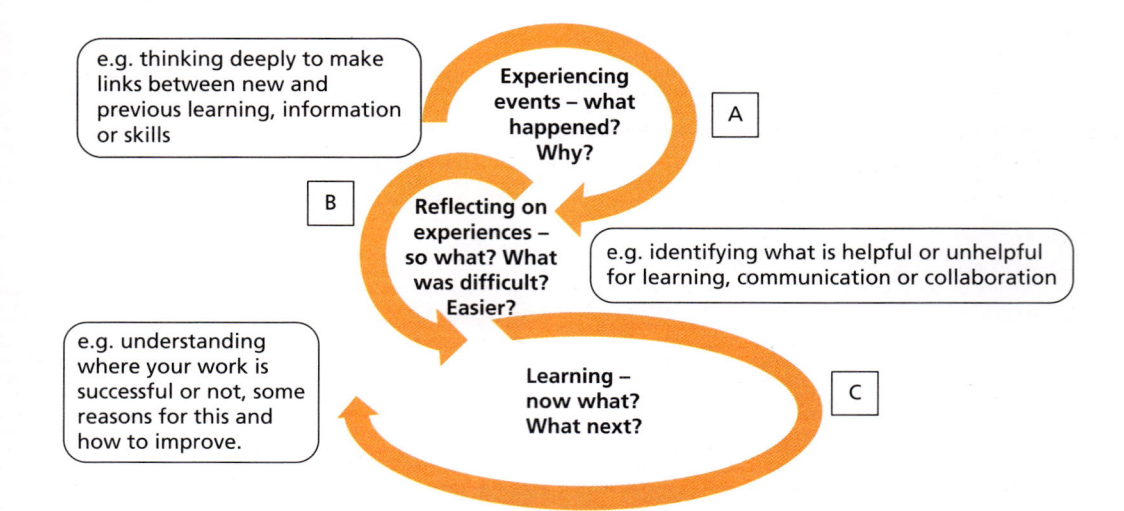

B — Reflecting on experiences – so what? What was difficult? Easier?
- e.g. identifying what is helpful or unhelpful for learning, communication or collaboration
- e.g. thinking deeply to make links between new and previous learning, information or skills

C — Learning – now what? What next?
- e.g. understanding where your work is successful or not, some reasons for this and how to improve.

Activity 1: Identifying the elements of a reflective log

a) Read these extracts from a student's reflective journal and identify which parts of the reflective learning cycle above they illustrate, A, B or C. The first paragraph has been done as an example.

> Nobody could agree on which different perspectives to use (A). I thought that the team would be better at deconstructing the sources we could use (B). I felt frustrated that our teacher had to push our team very hard (A). I/We need to meet and work out our sources and perspectives together (C).
>
> Next time, I will try to listen more and speak less. I intend to propose a different team leader and give others more space. I shall suggest task deadlines. I'm going to add diagrams and abbreviations to make my notes more visual.
>
> I achieved the learning objectives and learned from listening to others' ideas for reconstructing the arguments. My note-taking skills are getting better. I understood how important it is to communicate effectively in teamwork to achieve a shared goal.
>
> It was our team's turn to present three local problems that we identified as having significant global relevance for the class to evaluate. Two of the team did not contribute to the work. I gave the presentation and tried to involve them along the way. Nobody knows we are not collaborating effectively but me.
>
> The presentation went well, and the class gave us some feedback on how relevant they thought the issues were globally. The team members who hadn't contributed felt a bit ashamed. The communication within our team is tense outside class, but in class we are OK with each other.

b) Work with a partner to discuss if the writer demonstrates the 'ability to reflect on their own learning, their judgements and on their work with others' or not. Compare your ideas.

Activity 2: Writing a reflective log entry

a) Identify a recent learning experience, for example, the recording you made in Unit 4.2. Use the information from the diagram on page 74 and Activity 1 to help you write an entry to your reflective log.

Final task: Reflecting in groups

Think about and answer these questions. Discuss and make notes to communicate your findings with others.

a) What do you know now about reflection that you didn't know before?
b) What questions about reflecting do you still have? Can you find any answers?

Quick task

In pairs, discuss the purpose, format and writing style of your reflective log.

Reflective plenary

Read a partner's reflections. What additional strategies or ideas can you suggest?

Chapter 5

Reading and responding to sources

In this chapter, you will be looking at a range of thought-provoking sources around a global topic related to space travel. You will develop skills related to tackling unfamiliar sources (ones which may be outside your own chosen interests or knowledge), ranging from picking out key information to evaluating perspectives and evidence. You will also compare the relative merits of the texts, explaining how convincing arguments are. In particular, you will learn techniques that will enable you to approach these 'unseen' texts without fear, engaging with them so that the deconstruction process is clear and useful.

5.1 Reading unseen sources
5.2 Identifying key points and issues
5.3 Writing about evidence from an unseen source
5.4 Evaluating arguments and perspectives from two sources

5.1 Reading unseen sources

In this unit you will:
- learn how to engage with unseen sources.

Critical Path
You will need to:
- read and deconstruct unseen sources.

Deconstruction	Reconstruction	Reflection	Communication	Collaboration
✓				

It is essential to develop skills to read through sources quickly and find information you are asked for. You will also need to be clear about the terms referred to in any questions, so that you focus your energies on the right elements of the sources in question.

Starting point

How do you approach an unseen or unfamiliar text for the first time if you have limited time to read it? Discuss with a partner any core techniques you use and agree on the ones you find most useful.

How can 'reading pointers' help with tackling unseen source texts?

When facing one or more unseen texts for a task, you can use a range of pointers to help you read and focus on the relevant information.

Pointer 1: The general topic. When you are looking at two sources, look out for the common topic that the two sources share (for example, 'climate change'). If you are asked to identify issues, they may be linked to that topic – for example, 'rising sea levels' or 'food shortages'.

Pointer 2: Key words in questions. In a task, you may be asked about 'evidence', the 'impact of the evidence on a perspective' and to 'evaluate' how 'convincing' the two 'arguments' and 'perspectives' are. All these terms should be familiar to you, so as you read, bear in mind that this is ultimately what you will be writing about.

Pointer 3: Reading skills. Knowing what to look for helps you read efficiently. For example, you might *scan* a text to find factual information or data – something that is often used as evidence for an argument – or for the name of a quoted expert. Then, you might use close reading skills to *infer* from given details.

Pointer 4: Textual clues. Most longer texts are organised in ways to help the reader follow the writer's train of thought. So, you could look for how a title or an opening introduces a debate or issue, or consider how particular paragraphs cover different aspects, or how a topic sentence suggests a particular assumption or perspective. The authors' roles or the context may also provide clues. (See Chapter 2.)

Beyond these particular reading skills, when you engage with the text itself you will also need a process for breaking down the text before you answer any questions. This might involve highlighting key points or language that stand out or raise questions.

What is a good way to work through a reading for the first time?

Below is the introduction to a task based on two unseen sources, and the first paragraph of the first source. You will read the second source on page 81 of Unit 5.2. Look at the notes a student has made around it.

> The documents below consider issues related to scientific innovation. [1] Read them **both** in order to answer **all** the questions.
>
> **Document 1:** From 'Do we really need to send humans into space?' [2], an article written by Donald Goldsmith and Martin Rees for a blog on the website www.scientificamerican.com from 2020. One of the authors is a science writer, the other is Astronomer Royal of the UK and former president of the Royal Society. [3]
>
> What future lies ahead for humans in space? [4] Last year, the 50th anniversary of the first moon landing found a host of private and governmental projects that aim to [5] send astronauts far beyond the near-Earth orbits that have limited human space exploration since 1972. China [6], which landed the first spacecraft on the lunar far side in 2019, has plans to [5] place astronauts on the moon. India, which crashed a lander on the moon in 2019, dreams [5] of doing likewise. Russia, which doesn't seem to have much of an ongoing astronaut program, still provides the rockets and launch facilities that provide astronauts with access to the International Space Station. The Trump administration proposes to [5] create a lunar base as a key step in sending astronauts to Mars. Elon Musk and Jeff Bezos have spent large sums on future human space missions. Indeed, Musk has already created a thriving rocket business, which NASA uses to resupply the Space Station, 250 miles above Earth's surface.

[1] This is the topic.

[2] This is the title – it's a rhetorical question: what does it tell me about the perspective of the writers?

[3] The writers – at least one is a specialist science researcher.

[4] Topic sentence – does this give a clue about the writers' perspective?

[6] Specific example – evidence of what?

[5] These are similar phrases about the future – does this link to the writers' argument?

You may need to comment on:
- the core content (key information in the text, including issues)
- what the writers' perspective is
- the strengths or weaknesses in the evidence used in support of an argument
- how convincing the argument is.

Activity 1: Establishing the gist

This is only the first paragraph, but what can you learn about the **gist** of the whole article from it?

a) First, add your own notes, questions and annotations in the way the student has so far. Your highlighting could focus on:
   - any further examples or factual details/evidence referred to
   - any other aspects that give a clue to the focus of the text.

b) What conclusions about the text can you draw from this first paragraph? Copy and complete the summary notes below.

The opening question suggests that the text concerns…

The rest of the text gives examples of…

So, the overall gist is that lots of countries think…

> **Key term**
>
> **gist:** the overall focus or meaning of a text

> **Key advice**
>
> Your teacher may be able to provide you with more examples of texts to practise with from the Cambridge International past papers.

Now read this later paragraph from the same source. Go through it using the same reading skills to pick out any points, details or uses of language that will help you get a sense of the writers' perspective and the overall gist.

> But the past five decades have taught a clear lesson about how best to explore the cosmos. People venturing into space are fragile: They require a continuous supply of oxygen, water, food and shelter. They must endure long intervals of weightlessness. Their physical capabilities remain constant across generations. And their loss, when it occurs, casts a **pall** over our would-be joy of identifying with their exploration. In contrast, automated spacecraft require only a power supply. They cost far less than humans do, and we know how to improve them every year. And if they fail, we lose only dollars and scientific results.

*Glossary
to cast a pall over something: this means something unpleasant happens that makes an event gloomy

Final task: Building understanding

How does the second paragraph add to your understanding? Answer these brief questions about it as part of the thought process of reading source texts.

a) Is there a topic sentence that tells us the perspective of the writers here? If so, which one and what does it tell us?
b) Is an argument put forward here? If so, what is it and where?
c) What evidence is there to support the argument? Identify this in the text.
d) What, then, is the overall gist of this paragraph? Complete this statement:

The writers are suggesting that because of…

Reflective plenary

What have you learned about tackling an unseen source for the first time? Discuss with a partner or small group how the text itself, any questions provided and the reading skills you have employed could help you.

5.2 Identifying key points and issues

In this unit you will:
- identify key information from unseen sources
- communicate what you know concisely and clearly

Critical Path

You will need to:
- deconstruct specific elements from a source.

Deconstruction	Reconstruction	Reflection	Communication	Collaboration
✓			✓	

Your exploratory reading of the extracts in the previous unit ('Do we really need to send humans into space?') has helped you unpick the text so that you are ready to answer questions about it.

Starting point

What is the most effective way to identify key information in a text?

How would you approach a question asking you to identify two countries in the extracts from Unit 5.1 that have specific plans to put people into space?

Here is a suggested process:
- First, scan the text for references to key words from the question ('countries', 'plans', 'people into space').
- Now, check if they give you the answers you want.
- Note down your answers simply and concisely.

Key advice: Skimming and scanning

Choose the appropriate reading skill for the task. If asked to locate specific information, use *scanning* to run your eyes over the text, line by line, looking for any references that match what you are searching for. *Skimming* a text is more likely to be a skill you adopt in your coursework – for example, quickly checking the title and content of a web text to see if it fits what you are looking for in general.

Activity 1: Sample response

A student has noted down the following:
India and Russia.

a) Which one of these is *not* a country with a 'specific plan'?
b) What should the answer have been?

What is a good way to identify less explicit information in a text?

Sometimes, when you look at unfamiliar sources, you may be asked to identify particular issues, often problems or matters the author is addressing. Imagine you are trying to identify a range of potential issues with sending people into space. What would you look for? Does this demand the same sort of approach as when you are looking for factual information?

In fact, this is slightly more demanding, as the word 'issue' might not be used in the extract. In this case, it is a matter of looking for information from which you can infer what the issues are.

For example, here are two phrases used in the second part of the source:
- 'continuous supply of oxygen, water, food and shelter'
- 'long intervals of weightlessness'.

These give you a clue to one issue: the physical unsuitability of humans for space travel.

Activity 2

a) Look at this further quotation from the extract:

'their [humans] loss, when it occurs, casts a pall over our would-be joy of identifying with their exploration'

What is the issue or problem here with human space exploration? Write down your response in a simple sentence.

Final task

Read this second extract on a similar topic. It is from a speech about the race to the moon made by John F. Kennedy, then President of the United States, at Rice University in 1962.

> We set sail on this new sea because there is new knowledge to be gained, and new rights to be won, and they must be won and used for the progress of all people. For space science, like nuclear science and all technology, has no conscience of its own. Whether it will become a force for good or ill depends on man, and only if the United States occupies a position of pre-eminence can we help decide whether this new ocean will be a sea of peace or a new terrifying theater of war. I do not say that we should or will go unprotected against the hostile misuse of space any more than we go unprotected against the hostile use of land or sea, but I do say that space can be explored and mastered without feeding the fires of war, without repeating the mistakes that man has made in extending his writ around this globe of ours.
>
> There is no strife, no prejudice, no national conflict in outer space as yet. Its hazards are hostile to us all. Its conquest deserves the best of all mankind, and its opportunity for peaceful cooperation many never come again. But why, some say, the moon? Why choose this as our goal? And they may well ask why climb the highest mountain? Why, 35 years ago, fly the Atlantic? Why does **Rice play Texas**?

*Glossary
Rice play Texas: a reference to inter-university sport

> We choose to go to the moon. We choose to go to the moon in this decade and do the other things, not because they are easy, but because they are hard, because that goal will serve to organize and measure the best of our energies and skills, because that challenge is one that we are willing to accept, one we are unwilling to postpone, and one which we intend to win, and the others, too.

a) Make notes or annotate a copy of the extract, picking out:
- any significant phrases or uses of language that suggest a perspective
- any content that looks like evidence to support an argument
- what you think is the gist of this extract (the main or overall focus of what Kennedy is saying).

b) Then, write answers to these questions.

1. What two examples of human achievements does Kennedy refer to?

2. What issues does Kennedy raise in relation to going (or not going) to the moon?

Reflective plenary

How would you describe the difference between explicit information and implicit information (information that you have to infer)? Jot down how this would affect the way you approach a source.

5.3 Writing about evidence from an unseen source

In this unit you will:
- identify strengths and weaknesses in the evidence of an unseen source
- develop skills to help you write more detailed responses.

Critical Path

You will need to:
- communicate in a coherent way the deconstruction you have done.

Deconstruction	Reconstruction	Reflection	Communication	Collaboration
✓			✓	

You have already learned how to assess the strengths and weaknesses of evidence in support of an argument. This unit is about putting those ideas into a coherent written response.

Starting point

Work with a partner to review what makes evidence strong or weak. Note down factors for making a judgement. For example, the use of expert sources and relevant evidence would be strengths, whereas unreliable sources or a lack of knowledge on the writer's part might lead to weak or unrepresentative evidence.

What is a good way to explore an unseen source's evidence?

Look at this question:

Assess the strengths and weaknesses of the evidence used by the authors of Document 1 ('Do we really need to send humans into space?') to support their claims about the desirability of sending humans into space.

In your answer, include the impact of the evidence on the authors' perspective.

Now read this further extract from the article you started in Unit 5.1. You will also need to keep in mind the earlier extracts you read. Look at the initial annotations a student has made.

> The contrast between astronaut and automated space missions will grow ever stronger as we improve our miniaturization, virtual-reality and artificial-intelligence capabilities. Today a trained geologist on the moon can perform as well as a robotic explorer, but the future of geologic investigation of other worlds lies with highly improved versions of our Mars rovers. These explorers will deploy numerous tools to probe rocks and minerals, using a memory equal—and soon superior—to any human's. They will traverse the lunar or Martian surface for decades, continuously learning about the topography, seismographic activity and distribution of geologic strata in bulk and in detail. Conceptually similar robots will eventually be able to repair spacecraft at the L2 point, while others could construct complex structures in space, including an array of radio telescopes on the radio-quiet far side of the moon.
>
> […] Those who feel that our automated planetary explorers can never come close to the human experience in uplifting our spirits may find a modest rebuttal in our robotic explorers on Mars, which have commanded widespread attention and even some human identification during their years on the red planet. NASA's Opportunity rover, for example, spent more than 15 years on Mars and traversed complex topography for more than two dozen miles, at a price tag that is almost certainly less than 1 percent of what a comparable human expedition would cost today.

Annotations:
- claim made by authors
- examples of human technological developments
- some balance of evidence?
- possible evidence of past success?

Activity 1: Understanding the gist and key points

Make brief notes on the following:

a) What is the context from, or in which, the authors are writing? (The context might relate to: the authors' situation; the general area of interest; the medium in which the source was produced; or a particular event or development politically, socially or culturally.)
b) What is the overall perspective of the writers about space travel?
c) What other evidence (in addition to what they say about the effects on human physical and emotional capacity) do they cite to support what they say in this extract? (For example, examples of NASA's unmanned space exploration.)
d) In your initial view, how strong or weak is the evidence the writers have provided in this extract and the earlier ones?

Exploring responses

A response to a question on the strengths and weaknesses of evidence must address the factors listed in the table below. Copy and complete the table, building on your initial reading to add comments based on all the extracts from this source.

Factors to look for	Strengths	Weaknesses
Status/reliability of authors, motive to be accurate	One author is former President of Royal Society	This could be perceived as a Western-centric article, with the authors writing from a position of academic privilege.
Purpose or context of article	In a scientific journal	
Use of expert or official sources		
Range/balance of evidence		
Relevant or plausible evidence		
Use of statistics or data (vague or specific, relevant, etc.)		

Now, read the opening to a response by the same student.

The authors of the article make the assumption that improved technology will increase the potential for unmanned space missions. They cite three areas – 'miniaturization, virtual-reality and artificial-intelligence capabilities' – which are all relevant examples of factors that can affect automated space exploration. However, the authors acknowledge current evidence that 'a trained geologist on the moon can perform as well as a robotic explorer'. The use of technical language, examples of past space missions (the Mars rover) and the authors' journalistic credibility all strengthen their perspective further.

It is fair to say, then, that because this article sits in a scientific journal, there is a sense that its audience (likely to be academic) will take the evidence of the writers as reliable. However, it is not perfect.

Annotations:
- Opening sentence summarises a key aspect: the assumption made, but the question asks about evidence.
- Selected quotation provides detail of evidence authors mention.
- Signposts balanced evidence.
- Good summary of the positives.

Activity 2: Identifying strengths and weaknesses

a) Compare/share your findings with a partner, and agree on the overall strength or weakness of the evidence.

Final task

Write a further paragraph explaining the strengths or weaknesses of the evidence in the rest of the article. You could comment on:
- the amount of statistical evidence provided (or not provided)
- the use (or lack of use) of official sources
- anything else you can think of.

Try not to stray into discussing aspects like assertions or assumptions. These relate particularly to the expression of the *argument* which, whilst important, is not the focus here.

You could start:

A further strength/weakness of the evidence provided is that…

Reflective plenary

What key factors are you likely to write about when assessing the strengths and weaknesses of evidence? Write down at least three aspects you can recall (without looking at the table on page 84). Work with a partner to create a mnemonic (memory aid) to help you remember them.

5.4 Evaluating arguments and perspectives from two sources

In this unit you will:
- read two longer sources and respond to the arguments in them
- learn how to structure and convey your points coherently.

Critical Path

You will need to:
- deconstruct the key elements of two sources
- communicate your findings clearly.

Deconstruction	Reconstruction	Reflection	Communication	Collaboration
✓			✓	

Starting point

Read the following task. Highlight or note down the key words or phrases from the question that give clues as to what you have to do or focus on. The notes have been started for you.

The two sets of authors present different arguments and perspectives on whether we should continue sending humans into space. Evaluate the arguments and perspectives of both sets of authors.

In your answer, include a reasoned judgement about whether one set of authors is more convincing than the other.

Notes

- 'both sets of authors' – I need to refer to both documents A and B
- 'different arguments and perspectives' – this tells me the authors have different views and opinions

What skills need to be demonstrated?

You will need to:
- identify and compare key elements of the two arguments
- analyse and compare the two perspectives
- evaluate the key elements of the arguments in a balanced way
- make a judgement or come to reasonable conclusions about the arguments, supported by evidence from the text(s)
- write in a well-structured, logical way, sustaining your viewpoint.

If necessary, check your understanding of the terms here based on your previous study.

Activity 1: Engaging with the two texts

a) You have already read extracts from Document 1, but read it again below and then read Document 2. For Document 2, follow the same process as when you first read the extracts from Document 1. Highlight or note down:

- any significant key phrases or uses of language that suggest a perspective
- any content that looks like evidence to support an argument
- what you think is the gist of the extract (the main or overall focus of what the author is saying).

Document 1: This is an abridged version of 'Do we really need to send humans into space?', an article written by Donald Goldsmith and Martin Rees for a blog on the website www.scientificamerican.com from 2020. One of the authors is a science writer, the other is Astronomer Royal of the UK and former President of the Royal Society.

Do we really need to send humans into space?

What future lies ahead for humans in space? Last year, the 50th anniversary of the first moon landing found a host of private and governmental projects that aim to send astronauts far beyond the near-Earth orbits that have limited human space exploration since 1972. China, which landed the first spacecraft on the lunar far side in 2019, has plans to place astronauts to the moon. India, which crashed a lander on the moon in 2019, dreams of doing likewise. Russia, which doesn't seem to have much of an ongoing astronaut program, still provides the rockets and launch facilities that provide astronauts with access to the International Space Station. The Trump administration proposes to create a lunar base as a key step in sending astronauts to Mars. Elon Musk and Jeff Bezos have spent large sums on future human space missions. Indeed, Musk has already created a thriving rocket business, which NASA uses to resupply the Space Station, 250 miles above Earth's surface.

But the past five decades have taught a clear lesson about how best to explore the cosmos. People venturing into space are fragile: They require a continuous supply of oxygen, water, food and shelter. They must endure long intervals of weightlessness. Their physical capabilities remain constant across generations. And their loss, when it occurs, casts a pall over our would-be joy of identifying with their exploration. In contrast, automated spacecraft require only a power supply. They cost far less than humans do, and we know how to improve them every year. And if they fail, we lose only dollars and scientific results.

[...] The contrast between astronaut and automated space missions will grow ever stronger as we improve our miniaturization, virtual-reality and artificial-intelligence capabilities. Today a trained geologist on the moon can perform as well as a robotic explorer, but the future of geologic investigation of other worlds lies with highly improved versions of our Mars rovers. These explorers will deploy numerous tools to probe rocks and minerals, using a memory equal—and soon superior—to any human's. They will traverse the lunar or Martian surface for decades, continuously learning about the **topography**, **seismographic** activity and distribution of **geologic strata** in bulk and in detail. Conceptually similar robots will eventually be able to repair spacecraft at the L2 point, while others could construct complex structures in space, including an array of radio telescopes on the radio-quiet far side of the moon.

[…] Those who feel that our automated planetary explorers can never come close to the human experience in uplifting our spirits may find a modest rebuttal in our robotic explorers on Mars, which have commanded widespread attention and even some human identification during their years on the red planet. NASA's Opportunity rover, for example, spent more than 15 years on Mars and traversed complex topography for more than two dozen miles, at a price tag that is almost certainly less than 1 percent of what a comparable human expedition would cost today.

From scientificamerican.com

*Glossary

topography: the way a landscape and its physical features are arranged

seismographic: describes the movement of earth or ground

geologic strata: layers of rock

Document 2: The following article, 'Space colonisation is not only desirable, but essential', comes from an Indian blogger, writing on her own personal website.

Space colonisation is not only desirable, but essential

We live in challenging times. A global pandemic, continued problems with conflict, poverty and the sheer pace of climate change, have led many ordinary people and policy makers and leaders to re-evaluate our priorities, and what the future holds. It is in that context that we should welcome the initiatives of Elon Musk and Jeff Bezos in the arena of space travel, and the renewed interest from countries as diverse as China, Russia and my own country, India, in putting more people into space.

In August 2018, a group of 60 prominent scientists and engineers met behind closed doors at the University of Colorado Boulder to discuss an issue which smacks more of Star Wars than an academic discussion – Mars colonisation. The conference was organised by Elon Musk's SpaceX but was attended by members of NASA's Mars exploration programme. It had a serious objective – to begin putting into place plans for landing, building and sustaining a human colony on Mars within the next 40 to 100 years.

But why? Surely the difficulties humans face in surviving in a space environment makes this a pointless exercise? And why, too, risk the potential of conflict with other nations outside our old friends the USA, who might view such a plan as an exercise in empire building? Even surveys suggest it's not top of anyone's list of priorities. A **PEW** centre study in 2018 of US adults found that of NASA's current programmes, putting humans on Mars ranked only 8th out of the 9 programmes listed.

But that was then, this is now. The truth is that many of us already believe that humankind's future on Earth cannot be sustained. The late great Stephen Hawking, speaking to the BBC on their *Tomorrow's World* programme in 2016 said he believed that climate change, potential asteroid strikes, epidemics and population growth would mean humans would need to find a new planet to populate within the next 100 years or so. He said, 'I strongly believe we should start seeking alternative planets for possible habitation. We are running out of space on earth and we need to break through technological limitations preventing us living elsewhere in the universe.' Elon Musk has talked about the need for what he calls a 'back-up' planet. Well, if they said so, then who am I to argue? Our own Prime Minister, Nahendra Modi, in his annual Independence Day speech in 2018 also stated, 'We have decided that by 2022, when India completes 75 years of independence, or before that, a son or daughter of India will go to space with a tricolour [Indian flag] in their hands.'

Manned space travel and exploration is about humanity's future, but it is also to do with national pride and achievement – to demonstrate what we are capable of. 50 years after we put a man on the Moon, surely we can go one better and put a whole community there or on another planet?

*****Glossary**
PEW: a 'think-tank', named after the family who founded it, that conducts research into issues, trends and attitudes in the world today

This read-through and note-taking is only your quick first response. To answer the more detailed question above, you will need to focus on the specific elements you have been asked about.

Here are one student's notes on the two arguments that she has identified so far.

Document 1	Document 2
• Lots of evidence about countries wanting to send more manned flights into space • NASA already involved with private investors • The past 'five decades' prove humans are 'fragile' • Supplies, weightlessness • Emotional cost • Automation is better because…	• 'Challenging times', problems facing the world • Lots of businesses and countries think future is in space • Conference in Colorado in 2018 – Mars colonisation • But, survey of US adults…

Activity 2: Identifying the arguments

a) Complete the notes, adding any further points in support of an argument or perspective. Then, jot down what you think the perspective of each set of authors is.

b) You will have already assessed how strong or weak the evidence is for Document 1. Make some brief notes about the relative strength or weakness of the evidence in Document 2. For example:

- 'Conference in Colorado' – strong because scientists from NASA so has authority, but weak in that it's US-based, so not necessarily balanced. Also, does not indicate whether they all agreed with proposition to colonise Mars.

Structuring a response

There is no set way to structure your response to the task, but you will need to:
- logically set out your views
- refer to the two texts
- compare the two texts
- draw conclusions, both along the way and at the end.

Here is a possible plan you could follow:

Introduction
A brief summary of the topic and the two different articles.

Body of the essay
The particular arguments made against manned space travel in Document 1.
The particular arguments for space travel in Document 2.
An evaluation of these arguments and perspectives.

Interim conclusion
How convincing Document 1 is and why/why not.
How convincing Document 2 is and why/why not.

Conclusion
Sum up your overall, balanced view, saying which of the two articles is the more convincing.

What could an introduction look like?

Read this example of a simple, clear opening to the essay.

Both [3] articles address the issue of humans continuing or planning to travel in space [1] with Document 1 detailing the particular effects of space travel on humans, and its benefits or problems [2], whereas [3] Document 2 tackles the wider needs and desires of nations and societies. [2]

[1] A general summary of the over-arching topic.

[2] Concisely explains the focuses of Documents 1 and 2.

[3] Signposting terms help compare and contrast.

> **Quick task**
>
> Does the essay opening give a hint at the different perspectives of the two sets of authors? If so, what is it?

How should paragraphs in the body of the essay be constructed?

Read this first paragraph from one student's response. Look at the way they have identified a key argument in one document and compared it with a point from the other.

Document 1 argues that past history of space travel has proved that humans do not cope with it well. [1] The authors cite the constant requirement to supply 'oxygen, water, food and shelter' [2] and also the financial cost [3] of sending humans into space. They support this with reference to the ability of improved versions of the Mars Rover [4] to carry out complex research for 'decades'.

Document 2, on the other hand, [5] counters this argument [6] directly. The author asks, 'Surely the difficulties humans face in surviving in a space environment makes this a pointless exercise?' but then goes on to dismiss this, not through arguing humans can do as good a job as machines, but by suggesting people will have to travel in space, regardless, due to the threats to Earth. [7]

[1] A clear statement of one argument.

[2] Apt quotation fluently embedded in text.

[3] [4] further point/evidence supporting the argument.

[5] Signals a contrasting, but related point.

[6] Points out use of counter-argument.

[7] Explains the counter-argument in Document 2.

> **Key advice: Embedding quotations**
>
> When you include a direct quotation (the actual words written by an author from a source), remember to put them in speech marks. You should always insert them into the sentence so they work grammatically. You will sometimes need to edit or reduce the quotation to fit your sentence style.

> **Activity 3: Structuring paragraphs on the arguments**
>
> a) Referring to both documents, write a paragraph (or two if you have the space) in which you explain these further two arguments. If you can see a direct link or contrast between them, then use signposting words or phrases such as 'on the other hand' to introduce the contrasting point. You can also link between them if the points are different, if not actually contrasting.
>
> **The argument points:**
>
> A: Humans die during space exploration – creates suffering – reduces enjoyment of human exploration
>
> B: Travel in space – national pride – India's PM – achievement

Quotations you could use:

Document 1: 'And their loss, when it occurs, casts a pall over our would-be joy of identifying with their exploration.'

'… automated spacecraft… cost far less than humans do, and we know how to improve them every year. And if they fail, we lose only dollars and scientific results.'

Document 2: ' "We have decided that by 2022, when India completes 75 years of independence, or before that, a son or daughter of India will go to space with a tricolour [Indian flag] in their hands." '

'Manned space travel and exploration is about humanity's future, but it is also to do with national pride and achievement – to demonstrate what we are capable of.'

You could start:

The authors of Document 1 highlight one harsh reality of space travel, which is that…

What is a good way to sum up how convincing an argument is?

You will already have addressed the strengths and weaknesses of the arguments in terms of the evidence provided, the particular assumptions, and so on. Here are some other aspects you need to consider.

How well structured the argument is. For example:
- Is it logical and sustained? Can the line of thinking be traced clearly from start to finish? For example, you might argue that the reference in Document 2 to Modi's desire to put someone from India into space is not necessarily a logical part of an argument about *why* it should be done.
- How strong or well-argued is the conclusion? You could look at the extent to which a final paragraph makes a further appeal to the reader or draws together the core ideas that preceded it. For example, you might feel the final paragraph of Document 1 just provides a new point rather than really reaching out to the reader or drawing things together.

How well the argument appeals to the reader emotionally. For example:
- Are there first-hand accounts? Abstract, general observations or accounts can sometimes have less impact than a specific person's 'story' or views.
- Is there effective rhetorical language or imagery? Writers often use rhetorical flourishes – grand statements or powerful pictures that lodge in the reader's mind. For example, in an article about space, a writer might ask you to picture Neil Armstrong placing a foot on the moon's surface.
- Does the author use personal or human appeal? You could look out for the use of 'I' or 'we' as a form of inclusiveness – we are all in this together.
- There might also be a call to action – an appeal to the reader to act or not let an opportunity pass.

Activity 4: Identifying further convincing factors

a) Document 2 could be considered to be more convincing in terms of some of these factors. Find each example and note down a suitable quotation or phrase from the extract that you could refer to in a response.

Factor	Example
Final paragraph concludes argument with a rhetorical appeal to the reader	'50 years after we put a man on the moon…'
Direct quotation from respected figure(s)	
Strong imagery or vision	

How would this be summed up in writing?

If you can, summing up ideas as you progress through your essay is effective, as you are continually drawing things together. In order to do this:

- state clearly what you do and don't find 'convincing'
- use language that synthesises or draws points together
- continue to refer to points from the text, but don't repeat word for word anything you have said earlier.

For example, note how this student has commented positively on the strengths of Document 2 in relation to one of the factors above.

I find the structure and emotional appeal of the author of Document 2 more convincing. She proceeds from setting out the context in which manned space travel is being considered, and then raises counter-arguments before referring to a number of well-known figures directly to support what she says. The final paragraph is convincing because it makes an emotional appeal to the reader by rhetorically asking why shouldn't it be possible to put a 'whole community' on a planet.

— The factors drawn together.
— Clear statement of what the student thinks.
— Further reference to points in the text to exemplify conclusions drawn.

Activity 5: Summing up

a) Write an interim summative paragraph, drawing conclusions about how convincing the technological evidence/expertise of the authors of Document 1 is.

Use this structure to help you:

- *One area in which the authors of Document 1 are convincing is that of…*
- *For example, they…*
- *They are particularly convincing when referring to…*

Writing a conclusion

In addition to interim summative conclusions summing up particular aspects or areas, you will also need an overall conclusion. In this, you will need to:

- look back over the two documents *as a whole*
- draw together the aspects you have highlighted as strengths in what has been said
- compare the two documents using suitable comparative language.

Final task

Using this framework, write a concluding paragraph summing up the arguments and why you found them convincing.
- *Overall, I thought that Document 1 was convincing in...*
- *Document 2 was equally convincing in...*
- *However,...* (You could use this to set out any specific differences or strengths of one or other of the documents.)

Reflective plenary

Compare your conclusion with a partner's and check to see if both yours and your partner's effectively meet the criteria set out in the Final task. If necessary, rewrite your conclusion.

Chapter 6

Planning and researching a coursework essay

In this chapter, you will explore topics that interest you and provide opportunities for an essay investigating global perspectives on your chosen issue. You will develop an effective question for the title of your essay that will enable you to research productively. In addition, you will learn how to manage your time efficiently so you can plan, write and edit your essay successfully to meet a deadline.

The most important aspects of the Critical Path for this chapter will be deconstruction, reconstruction and reflection. When selecting a topic and research question, you will consider your own perspective and those that others hold on an issue. Then you will analyse and evaluate the sources you identify.

6.1 Choosing a topic
6.2 Time management
6.3 Research for your coursework essay

6.1 Choosing a topic

In this unit you will:
- explore and identify global topics of particular interest to you
- construct an appropriate question for an essay title.

Critical Path

You will need to:
- reflect on areas of interest to you and evaluate why you find these topics interesting
- understand your original perspective on these topics in order to shape your response when you deconstruct different sources of information.

Deconstruction	Reconstruction	Reflection	Communication	Collaboration
✓	✓	✓		

The focus in this unit is on finding a suitable issue of interest to you and formulating an appropriate question that sets up a 'yes/no' discussion for the essay. This is important, because choosing a high-quality question and topic will enable you to exploit fully your skills and knowledge.

Starting point

Checking out potential topics

What particular issues or concerns interest you? Perhaps you find fast-fashion trends worrying, or you are interested in how gaming has become a multi-million dollar industry? Or you might just have a more general interest in conservation or climate change. It may be a news story or something connected to a subject you enjoy, or even a desire to explore the work or life of someone you know.

Take a few minutes to reflect on what *really* interests you. Note down two or three ideas. For the time being, don't edit or limit what you consider.

Syllabus links

The ideas you have may be stimulating and rich in potential, but they will need to link with the themes provided in the syllabus.

Activity 1: Making connections

a) Try linking your topics to the list of themes provided in the syllabus: Environment/Politics/Economics/Ethics/Culture/Science/Technology. What connections can you make? Share your ideas with a partner and see if you can help each other find new connections.

This is very much a first chance for you to 'test out' ideas, so you may find you need to start again, refine or develop your first thoughts.

Exploring topics

The topic area you select for your essay should be one that you are going to enjoy exploring and writing about. In addition, it should allow you to easily access content to use for further research. It may link with your other subjects or interests, but it must expand on them. For example, you might be studying History and be interested in how dictators came to power at that time of the Second World War. Your global essay could branch out from this to engage with perspectives on modern dictators.

General topic (from syllabus)	News or current affairs focus
Health issues Themes: Science/Economics/Ethics/Culture	Global diseases: Coronavirus, Ebola, Zika
Industrial pollution or **Climate change** Themes: Environment/Politics/Economics/Science	Plastic waste and how countries are tackling it
Global inequality Themes: Politics/Economics/Technology/Culture	Access to higher education and its costs – how in some countries education is free, but in many, costs are prohibitive

Remember – whatever topic and focus you select, you will need to consult a range of global sources, so make sure your selected topic has enough material to support your research.

Exploring your own interests

You have already begun to consider your own interests in relation to the topics listed in the syllabus. You could also think about how these interests link with the subjects you are studying. For example, you could link:

- Geography studies with the environment/**demographics**/global business
- Science studies with robotics/disease prevention/renewable energy
- History/Art/English studies with education/human rights/global law.

A further step is to consider what you might want to study in the future, and use this opportunity to do some initial research. For example:

- if you are planning to study International Relations, you could consider questions relating to disease, pollution, business, energy, mining or transport
- If you are planning to study an Art and Design course, you might consider questions in relation to town planning/architecture, access to or funding for the arts, well-being, public **policy**, and so on.

> **Key terms**
>
> **demographics:** data relating to population or groups in a population, such as age, wealth or what people spend money on (used by governments or other authorities to drive or justify policy)
>
> **policy:** a course of action taken by an individual or organisation, but usually intended to mean a planned strategy or approach

> **Activity 2: Linking study to topics**
>
> a) What links can you make between the topics and issues you selected in the starter activity on page 95 and the subjects you are studying now? Make a note of any connections you identify. Present these to a partner and see if you can identify further connections.

Other considerations when selecting a topic

Beyond those topics that you have an interest in, or link to subject areas, you also need to consider whether the selected topic allows for genuine debate.

You need to:
- ensure your issue is reasonably **controversial** or provocative, so that you can engage contrasting perspectives. This will help you create a strong line of argument in your essay.
- ensure you can look at the topic both *objectively* and *empathetically*. You should avoid choosing a topic that you feel so strongly about that you would be unwilling to engage with contrasting viewpoints.

Consider as a topic the divide between the secular values and religious beliefs. This often stirs up deep feelings and may make it difficult for a student to put themselves in the shoes of those with contrasting views. Selecting such an emotive topic could lead to a one-sided essay that does not fulfil the requirements of this kind of writing. This does not mean it should be avoided, but you may have to work harder to present the range of perspectives in an objective way.

> **Key term**
>
> **controversial:** likely to invoke strong opposition; the term 'controversy' is often applied to a particular issue or the actions of a particular person; controversial figures might be those who are seen to go against social norms or conventions

Activity 3: Are any topics off limits?

a) Work with a partner. Make a list of topics or issues you consider off limits.

b) Compare and justify your ideas with another pair.

Note: Think carefully – some ideas might prove to be topics that provoke really interesting debates, so do not dismiss them without considering why exploring alternative perspectives will help your critical-thinking skills.

What types of questions work best?

The best sort of question is one that invites a response that varies depending on the respondent's perspective or knowledge. You could think of these as 'yes/no' questions.

For example: Should governments place renewable energy at the top of their agenda?

If you think about this, you could argue:
- Yes: because of the lack of primary energy resources and the need to save the environment.
- No: because some countries are at a stage in their development where they still need to use fossil fuels to catch up economically.

You might hold one point of view, but you can easily see that someone else might have a different perspective. As a result of this difference in opinion, a line of argument can be constructed.

Consider this question: *Has the internet changed society?*

You need to ask yourself: does this question provoke debate? The answer is, probably not. Few, if any, would argue that the internet has not changed society. If the question does not allow you space to consider a range of perspectives, there is also the danger you will go off topic into other, unrelated areas.

A better question, linked to a 'Human rights' or 'Political power and resistance' topic, might be: *Have social media platforms helped or hindered oppressed groups?* This is both a narrower focus (not just about the internet in general) and more open to debate.

You also need to avoid questions with a focus that is insufficiently global, or too local. For example:
- Should Florida ban plastic bags?
- Is demolishing the slums the best way to address Mumbai's inequalities?

What questions encourage effective research?

Think carefully about the topics related to the questions you select. You need to be certain that you can access suitable source material to research in order to write an effective answer. This material could be composed of newspaper articles, academic research, published books and journals, and websites from reputable sources.

It is clear that governments' attitude to conservation and its impact is an issue for which there is plenty of content, but consider the following question:
- Does music have a negative effect on listeners?

Not only is this question very wide and general in scope (What are 'negative effects'? What music? What particular songs/bands – all of them? All listeners?) It is also one for which finding concrete evidence will be challenging, even if there are differing opinions on the issue itself.

Activity 4: Testing out questions

Decide for yourself what you think about the following questions, using the rationale established above, namely:
- Will they allow you to have a genuine 'yes/no' debate?
- Do they avoid being too 'local'? Or too vague and general?
- Can you research them? Would there be sufficient source material?

a) First, rank the questions below from 1 (best) to 10 (worst) in the order you think would work best.
b) Share your ideas and decide which are effective or not, and why.

- Should capital punishment be outlawed?
- Should conservation be placed higher on political agendas in sub-Saharan Africa?
- University education: a good or bad thing?
- Should there be a moratorium on social media companies' use of AI development?
- Is fracking the answer to our energy crisis?
- Should our local government invest more in leisure facilities?
- Can the crisis in Syria be solved by the United Nations?
- Do national security issues justify governments limiting access to information?
- Should cities become traffic free?
- Should we protect nature where it is possible to do so?

c) Rewrite and improve any questions that don't fulfil your requirements.

How should questions be worded?

There is no absolute right way to word questions but if you are struggling to construct them, then you could consider starting with the verbs "Should", "Is", "Are", "Do", "Does". Think carefully about whether words and phrases such as 'How' (descriptive), 'How far' (discursive) and questions involving 'either/or' (choice that does not invite a direct 'yes/no' response) will deliver the sort of argument you wish to make in your essay.

Activity 5: Practising wording questions

a) Imagine you are considering people paying for basic healthcare – for example, routine visits to a doctor or emergency visits to a hospital – as a topic. Work with a partner to create an effective question, using the advice above. Compare your wording with others, and suggest ways to improve questions.

Reflective plenary

What have you learned so far? Write down the two or three most important points about selecting topics and questions in your reflective journal or Workbook.

Key advice

As early in the essay writing process as you can, do some basic library and online searches to see how much information is readily available to you. If you are struggling to find material, then it is unlikely to be a suitable topic to pursue. Once you have identified a topic that engages you, you should test it by asking your teacher, classmates, parents or relatives about it, and start to assess which themes can reveal different perspectives.

Key advice

The skills you develop here in relation to suitable and available sources of research will help prepare you for the Team Project and the Cambridge Research Report, in which even more extensive research will be needed. Keep a note of websites or reputable sources which you can return to in later units. (See Chapters 8, 10 and 11.)

Special focus: Case study

A student called Tatenda is trying to come up with a question for her essay. This is the process she follows.

Stage 1: Selecting a broad topic

Using the first phases of the process above, Tatenda has decided she wants to explore the topic of plastic waste and the environment. She is studying Geography A Level and wants to pursue Conservation at university.

Stage 2: Exploration

Through class discussion and basic research, Tatenda begins to think about what the topic means to her. This is what she comes up with:

- recent whale deaths on local beaches (local news feeds)
- plastic bags clogging up local rivers (a discussion about pollution)
- news stories about local clean-up groups, which complain about fast-food outlets.

Stage 3: Development

As she progresses, Tatenda logs her ideas in her reflective journal.

- My initial response: Plastic waste is destroying the oceans and rivers and making a mess of the environment.
- I need to research what constitutes 'waste'.
- I need to research specific examples of such waste globally.
- I will draw up a schema of plastic waste.

Example schema

[Schema diagram centred on "Plastic waste" with four connected bubbles:
- bags, cotton buds, disposable nappies, drinks bottles, food packaging, straws, coffee on the go, plastic cutlery, feminine hygiene products
- vegetables/fruit storage, fashion multibuys, meat/fish, carrying shopping, rubbish receptacles, travel convenience, water
- recyclable, health, edible, cleanliness
- economics, science, technology, culture]

Stage 4: Evaluation

By looking at Stages 1 and 2, Tatenda starts to decide how suitable and achievable the topic is for her. Can she research and write a 2000-word essay on it?

- Is it global? Yes – examples of river and ocean pollution can be found in all areas of the world. Areas researched could include the Ganges and rivers in Pretoria, South Africa.
- Are there different themes involved? Yes, though be aware you don't have to cover everything. Clearly economics, environment, politics, science and technology, culture, and even ethics can all illuminate the topic.
- Does the topic engage discussion when raised? Yes, some classmates argue for convenience and cleanliness when shopping. Some argue about the culture of using straws to avoid touching a glass. Others argue that wildlife is vital to our planet and discuss pictures of starving sea birds with plastic rings around their necks. They, too, argue about the ethics of dumping rubbish without thought.

Stage 5: Narrowing the topic

Tatenda now feels she is in a position to start to narrow the topic into an issue that could set up a question.

- Using the schema drawn up, Tatenda starts to isolate areas and themes that are of particular interest or that she knows she can research.
- Tatenda notices that environmentally there is much evidence of plastic waste killing marine life and polluting freshwater supplies.
- She also notices that there is an economic perspective, where employment and trade are involved with the manufacture and distribution of plastic.

Stage 6: Working towards a question

Tatenda starts to pose questions to explore, trying to use the correct command words.

- Is plastic waste the primary source of environmental pollution?
- Should governments increase their spending on reducing plastic pollution?
- How far is plastic waste damaging our environment?
- Plastic waste is the main cause of oceanic pollution. Discuss.

Final task

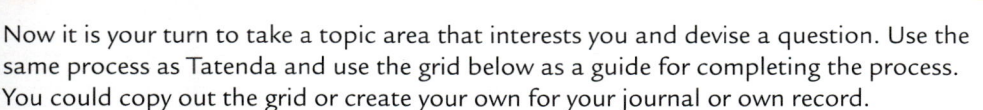

Now it is your turn to take a topic area that interests you and devise a question. Use the same process as Tatenda and use the grid below as a guide for completing the process. You could copy out the grid or create your own for your journal or own record.

Stages	Focus	My notes	Done?
1 Selecting a broad topic	Consider interests, news, further study		
2 Exploration	What does the topic mean to me?		
3 Development	Log ideas – what are my initial reactions? What do I need to research? Have I done a schema?		
4 Evaluation	Test the suitability of your topic. Is it a global issue? Does it engage different themes? Does it set up some form of argument/discussion?		
5 Narrowing the topic	Narrow the topic into issues that could engage a 'yes/no' discussion. Use the schema to select areas of interest. What themes arise? Do the themes lead to contrasting perspectives?		
6 Working towards a question	What possible questions could I use? Log them and decide which offer most in terms of my essay.		

Selecting the final question

At the end of the process above, you should be ready to decide what question you will write about. Draft it now and then evaluate it against the criteria below.

Success criteria

Make sure you have:
- chosen a topic that is meaningful or enjoyable to you
- selected a global topic that will invoke controversy or debate (without being offensive to faith or ethnicity)
- checked there are alternative perspectives
- checked there are sufficient resources you can access
- considered how to make the question clear and simple, with a 'yes/no' response.

> **Reflective plenary**
>
> Write up your initial ideas for your essay in your journal or Workbook, and add your key action points to take forward from this point. Make a note of any further obstacles or issues that you are unsure of, or which you feel you need to further explore – whether these are practical ones (such as access to sources) or academic ones (such as concern over the process or the style of question you have settled on).

6.2 Time management

In this unit you will:
- plan your time for researching, developing and writing your essay.

Critical Path
You will need to:
- balance time spent on developing your question, research, writing and editing.

Deconstruction	Reconstruction	Reflection	Communication	Collaboration
✓	✓	✓	✓	✓

How do you plan your time?

The focus in this unit is on developing a plan that suits the way you work and the time you have available for your coursework essay. You may start by thinking you have unlimited time, but the year passes quickly, and you need to manage your time carefully to balance research, writing and editing the essay.

Starting point

What kind of time manager are you? Do you leave everything to the last moment or do you meticulously set out a step-by-step approach on day one of a project?

Work with a partner to discuss these questions:

1. How do you organise your assignments/your day/week?
2. Are you a morning or an evening person?

How could your answers affect your coursework essay? Note ideas for how best to schedule *your* tasks and time effectively.

Key advice

As the deadline for your coursework essay is absolute (your teachers will give guidance on use of time in your particular setting), time management will be essential. Ultimately, it is your responsibility to work efficiently and ensure you submit a well-researched, well-structured, polished, effectively supported essay that is mechanically correct by the deadline set by your school or college.

Activity 1: How will you plan, log and check your progress?

a) Following on from the starter activity, work with your partner to decide how the following might help you:
- notebook or note-taking app
- diary planner or scheduling app
- log for keeping research details
- checklist of requirements.

b) What other useful planning tools could you recommend?

How much time should you spend on each stage of the project?

Look at the table below showing the stages you need to work through in order to complete this assignment. Notice that the majority of your time will be spent in preparation and editing rather than actual writing.

The table is simply a guide, but you should notice how many tasks are in each section and plan your time accordingly.

Quick task

Read the table below. How could you use it to help you plan and manage your essay? Discuss your reactions with a partner(s), e.g. *I didn't expect..., I didn't know that..., It surprises me to see that...*

Preparation	Topic selection Devising question Research Brainstorming Planning Drafting (with paragraph headings as a guide – these are removed later)	45%
Execution	Writing: Introduction/perspectives/reflection (synthesis)/conclusion	10%
Finalisation	Editing Proofreading (general sense/typographic errors/spelling) Editing (structure/word count) Checking references/inserting footnotes (if used) Production of bibliography Proofreading (layout/typographical errors/spelling) Referencing	45%

What sort of weighting should you give parts of the essay?

Look at the suggested weighting of each part of the essay here. This is not a firm rule, but simply guidance to help you manage your time.

- Introduction   (360–460 words)
- Research/perspectives (700–800 words)
- Reflection/synthesis (600–700 words)
- Conclusion   (100–140 words)

Key advice

In your Workbook or notebook, keep a checklist like this and then mark off red/amber/green as you cover each point. Remember, this does not have to be an entirely linear process within each section.

How can you make sure your plans are achievable?

The SMART test is a tool that will help you judge how achievable your plans are.

Activity 2: Is your planning SMART?

a) Use the following table to check your work so far.

Specific	Is my chosen question sufficiently specific but also likely to generate an effective discussion which supports the syllabus criteria?	☐
Measurable	Have I set appropriate boundaries on my time (that I can measure)? How have I measured the effectiveness of the time I spent researching?	☐
Achievable	Am I in a position to fulfil all parts of the assignment (the requirements of the tasks in the checklist) – e.g. have I found a sufficient range of material?	☐
Realistic	How realistic has my planned schedule of research and preparation for the essay been in terms of my other studies and time commitments?	☐
Time-based	Have I completed the tasks on the essay checklist in the time I allocated for myself?	☐

Key advice

The SMART acronym provides a useful way to help you ensure that you manage your time effectively and – more importantly – continue to enjoy your work on the essay, developing your interest in your chosen topic. Use research on your topic as a break from other work.

Final task

a) Now draft a plan to help you manage your time allocation for the essay. Look at the table on page 104 and schedule your time, adding deadlines for the completion of your next tasks.
b) Evaluate your draft plan with a partner(s) using the SMART tool.

Reflective plenary

In pairs, discuss what you will need to consider when managing your time, and share any issues that have been raised as you worked through this unit.

Create a reflective digital or sketch poster. Include images of yourself in the process of undertaking all the tasks this essay involves. Incorporate everything you have learned about your own organisational and time-management strengths and challenges.

6.3 Research for your coursework essay

In this unit you will:
- apply your understanding of research and evaluation to the coursework essay.

Critical Path
You will need to:
- deconstruct information from your chosen sources
- evaluate perspectives
- evaluate reliability and usefulness
- begin the reconstruction process through effective note-making.

Deconstruction	Reconstruction	Reflection	Communication	Collaboration
✓	✓			

Strong research skills are central to your development as a student, allowing you to gain a deep understanding of your subjects, independence of thought and confidence. Now is the time for you to put into practice all that you learned in Chapter 3. You will use key search terms for your chosen topic, find possible sources of information to research, identify relevant material, and assess and evaluate these sources to ensure that your support material is credible.

Special focus: Case study

This case study continues from Unit 6.1, where Tatenda worked on her essay question.

Tatenda has settled on the following question:
- **Is plastic waste the primary source of environmental pollution?**

She is preparing her research. Here is the process she follows.

Stage 1: Looking for sources

Tatenda considers the range of material available. She decides to concentrate her search on international magazines that focus on the environment, newspapers and television news channels from geographic areas of specific interest to her, and government/public health websites.

Tatenda starts the search in her library to see which magazines and newspapers are available. She then moves on to using keywords in the hope of finding relevant sources online.

Stage 2: Using keywords

Tatenda breaks down her question and decides to search for information on 'plastic waste' *and* 'pollution'.

Using these keywords and the guidelines given in Unit 3.2 for evaluating source material, she identifies the following sources of information to interrogate:
- a local government website – no date but relevant for nearby problems
- a recent National Geographic article referring to oceanic pollution
- a world data website giving statistics on plastic pollution
- a current UK newspaper article on an alternative marine pollutant – noise
- a current international news report on the increase in plastic waste due to the global coronavirus pandemic
- an activist website on reducing plastic usage
- an article from the WWF – no date
- a world data website giving statistics on air pollution
- a National Geographic encyclopaedia entry with details of recent updates
- a definition in an encyclopaedia
- a scientific information website on types of pollution.

As Tatenda progresses, she logs the basic details of the sources in her reflective journal. She is particularly careful to keep a note of any URLs and the dates she accessed the information. She will add to this log once she has interrogated the material.

Stage 3: Interrogating material

Tatenda initially scans her search results for potential information sources, then skims two articles to assess their potential before diving more deeply into them for closer exploration.

While skim reading and highlighting the main points, she notices that two articles are from the same source, the National Geographic, so she decides to explore them both in more detail.

Initially, she uses the RAVEN test (see Unit 3.2).

R: The magazine is both reputable and reliable.
A: The article is written by someone who has researched the issue first-hand.
V: The magazine is not linked to any particular organisation.
E: The magazine is written for a non-specialist readership, but uses research-based evidence/facts.
N: The articles in the magazine are objective but the photographs make these emotive.

She decides to do a partial CRAAP test (see Unit 3.2) on all the sources first, to establish their currency.

The articles are recent and therefore current, but the encyclopaedia entry is nearly ten years out of date, so she decides to look for a definition from a different source.

She is further intrigued by the activist website but notes that it might not be reliable as it has a strong bias. She decides that she will need corroboration from more reliable sources if she is to use the information or data supplied in this source.

Stage 4: Note-making

Tatenda starts to read some of her sources and takes brief notes. She knows these notes will be essential in helping her understand, analyse and incorporate information from these sources into her essay. It will also help her keep track of where each piece of information came from. She needs to paraphrase and summarise information as she reads (as discussed in Unit 3.3) and cite it correctly. So, now she copies basic details of the source into her Workbook, including the form of the source (article, report, etc.), title, date and authorship. She also notes the key information she has taken from it. Here are her initial annotations and notes on one source.

Cacophony of human noise is hurting all marine life, scientists warn [1]

Major assessment concludes that ocean soundscape is being drowned out by human activity

By Damian Carrington, Environment Editor [2], Feb 4th 2021 [3], The Guardian

A natural ocean soundscape is fundamental to healthy marine life but is being drowned out by an increasingly loud **cacophony** of noise from human activities, according to the first comprehensive assessment of the issue.

The damage caused by noise is as harmful as overfishing, pollution and the climate crisis, [4] the scientists said, but is being dangerously overlooked. The good news, they said, is that noise can be stopped instantly and does not have lingering effects, as the other problems do.

Marine animals can hear over much greater distances than they can see or smell, making sound crucial to many aspects of life. From whales to shellfish, sealife uses sound to catch prey, navigate, defend territory and attract mates, as well as find homes and warn of attack. Noise pollution increases the risk of death and in extreme cases, such as explosions, kills directly.

Carbon dioxide emissions from fossil fuel burning [5] are also making the oceans more acidic, meaning the water carries sound further, leading to an even noisier ocean, the researchers said. But the movement of marine mammals and sharks into previously noisy areas when the Covid-19 pandemic slashed ocean traffic showed that marine life could recover rapidly from noise pollution, they said.

'Everything from the tiniest plankton up to sharks sense their acoustic environment,' said Prof Steve Simpson at the University of Exeter in England, [6] and part of the review team. 'As a result, the animals have to produce sound to communicate, but also to receive sound.' He said noise pollution was like an 'acoustic fog' in the ocean.

Annotations:
- [1] Refers to academic report.
- [2] Specialist reporter.
- [3] Current information.
- [4] Alternative perspective?
- [5] Different form of pollutant.
- [6] Academic secondary evidence.

*Glossary
cacophony: a harsh mixture of loud sounds

Tatenda realises that this source challenges her prevailing argument about how damaging plastic is in comparison to other pollutants. She paraphrases this information using note form for a research log entry.

Stage 5: Keeping track

Tatenda has already started her log of resource material. She now expands the log to include her notes on material she has read so she can use and cite it accurately.

She knows that that all data (e.g. numbers, facts) must be referenced. She also remembers that the only time she can safely cut and paste from the internet is for URLs. She chooses to add her notes as bullet points to her log, but she will use a separate page for this source at a later stage.

She has a table in her Workbook which she updates as she reads. (This may be paper-based or a digital portfolio.)

Source and date	Author	URL/publication	Accessed	Notes
The Guardian newspaper 04/02/2021	Damian Carrington	https://www.theguardian.com/environment/2021/feb/04/cacophony-human-noise-hurting-marine-life-scientists-warn	15-02-21	<ul><li>Other type/s of marine pollution – noise.</li><li>Neutral source quoting new report (Uni of Exeter) Importance of sound to marine animals.</li><li>Problem easier to fix than others.</li></ul>

Summary

Tatenda will repeat this process as she continues to explore her topic. She checks her notes to ensure that she is finding global sources that show contrasting perspectives. She uses her log to evaluate the sources of information she finds to support her argument.

Final task

Take your own question and try working through the research and evaluation stages outlined in the case study above.

Key advice

You will be asked to sign a Statement of Originality to be sent off with your essay. This is to confirm that you have actively produced the essay yourself. Keeping close tabs on your research will assist you to be accurate with your referencing.

Reflective plenary

Work with a partner(s) to discuss solutions or advice for overcoming any challenges you may have found either in researching or making effective notes on your reading.

Chapter 7

Structuring and writing a coursework essay

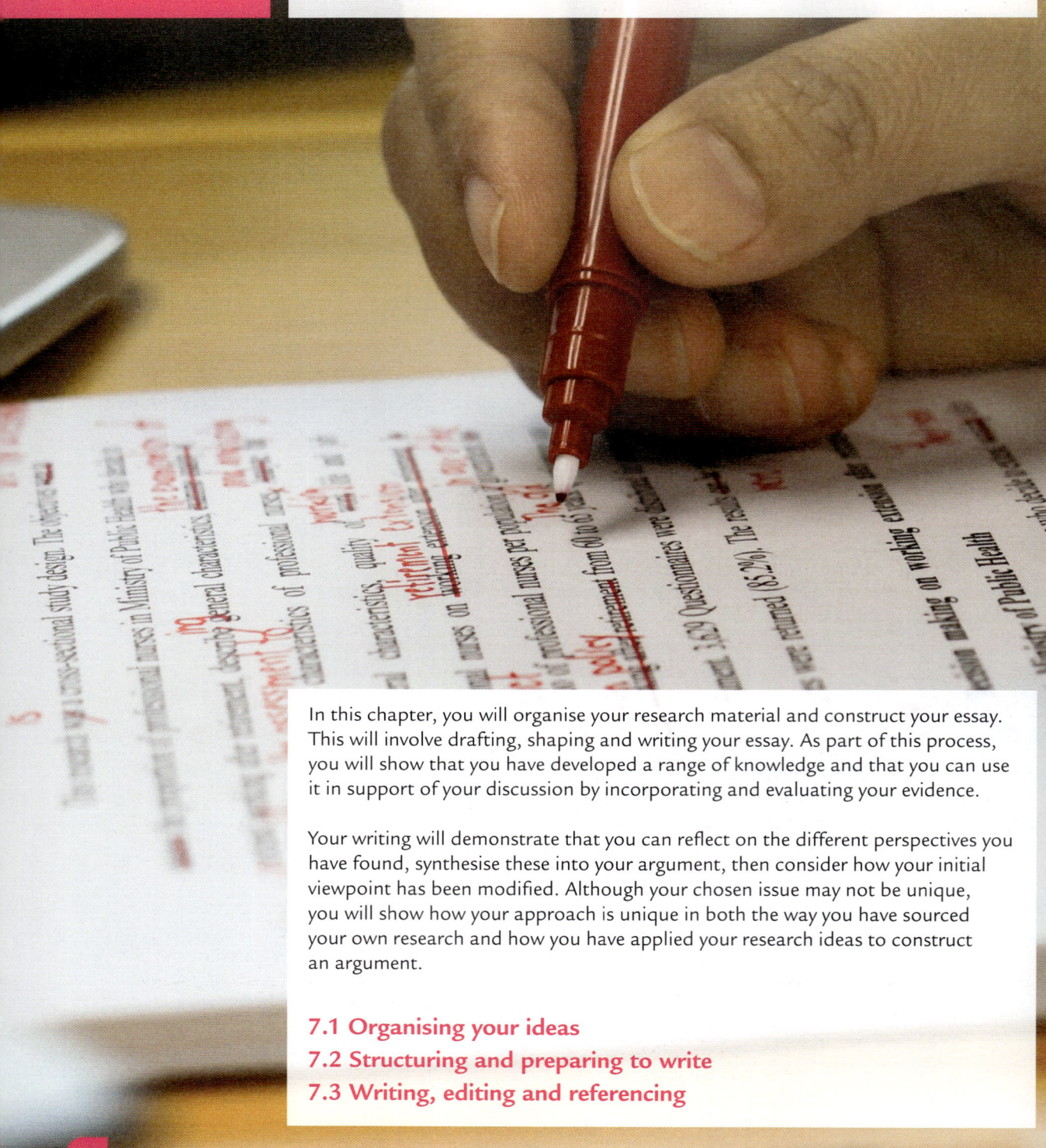

In this chapter, you will organise your research material and construct your essay. This will involve drafting, shaping and writing your essay. As part of this process, you will show that you have developed a range of knowledge and that you can use it in support of your discussion by incorporating and evaluating your evidence.

Your writing will demonstrate that you can reflect on the different perspectives you have found, synthesise these into your argument, then consider how your initial viewpoint has been modified. Although your chosen issue may not be unique, you will show how your approach is unique in both the way you have sourced your own research and how you have applied your research ideas to construct an argument.

7.1 Organising your ideas
7.2 Structuring and preparing to write
7.3 Writing, editing and referencing

7.1 Organising your ideas

In this unit you will:
- sift and evaluate your research material in the light of your essay title
- develop your arguments.

Critical Path
You will need to:
- deconstruct information and data from your sources
- start to reconstruct the insights and knowledge that will inform your essay.

Deconstruction	Reconstruction	Reflection	Communication	Collaboration
✓	✓			

In this unit, you will be working through your research materials, sifting, organising and thinking about how you could use them to develop the discussion that you will work into your essay.

First, remind yourself of the coursework essay task.

You will be writing an academic essay of between 1750 and 2000 words that explores various perspectives on a question of your own devising, and coming to a conclusion in answer to that question.

In your essay, you should:
- look carefully at what your chosen question means
- use a range of sources and consider how appropriate they are
- build up contrasting perspectives by analysing arguments
- compare and evaluate these contrasting perspectives
- develop your own views by reflecting on and developing the perspectives you've considered
- suggest how you might develop your view and understanding with additional research.

(See the Cambridge International AS & A Level Global Perspectives and Research syllabus.)

> **Key advice**
>
> Ensure that the word count of your essay does not exceed 2000 words.

Starting point

Before you start to engage with research and how others view your topic, you need to think about what your first response was to your question and why.
a) Write down your chosen essay title.
b) Highlight key words in your essay title. Then around the essay title, write down your initial answer, and the first four or five thoughts that come to mind in response to your title. For example:

Should city centres become traffic free? → YES!

- But how will this affect commerce/deliveries to shops?
- Less noise pollution
- Would it deter businesses from attracting workers from outside the city?
- Is public transport sufficient to move people around efficiently?
- health issues!!
- Air quality would improve – lives will be saved

c) Next, share your title with a partner and ask for their initial reactions. Discuss the similarities and differences in your viewpoints. Explain and defend your points, and take note of your partner's thoughts.
d) Before moving on, make a careful note of your initial answer to the question (in the example above it was 'Yes'). Part of your eventual reflection will arise from how this viewpoint has changed or been confirmed. Your original viewpoint will also help you to see *where* and (importantly) *why* another viewpoint might be a contrast.

How do you organise your research?

At this stage, you will have completed much of your research and may find that you are confronted with a lot of material that needs organising in relation to your essay question. You will need to sift through your information sources, notes and ideas, to decide loosely which side of the argument they support and how much value to give each one.

The first step in this organising process could be to create graphic/visual organisers, for example a mind map or spider diagram, with your question and your initial response at the heart, and research branching off.

As you produce your own diagrams, you will notice that you are beginning to interrogate your research. You are asking what function it performs and so identifying what you can (or cannot) do with it.

- Where? (Geographic locations)
- What? (Types of pollution/types of plastic)
- When? (Historic versus current plastic pollution)
- **Is plastic waste the primary source of pollution on Earth? Yes?**
- How? (Problems caused)
- Who? (Case studies/stories of the effects of pollution on people and animals)
- Why? (What problems does plastic pollution cause and why?)

What are you looking for?

In order to complete your essay effectively, you need to be sure that you can explore the following:

Global reach: Do you have examples from at least two contrasting parts of the world? A beach in Mozambique and a river in Pretoria, South Africa, is not really 'global' (Why not?) but a beach in Portugal and a river in Pretoria is.

Alternative perspectives: Do you have examples that show other ways of looking at the issue? For example, the economic collapse caused by tourists staying away because of pollution in Pacific Island communities, versus the cultural impact of pollution on the Ganges, versus ethical concerns of European animal protection groups.

Or, **alternative takes on the topic** – such as the views of marine biologists versus the views of different players in the tourism industry, or the view that ocean noise pollution is central.

Information and evidence to support your argument – can you support the idea that plastic is more damaging than sewage, for example? You could use the dangers of microplastics entering the food chain (e.g. in fish or plants) from plastic waste in the oceans and contrast this with cholera outbreaks in a poorly serviced slum area.

Finally, can you be sure that you have information to help you clarify any possibly confusing terms – for example, **definitions** of types of plastic waste and definitions of types of pollution?

So, the next stage is to 'code' the information contained within the 'bubbles' on your spider diagram (if that was the method you used), using different colours or numbers to help you see what types of information you have. This will help you 'cluster' and, if needed, add to your research.

Here is a diagram with information 'coded' using the different colours to pick out particular types of information.

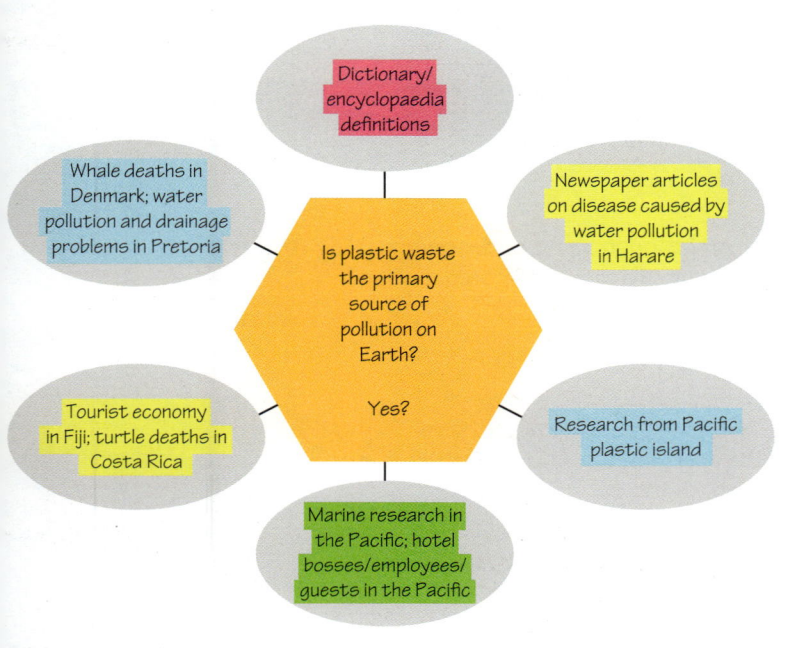

- Dictionary/encyclopaedia definitions
- Whale deaths in Denmark; water pollution and drainage problems in Pretoria
- Newspaper articles on disease caused by water pollution in Harare
- Is plastic waste the primary source of pollution on Earth? Yes?
- Tourist economy in Fiji; turtle deaths in Costa Rica
- Research from Pacific plastic island
- Marine research in the Pacific; hotel bosses/employees/guests in the Pacific

Once you have coded your work, you should be able to see which information most effectively allows you to investigate and explore your question.

Key advice

It isn't always possible to retain or add to your initial ideas. Sometimes you will need to remove less important information; for example, you may not be able to cover everything within the word limit of the essay.

Key advice

Spider diagrams and mind maps are not the only way of ordering your information. You can use any system that suits you best, including a spreadsheet or vertical columns in a notebook.

Whatever format you prefer, you will notice that it must allow for at least two stages. The first notes all your ideas and the second starts to sort them.

Final task

Start ordering your own research using a method that appeals to you. See if you can identify:

- surplus information or gaps
- gaps in geographic or global reach
- whether you focus on only one perspective too much.

Explain the issues you identified above and decide if any further research is needed and how you will carry this out.

Reflective plenary

Work with a small group. What have you learned about your ability to organise material that you have researched? Compare and evaluate the organisational strategies used (i.e. visual, linear, listing). Give any suggestions for improvement and ways of organising your research more effectively.

7.2 Structuring and preparing to write

In this unit you will:
- learn how to structure your essay
- learn about the drafting process.

Critical Path

You will need to:
- communicate your ideas clearly in writing
- reconstruct your research material to add detail and support to your essay.

Deconstruction	Reconstruction	Reflection	Communication	Collaboration
	✓		✓	

Now that you have sifted through and organised your thoughts and evidence, you are in a position to start structuring your essay and identifying which material will go in each section.

Starting point

Think about how you have written essays in the past. The standard structure is introduction, body and conclusion. Work with a partner(s) to discuss and note:

a) What are the functions of these divisions? What should be included in each?
b) What else might be needed in this global essay?

Compare your answers with another pair. Share ideas and questions with the class.

Will this structure work for the type of essay you are going to write in this instance?

Essay types

When establishing the question for your essay (see Unit 6.1), you devised one that encouraged a 'yes/no' (or somewhere on that line) answer – for a **discursive essay**. You are aiming to discuss and debate an issue in this essay, not simply to describe or explain one.

What makes an effective discursive global essay?

There are a number of key elements to keep in mind to ensure you take a clear discursive approach:
- Having a topic that encourages differing positions.
- Being objective and analytical of information, sources and topics.
- Being perceptive about cause and effect – and how the same cause can have different effects.
- Having a strong reflection on the alternative perspectives, which leads to a considered conclusion that clearly answers the question.

> **Key term**
>
> **discursive essay:** a structured, balanced, written debate made up of arguments exploring various perspectives on a particular topic that weighs up the perspectives and comes to a conclusion

How do you structure your global essay?

In Unit 7.1, you began to organise your information. In this drafting stage, you will see how this organisation fits into the essay structure. The structure of an essay on a global issue will be more complex than the typical three-part structure. Each part will have several sub-sections, and you will include a bibliography.

> **Essay structure**
>
> **Introduction:** Shows clearly where the essay is going to lead the reader, and should include:
> - a strong, engaging opening sentence
> - your motivation for choosing the topic
> - the purpose of your exploration (the question)
> - the controversy that exists
> - your initial opinion prior to research
> - any relevant definitions.
>
> **Body:** Shows identified perspectives, analyses and evaluates sources, synthesises the argument and reflects on perspectives on your issue. The body usually falls into three parts, with the important reflection section leading into the (short) conclusion.
>
> **Body Part 1: Perspectives** on the topic, supporting the work with:
> - identification of theme and perspective
> - link to global area
> - evaluation of sources
> - use of case studies/evidence.
>
> **Body Part 2: Synthesis** of the perspectives covered, linking or contrasting themes and global areas.
>
> **Body Part 3: Reflection:** Reflecting on your work is the key part of your essay. It is here you set up for your conclusion – can the answer be 'yes' from one point of view and 'no' from another? Is there a prevailing viewpoint? Has your initial opinion been modified or not and why?
>
> **Conclusion:** Here, you must *answer the question* but you also need briefly to acknowledge the limitations of the essay and suggest further areas of exploration.
>
> **Bibliography:** This is where you provide the full details of your cited research. This is not part of the word count, but is a required and vital part of your coursework.

Key advice

To begin with, you may find it easier to write some parts of each section in a different order to the linear sequence shown here. For example, the motivation for choosing your topic is often the easiest to write because it forms your inspiration. The engaging opening sentence may in fact be the last thing you write.

Special focus: Sections of the essay

This section contains examples of what might go in each of the essay sections outlined above. Here, the content is based on the essay title:
- **Is plastic waste the primary source of pollution on Earth?**

Activity 1: Evaluation

a) Read the examples of student work below. For each section, evaluate what you think works or does not work, referring back to the structure outlined on page 115.

Introduction

There are six elements to consider including in your introduction. These are:
- your opening sentence – how you 'hook' the reader
- your explanation of a central controversy or differing views
- your motivation – why you are writing this
- your personal opinion
- any key definitions
- any limitations you need to acknowledge.

Let's look at each one in turn.

Opening sentence: This is where you grab your reader's attention. Compare the three examples below.

A

> This essay explores whether or not plastic waste is the most prevalent source of pollution.

A Factual, but does it excite the reader?

B

> Plastic waste. Is it the primary source of pollution in the world? Or is it simply a myth that it is clogging our oceans? In this essay, I will be exploring different perspectives.

B While not strictly one sentence, this entices the reader with contrasting rhetorical questions.

C

> From 'the plastic age' to oceans becoming the 'plastic super-highways' (Parker & Olson, 2019), it seems we are surrounded by plastic.

C Using dramatic quotations, this immerses the reader.

Quick task

Which do you think is the most effective opening: A, B or C?

Controversy: This is where you show you understand that there are different viewpoints on the topic. How has this been done in the following extract?

> The 21st century has seen the rise of concern about what humanity is doing with the planet. Many argue that we are using and throwing away too much plastic and so damaging our environment by killing the wildlife that gets caught in or eats plastic. However, others [1] living under the flightpath of busy airports will argue that CO_2 emissions from fossil fuels pose a far greater threat to the environment, leading to global warming and rising waters which could annihilate low-lying land.

[1] Clear contrast in views set out.

Motivation: Writing about why you chose the topic will ensure that both you and your reader become engaged in the essay. Again, there are several approaches you could employ. Look at these three examples.

A

> I recently attended a Model United Nations (MUN) conference and was on the committee for environmental management. I was struck by how much rubbish is generated globally and how much of it was plastic. I was further struck by the seemingly indestructible nature of plastic combined with its ubiquity in all lives from rich to poor, east to west. This led me to enquire whether plastic might not be the most dangerous pollutant in the world.

B

> On a recent visit to the beach, I was horrified at the level of garbage that covered the sand. I noticed that much of it was discarded plastic and wondered whether this pattern was repeated elsewhere.

C

> I have noticed how the kitchen cupboard door was hard to shut because of the plastic bags stored there with no hope of recycling, and this led me to this research on plastic as a global enemy.

> **Quick task**
>
> What is the difference between these three approaches? Is one more effective than the others, or do they all give a clear personal starting point?

Personal opinion: You discussed and noted your initial viewpoint in Unit 7.1. It forms a central part of your argument as you will revisit it in your reflection after you have evaluated your research. You will notice that personal opinion often links to motivation. All three of the examples above suggest the writer starts out by thinking of plastic as the primary source of global pollution.

Definition: Definitions provide essential information to inform understanding of key terms used in the essay, which might come with assumptions, depending on perspective. It is often important to identify and define these key terms right at the start of the essay. It is *not* about explaining or translating a word for the reader; it is about setting clear boundaries for its precise meaning you intend when using a term in your arguments. For example, you would probably want to define 'plastic waste' in your introduction, and acknowledge its source as shown here:

> Plastic waste is 'the accumulation of plastic objects (e.g. plastic bottles and much more) in Earth's environment that adversely affects wildlife, wildlife habitat, and humans.' (Wikipedia)

> **Quick task**
>
> Given what you know about this question/issue are there any other key words or terms you would define in the introduction?

Limitations: Finally, your issue should be so interesting that 2000 words can only cover a small portion of the potential scope for this area. You need to acknowledge this in order to narrow the amount of material included in your essay.

> The rising tide of plastic waste is formed from many items, such as packaging materials, microbeads in beauty products, fashion fabrics and accessories, and hygiene products. This essay focuses on rubbish created by plastic bags and bottles [1] as these are clearly visible, and countries such as Kenya and England [2] have legislated policies revealing different perspectives.

[1] Shows limitation in the kind of waste the essay focuses on.

[2] Shows geographic limitation.

You will revisit these limitations at the end of the essay to indicate where further work might take you.

Body

The **introduction** is vital to the force and clarity of your essay, but the real use of research and construction of argument comes in the **body** of the essay, where you explore alternative global perspectives.

The body of your essay broadly comes in three parts:
- Part 1: paragraphs outlining different perspectives on your topic
- Part 2: synthesis of your research material and evaluation of this information from a range of sources
- Part 3: reflections on what you have explored and learned.

So, what might this look like?

Part 1: Perspectives
What follows is a simplified example (it would need expanding with detail from research).

> In many countries access to clean water is limited, despite it being one of the key rights listed in the UN Declaration of Human Rights (United Nations Media Brief, 2010). This can be seen in Zimbabwe, where waterborne disease is endemic. [1] Families need to buy water in plastic bottles to survive, and the rubbish created is often a source of income for someone else who collects the bottles for re-use. [2] The primary source of pollution in these areas is not plastic but rather failed sewage systems. [3]

[1] Disease not caused by plastic.

[2] Alternative use for rubbish?

[3] Clear, alternative perspective.

Part 2: Synthesis
Here, you combine information and evaluation of evidence. For example, the above paragraph could be supported as follows.

> Evidence of the failed sewage system can be found in a BBC report, https://www.bbc.co.uk/news/world-africa-45546699, (Nyoka, 2018), which shows pictures of people walking beside an open ditch of sewage from a burst pipe. The BBC used a local reporter who actually saw the situation, but the real impact comes from the authority of an internationally recognised news organisation. [1]

[1] Uses first-hand evidence from a reputable source, supporting an alternative perspective that plastic pollution is not the primary cause.

Further synthesis inevitably merges into the reflection. This portion of the essay can only really come together once you have created the first part of the body.

The following shows a brief synthesis of findings on single-use plastic bags.

> There seems to be a global consensus on reducing the use of single-use plastic bags for shopping, as seen through the strict legislation from places as diverse as Kenya, the USA and most of Europe. [1] However, during the lockdown imposed in March/April 2020 as a result of the Covid-19 pandemic, shoppers became concerned that their 'bags for life' were able to harbour the virus and so transmit it easily. [2] The perspective of 'doing one's bit to save the planet' was frowned on. Instead, adopting single-use bags and disposing of them responsibly became the 'correct' thing to do, especially with regard to those people in a vulnerable category, i.e. the sick or elderly. [3]

[1] This sentence has been derived from perspective paragraphs that talked about legislation banning the use of single-use plastic shopping bags.

[2] This contrasting viewpoint comes from paragraphs dealing with research on the increase in the use of plastics, especially shopping bags at the start of the global pandemic in the UK.

[3] The writer combines ideas, contrasting irresponsible and responsible use of plastic to avoid health risks.

Part 3: Reflection

Reflection is a key part of your essay and is where your work gets really interesting. Part of your reflection should be about how your initial viewpoint has been affected by your research. For example:

> Initially, I considered plastic waste to be a major player in polluting the world. My research into the 'islands' of plastic in the oceans, together with the damage done to rivers in sub-Saharan Africa from blockages caused by plastic bags, seems to confirm this. [1] However, when considering the need for access to clean drinking water, [2] I realised that some uses of plastic waste in the form of bottles could potentially prevent the spread of disease.

[1] Original thought.

[2] Alternative perspective – through eyes of a slum-dweller.

Then you should look at the various perspectives you have researched and reflect on (think critically about) how contrasting views change or challenge previous ideas.

> The evidence of plastic waste in the ocean washing up on nearly every beach in the world, coupled with the horrific stories of bird life being destroyed by strangulation from plastic seemed to confirm that plastic is a global pollutant. However, evidence from slum areas shows that raw sewage remains a massive problem in terms of causing deadly diseases. [1]

[1] Weighing up two kinds of pollution.

Clearly, the body of the essay will be more extensive than the paragraph examples provided here, but you now have a style and structural guide on which to base your own work.

Conclusion

This section of the essay is generally short. It is the final weighing up of the reflection, giving an answer to your question.

Your answer does not have to be totally 'yes' or 'no'; it can fall anywhere along a scale from 0 to 100. This allows you to hold on to your opinion while acknowledging that the answer may be different if considering it from someone else's perspective.

The reflection above might conclude:

> The evidence considered in this essay shows that for beach-dwelling communities and marine life, plastic is the primary cause of pollution. However, people living in the townships around many cities in countries like Zimbabwe, India and Brazil would argue that raw sewage is a far greater problem. [1] **So, to answer my question, plastic waste would seem to be the primary source of pollution in the sea but not in urban areas, where more research needs to be carried out.** [2]

[1] Sums up gist of the debate.

[2] Strong, clear conclusion – around 50 on the scale.

The conclusion also needs to acknowledge that you have only touched on one small part of your topic.

Limitations/Further research

You have acknowledged in the introduction to your essay the word limitations (the essay only looked at plastic bags and bottles). In your conclusion, you will show where further research might be valuable.

This essay has only considered a small portion of the problems caused by plastic waste. It shows there is a balance in terms of pollution between bags and bottles and sewage. However, a significant source of pollution can also be found in the use of microplastics by the fashion industry, and this would need to be explored further to establish the full scope of plastic pollution. [1]

[1] Shows understanding of the nuances of this debate.

Final task

Using the examples you have just explored, copy and complete the table below to start to structure your own material.

Introduction	Question (Y/N format)		
	Catchy or engaging introductory sentence		
	Controversy		
	Motivation		
	My initial opinion		
	Definitions		
	Limitations		
Body	Perspective 1/Case study 1		
	Perspective 2/Case study 2		
	Perspective 3/Case study 3		
	Synthesis of perspectives/case studies		
	Reflection on what has been learned/observed		
Conclusion	Brief summary of evaluation of perspectives		
	Reflective judgement on the question		
	Change or confirmation of original view		
	Limitations leading to suggestions for further research		
	Answer		

Reflective plenary

Work with a partner to conduct an evaluation of each other's work. Use the following questions to guide you. Does the essay preparation contain:
- quality content that will be analysed and evaluated
- originality in the way the research is treated and the argument created
- a clear focus on the question
- a coherent argument
- deconstruction and reconstruction of sources
- an opportunity for reflection that shows how you arrived at your answer to the question?

Which of these do you already have in your preparations, and which are still to come as you write?

Now make an entry in your reflective log outlining your next steps.

7.3 Writing, editing and referencing

In this unit you will:
- look at strategies to help you write and edit your essay
- learn how to check your work to ensure it is well-structured, clear and accurate.

Critical Path
You will need to:
- structure your ideas coherently
- cite and reference your source material accurately
- communicate clearly, effectively and correctly.

Deconstruction	Reconstruction	Reflection	Communication	Collaboration
			✓	

In this unit, you will focus on writing, editing and referencing your essay so that you produce a structured, stylish, formal essay that is correctly cited.

You should now have an essay structure that broadly follows the format:
- Introduction
- Main body:
    o Perspectives
    o Synthesis
    o Reflection
- Conclusion

Starting point

Work with a partner(s). Check and discuss your essay structure plans using the grid in the 'Final task' on page 120 to make sure your plan is clear and covers all elements.

Written essay format

Once you have checked your plans, the next stage is to write your first draft. Remember, that this is exactly what it says – a first draft – so there will still be time for **content editing** and **proofreading**.

> **Key terms**
>
> **content editing:** checking and improving on the content, structure and clarity of your work
>
> **proofreading:** checking your work for more technical concerns, such as to correct errors of grammar and spelling and to confirm accuracy of referencing

Key advice

Your essay should be between 1750 and 2000 words and should be in an electronic format. You will need to include citations and a bibliography, but these elements won't be included in your word count.

Word count

The following diagram gives an outline of how the word count could be allocated across the structure.

Introduction
360–460 words

Main body
Body section 1: Perspectives, case studies, perspectives
700–800 words split evenly between perspectives
Body section 2: Synthesis/reflection
600–700 words

Conclusion
100–150 words

(**Bibliography** – outside word count)

> **Key advice**
>
> Don't worry if your first draft is over the word count – it is easier to cut work down and tighten the focus, rather than to add words in.

You want to be sure that you give enough attention to both synthesis and reflection, and that the conclusion falls within the word count.

How can you get started on your writing?

There are many strategies for getting started. Some students prefer to start with the main body of the essay by looking at evidence and perspectives, then come back and write an introduction later. One helpful strategy for getting started is to use **paragraph headings**. You can start by writing a list of headings for all the paragraphs you have planned. Putting a word or phrase as a heading for every paragraph can help you easily see how your essay connects logically and flows. These headings will be removed before you submit your final work.

As you write, keep in mind the following, which you can also use retrospectively to check your work.

- Use accessible language: this means language that can be understood by a general audience, and which avoids jargon and slang.
- Avoid generalisations: these are points that generate questions from a reader where context does not supply the answer. They are often used to increase the word count.

> **Key term**
>
> **paragraph heading:** a one-word/phrase summary of the content of a specific paragraph; useful in drafting to help highlight sequencing

Activity 1: Paragraph headings

a) Write your paragraph headings. Work in small groups, evaluate and share these, and discuss your strategies for getting started on an essay.

How to structure paragraphs

How you structure and link paragraphs, along with a helpful use of signposting words, will guide your reader through your essay, ensuring that your meaning is clear.

As you know, paragraphs should contain one idea which is introduced by a topic sentence setting out what the rest of the paragraph is about. Consider the following paragraph.

> We live in challenging times [1]. A global pandemic, on-going problems with conflicts, poverty and the sheer pace of climate change have led many ordinary people, policy makers and leaders to re-evaluate global priorities and what the future holds. It is in that context that we should consider the initiatives of Elon Musk and Jeff Bezos in the arena of space travel, and the renewed interest from countries as diverse as China, Russia and India in putting people into space.

[1] Here, the topic sentence 'sets up' what follows – by setting out what those 'challenging times' are.

Activity 2: Using signposting in an essay

Now look at these paragraphs taken from the essay in Unit 3.4.

a) Identify the signpost words and phrases that pick out a connection between the paragraphs.
b) Identify the topic sentences for each paragraph.
c) Identify other words that signpost transitions.
d) Work with a partner(s) to compare, check and clarify answers.

On the other hand, large cosmetics companies such as The Body Shop are beginning to change their attitude. A 2019 report shows that The Body Shop's profits went down by 20 per cent in 2017, only to recover after the company shifted to promoting products that had only been tested either on humans or via computer programs.

Away from cosmetics, however, there is an argument for the use of animals in medical research. Life-saving cancer drugs, such as Herceptin, have only been authorised by the FDA and BMA as a result of extensive safety checks provided by animal-based research before human trials.

So, whilst there is possibly a case for the continued use of animals in medical research, The Body Shop's experience suggests that we do not necessarily need to use them in cosmetics research, despite the arguments around profit. Therefore, animal testing should not be used in this specific area of scientific research.

Remember that transition words are those that contribute to the structure of your essay by clearly showing the reader what direction your argument is taking. For example, 'because' heralds an explanation; 'therefore' a conclusion; 'although' suggests a comparison. These words show sequence, cause and effect, and introduce quotations and paraphrases that need referencing. In effect, they show the reader how to deal with the information.

Citations and bibliography

In the essay, you are required to show the origin or sources of the information you researched, through careful referencing. You have kept a log of your research from the start of the process of planning and research. Now is the time to transform this into a list of citations that can then become both footnotes and bibliography.

Citations

Citations are either alphabetical or numeric indications within your text to show that you are using ideas or facts that are not originally yours. The format of your citations is up to you, but in the essay it may be preferable to use some form of numeric/footnoting referencing system due to the limitations of the word count. If you look back to Unit 3.5, you will find some examples of citations. Now you need to create citations for your own work. Below is a short reminder.

The use of animals in research on new cosmetics is a widespread but controversial issue. On one hand, a scientific perspective suggests that using animals in research is easier [1] (and therefore possibly cheaper) than the alternatives. On the other hand, animal lovers say it is cruel and unnecessary [2].

Footnotes: [1] Animal Testing on Cosmetics [Online]
[2] Alternatives to Animal Testing [Online]

Bibliography

Once you have completed your essay, you are required to attach a bibliography giving the full details of your sources, so that your reader can consult these to research further if they want to. A bibliography, or list of your sources or references can be constructed in several ways (see page 65). However, producing your bibliography can be time-consuming, so you will need to leave enough time before submitting your essay to complete it correctly.

Bibliographies are generally in alphabetical order of author as shown below:
> Cannington, J. J. (1979). *How to write Good Essays and Critical Reviews*. Toronto: Coles Notes.
> Cruelty Free International. (n.d.). *Alternatives to Animal Testing*. Retrieved July 14, 2020, from https://www.crueltyfreeinternational.org/why-we-do-it/alternatives-animal-testing
> Murnaghan, I. (2019). *Animal Testing on Cosmetics*. Retrieved July 14, 2020, from http://www.aboutanimaltesting.co.uk/animal-testing-cosmetics.html

Here you can see the full details of the sources used in the extract for referencing, including the date the website was accessed. While print dates are generally more stable, even print materials can be subject to change, for example, during reprints or when further editions are commissioned.

Post production

This is a vital stage of completing the essay, which is crucial to your success. The work is not over when you finish writing. You now need to:
- edit your work: make changes to the content and ideas, and make sure your essay is clearly organised and signposted; you may also make changes to words and expression
- proofread: this is a more mechanical process in which you check for errors in spelling, omissions, punctuation and referencing.

Proofreading is a skill like any other skill. It takes time and patience to go through your work again with an objective eye.

What you are checking falls broadly into three key areas, shown in the following three grid checklists.

Content editing (overall structure)

To check	Yes	No	Comment
Have I followed my plan (e.g. the right content for each section)? Effective introduction; main body with its analysis of different perspectives, synthesis of ideas and evidence in my arguments, my reflections? A strong conclusion?			
Are new ideas in separate paragraphs?			
Do my paragraphs link logically and sequentially?			
Have I answered the questions posed?			

Style and expression

To check	Yes	No	Comment
Are my points clear?			
Is there support for all points made?			
Have points been supported with appropriate evidence and/or examples, and, where appropriate, sources quoted fluently?			
Have I used PEEL (**P**oint, **E**vidence, **E**xplain, **L**ink) paragraph structures?			
Have I used signpost words to indicate:			
• new ideas			
• evidence			
• conclusions			

Proofreading

To check	Yes	No	Comment
Are all my sentences complete (subject/verb/capital letter/end punctuation)?			
Is my punctuation correct and are my sentences the correct length?			
Is my choice of vocabulary accurate?			
Is my use of pronouns clear?			
Have I used any jargon, slang or clichés which should be avoided?			
Have I spelled commonly confused words (there/their) correctly?			
Are quotations introduced by a signal phrase?			
Are quotations accurately cited and referenced?			

Final task

Now write your essay (if you feel ready to do so). Make sure you check with your teacher that you are in a position to write it.

Keep in mind everything you have learned in this unit (and the chapter as a whole). In particular:
- answer the essay question you have set yourself
- follow the plan you developed in Unit 7.2
- synthesise arguments to build contrasting perspectives
- use a range of sources and consider how appropriate they are
- compare and evaluate contrasting perspectives
- develop your own views by reflecting on and developing the perspectives you've considered
- suggest how you might develop your view and understanding further with additional research
- make sure your essay is clearly structured and includes effective referencing.

Reflective plenary

Reflect on what aspects of the essay you are clear about and make a list of anything you are not sure about. Compare your list with a partner(s), try to answer each other's questions then find answers to any remaining queries with the class/your teacher.

Chapter 8
Preparing and presenting the Team Project

In this chapter, you will focus on understanding what is required for the Team Project. You will identify and develop the skills that you need to engage in collaborative team development and to present your individual research successfully. You will expand on the research competences you attained earlier in the course to find solutions for a local problem that sparks your interest and has the potential for global impact.

The most important aspects of the Critical Path for this chapter are communication, collaboration and reflection.

8.1 What is the Team Project?
8.2 Selecting suitable problems to research
8.3 Preparing for your presentation
8.4 Organising your argument
8.5 Using language to present effectively
8.6 Supporting your presentation visually
8.7 Practice and evaluation

8.1 What is the Team Project?

In this unit you will:
- identify your individual role within the team
- understand the requirements of the Team Project.

Critical Path
You will need to:
- negotiate and explore individual roles for the Team Project in a collaborative way.

Deconstruction	Reconstruction	Reflection	Communication	Collaboration
			✓	✓

Introducing the Team Project

Teamwork is central to the Team Project. You will work in a group to investigate a local problem which has **global relevance**. Your team will investigate the problem from different perspectives, and will work towards the presentation of a variety of solutions.

> 🔑 **Key term**
>
> **global relevance:** when an issue of local or national importance affects people and societies internationally

Starting point: Exploring an example of a Team Project

Read the notes one group of students has made to clarify their team's different perspectives on a particular local problem. Does this project appeal to you? Discuss your thoughts with a partner.

Local problem Parents in our poorer rural areas are being duped by fashion industry recruiters who promise their daughters a comfortable life, with a well-paid job and education. The reality is, in fact, the opposite; children work in appalling conditions with no schooling.

Global relevance Internationally, around 170 million child labourers are used by multinational fashion brands across the globe to satisfy consumer demand. The supply chain is so complex that companies and consumers are not always aware of their involvement in exploiting vulnerable children, with low skills and no protection.

Nihal's perspective; global inequality.

- Exploring the effect of incomplete basic education in our country, i.e. low rates of literacy and skills in families – impoverished parents make bad choices for their children.
- Finding out how recruiters for the garment manufacturers exploit a family's hope of a better life for their children.

Tobi's perspective: international law.

- Researching why child labour in the 'fast' fashion industry continues in these regions of our country, although it is unlawful.
- Drawing comparisons with other countries in the region and the labour laws.

Diep's perspective: sustainable futures.

- Investigating how to meet international markets more sustainably.
- Analysing the effect on local water supplies, traditional clothing and textiles.

Activity 1: Identifying perspectives

a) Identify any perspectives implied in the description of the local problem and its global relevance. Can you think of any others?

Activity 2: What steps do you need to follow during the Team Project?

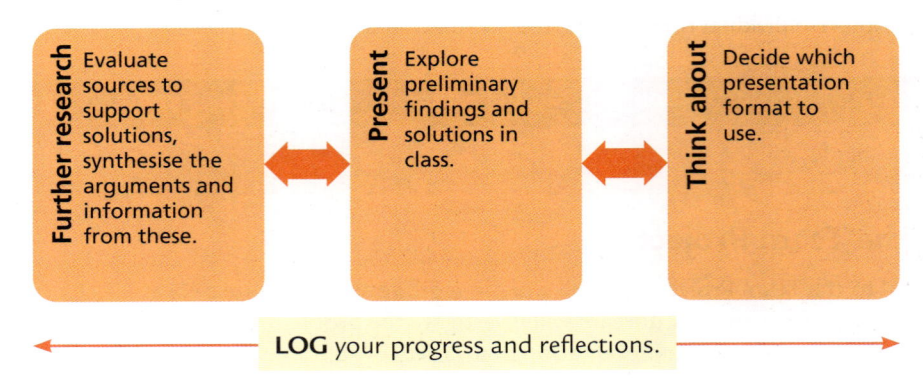

Further research: Evaluate sources to support solutions, synthesise the arguments and information from these. ⇄ **Present:** Explore preliminary findings and solutions in class. ⇄ **Think about:** Decide which presentation format to use.

LOG your progress and reflections.

a) Read the following messages. Which of the steps in the diagram are the team members focusing on?

> Hey @Diep_85 @Nihal110 I can't remember exactly what we did last week, or what I still need to do – lost my notes :-() can you screenshot or share your logs? Thank you forever and I'll bring you cookies!! Tobes
>
> @Tobi007 and @Diep_85 shall we try out that new presentation tool tonight? We could take two slides each, and it's quieter working at home (?!) I'll set it up and give you editing permissions, so we can feed back and chat. NB Do NOT delete any of my text like last time please, guys! And we need to be done before Friday, OK? N :-)
>
> @Nihal110 do you realise that the research for this source is funded by the biggest chain of garment manufacturers? Surely that makes it biased? Definitely not objective ;-) D
>
> Hi y'all (!) I need your feedback – I realised a bit late that the most important part of our project is finding a problem and perspectives that can hold everyone's level of interest over time. That passion I had at the beginning is beginning to grow a bit old, if I'm honest (sorry, reflective!) Is it too late now to switch perspectives? Do any of you feel the same way? D
>
> @Nihal110 @Diep_85 I can't find another source in English to add support for my suggested solution. Do you think it matters if I translate and synthesise info in the one we found in the local business report? Tobes

b) Work together. What potential problems are these students experiencing? How could you avoid the same issues?

Activity 3: Understanding the stages of development in the Team Project

Look at the following diagram, which shows the developmental stages your team is likely to experience as you work together.

Starting out:
- Excited <---> uncertain?
- Defining team roles?
- Identifying the local problem (with global relevance)?
- Understanding ways of working?
- Positive expectations?
- Beginning to build trust?

Working it out:
- Frustrated <---> anxious?
- Progress slow, or steady?
- Worry about meeting objectives?
- How are diverse skills and approaches met?
- How is disagreement handled?
- How are conflicts resolved?
- Critical of choices, skills or contributions?

Finding equilibrium:
- More realistic expectations?
- More flexibility?
- Comfortable with 'real' ideas feelings, opinions?
- More meaningful communication, sharing?
- Increasing acceptance of difference?
- Willingness to seek/offer help?

Operating:
- Better understanding and awareness of individual and team strengths and weaknesses?
- Confident that team is meeting requirements and deadlines?
- Comfortable communication?
- Taking different roles flexibly when needed?
- A helpful, 'can-do' attitude to problem-solving?

Work with your team to answer these questions.
a) Which stage are you currently at? Which of the issues in the labels are you likely to face?
b) How might the following factors affect a team's development (negatively or positively)?
- familiarity and friendship with other members of the team
- the knowledge that teamwork itself is not assessed, only reflections on it
- the size of the team (two or three members? four or five?)

How can individual roles help in developing effective teamworking?

> ❛Too many cooks spoil the broth.❜

In addition to the role of leader, manager or **facilitator**, other possible 'job' or team roles are researcher, note-maker or recorder, debater, timekeeper, reporter, IT expert, language expert, energiser or harmoniser, strategy analyst, or reflection coach. Every team needs someone to organise, motivate and delegate responsibilities. However, too many facilitators will lead to confusion! Other roles may be combined according to the task involved and number of team members present. Ideally, each team member will play to their strengths, and be prepared to take on alternative roles and responsibilities on different occasions, depending on the task.

"We have too many cooks in the kitchen."

Key term

facilitator: a person on a team whose role is to help everyone work together better by 'facilitating' or making it easier to understand and achieve common goals and objectives

Quick task

Research and discuss what you have to do in the job roles listed above. How can you avoid having 'too many cooks' spoiling your teamwork?

Activity 4: Evaluation of roles for the Team Project

a) In pairs, discuss which roles:
- might make a good 'fit' if combined (and in what ways)
- are the most important for the team project (and why)
- you feel most/least positive about/would be most happy to take on (and for what reasons).

Final task: What makes an effective team?

Effective teams reflect by thinking about these questions:
- How do I/we show our commitment to the team and the project?
- How are we developing as a team?
- How effective is my/our communication?
- What contribution(s) have I/we made to the team and the project?
- How effectively do we resolve any issues or problems?
- What do we need to re-evaluate, do or think about differently? Why?
- What do we need to encourage more/less of?

Identify the questions the following students answer. Discuss how the issues involve:
- communication
- collaboration
- research skills.

A 'I didn't keep a record of the sources for my research, so I don't know how to find them again. I need to synthesise and paraphrase information when I make notes – not copy!'

B 'Listening, talking! We recorded our discussion and after listening, I understood that some people speak too much, so others didn't have a chance to contribute!'

C 'We meet on or offline when we have questions or need help and find the best person for the job!'

Reflective plenary

Use the information above to help you negotiate, write and sign a 'team contract' with other members of your group. Include 5–10 core 'promises'. For example: *We will meet up weekly to check in on progress and swap skills.*

8.2 Selecting suitable problems to research

In this unit you will:
- analyse a local problem to identify issues and stakeholders locally and globally
- identify a local problem of global relevance to research from different perspectives.

Critical Path

You will need to:
- collaborate with your team to communicate and reflect on the suitability of problems.

Deconstruction	Reconstruction	Reflection	Communication	Collaboration
		✓	✓	✓

How to identify if a local problem is suitable for your team project

You will have to work with your team to decide whether an issue is of global relevance from different perspectives. Equally importantly, you will need to evaluate how much information from valid sources is available to you for effective research to help you solve the problem. This might involve thinking about the feasibility of team members conducting some 'live' research (i.e. interviewing interested **stakeholders** locally) as well as evaluating the availability of appropriate reliable sources published online or in print. You will need to discuss this with your teacher(s). Some efficient 'desk' research of published data will help your team to assess the practicality of researching the problem you identify.

> **🔑 Key term**
>
> **stakeholder:** someone involved in or affected by an issue (e.g. *local* stakeholders concerned in a global fashion supply chain might range from parents, siblings and other family members to the local community, schools and small business enterprises; *global* stakeholders include consumers of brands around the world, customer service and sales assistants, designers and distributors)

Activity 1: Exploring the suitability of a local problem: how is it relevant globally?

a) Read this team's analysis of a local problem identified as having 'global relevance'.

Problem	Global relevance?
• Our cultural heritage is being lost; archaeological sites are being destroyed by new buildings and road development. Newly discovered sites in our tourist regions have been concealed to avoid attention and so hotels can be constructed. • Historical artefacts are being looted and traded on the international market, often illegally. • Future generations are losing important cultural information when objects are removed from their original cultural context and traded purely for profit that does not benefit locals.	• Around the world, countries both rich and poor face similar threats to irreplaceable heritage sites and treasures from museums. • Such losses affect all of humanity – we lose the ability to understand the ways in which different societies operated. • There is a link between the sale of looted antiquities and the funding of terrorism on an international scale.

b) Work with your team to research and discuss: How suitable is this problem?

1. Is there sufficient global relevance to the local problem in your opinion? (Evidence?)
2. Which perspectives could be used to investigate the problem and provide a solution? Look back at Unit 1.2 for a list of topics to choose from. For example, *Changing identities* might be relevant here.

Considering a local problem: in what ways is it of concern to us?

According to the ancient philosophy of an Iroquois nation, to consider the true impact of an important decision, we must consider how it will affect *the next seven generations*. This timeframe could provide a useful way of looking at local problems. Equally important, perhaps, is thinking about how a local issue has developed over time to become important now. Speaking to family members and others in your learning community may inform your choice of problem to investigate. Being curious about and interested in your own and each other's research perspective for the project is crucial for the success of a team project.

Activity 2: Choose and explore the global relevance of a local problem

Look at the framework below, designed to guide individual thought and team discussion about a local issue.

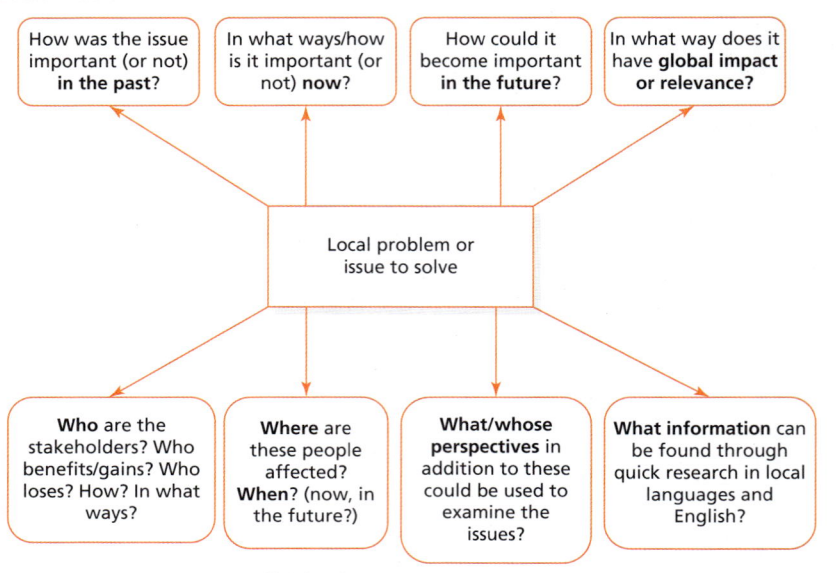

Framework diagram centred on "Local problem or issue to solve", with arrows to eight surrounding boxes:

- How was the issue important (or not) **in the past**?
- In what ways/how is it important (or not) **now**?
- How could it become important **in the future**?
- In what way does it have **global impact or relevance**?
- **Who** are the stakeholders? Who benefits/gains? Who loses? How? In what ways?
- **Where** are these people affected? **When**? (now, in the future?)
- **What/whose perspectives** in addition to these could be used to examine the issues?
- **What information** can be found through quick research in local languages and English?

a) **Silent thinking time:** divide the questions above for team members to consider individually first by making notes to inform a discussion.

b) **Individual mini presentation:** present the answers to the questions you considered to the team. Debate and decide:
   - What is the global relevance?
   - Is there a sufficient range of different perspectives of interest to team members? If so, select one each.

c) **Repeat the activity if needed.**

Final task: Team statement

Write a joint team statement describing the local problem you identified and justifying its global relevance for your teacher(s) to evaluate. Use the information on this page and the example Team Project outlined in Unit 8.1 to help you.

Reflective plenary

Reflective log entry
Work with a partner. Discuss:
- How effective was teamwork in making decisions and discussing the project? How did you contribute positively?
- What do you and your team need to do now?

Refer back to the stages of team development on page 129.

Use your reflections in answer to the questions above to write a log entry. For example:
Next time the team meets, I need to make more of an effort to contribute my own opinions as I was quite passive in the debate today. I will play a more active role by indicating when I'd like to say something.

8.3 Preparing for your presentation

In this unit you will:
- identify several information sources
- evaluate the suitability of sources.

Critical Path
You will need to:
- evaluate possible sources to research your problem from different perspectives
- communicate and reflect on your findings together.

Deconstruction	Reconstruction	Reflection	Communication	Collaboration
✓	✓	✓	✓	✓

You have decided on a local problem of global relevance for each team member to research from a range of perspectives. You explored research strategies in Chapter 3 and will be familiar with the need to select and evaluate sources before deciding which are suitable for close reading and detailed analysis, or *research*. Academic research requires sources of information (i.e. data) to be *scholarly*, *reliable* and *accurately dated*. You have learned how to identify *arguments*, *ideas*, *supporting evidence* and *opinions* from a *variety of information sources*. You will continue to develop skills that will build your awareness of *bias* from the *vested interests* of writers and producers of information; in other words, potential *sources*. In this unit, you will consider how and why to stay organised, focused and evaluate potential sources of information.

Starting point

Work with your team. Identify the differences between the concepts in *italics* in the text above. Define the terms and give examples. If you are unsure or there is disagreement, look again at Units 2.3 and 3.2 for a reminder.

Activity 1: Why do organisation and focused attention matter?

Investigating and reading online can lead to circuitous searches, an overwhelming amount of data and the danger of disappearing 'down the research rabbit-hole' like Lewis Carroll's Alice in Wonderland. When this is coupled with competing digital distractions (such as sounds and visual notifications) you may be at risk of ineffective and superficial ways of working.

a) Work with a partner or team to discuss these questions from your own experience. Share advice, reminders and tips.

   i)   How do you avoid digital distraction when reading and researching online?
   ii) Remind yourself how you decide if a source is sufficiently academic.
   iii) How do you note, bookmark and curate a list of sources to refer to or share?
   iv) How and why are the research skills in i)–iii) crucial?

b) Decide on helpful digital practices (e.g. switching all notifications off) as a team. Share tools you find helpful for note-making, bookmarking, citing, curating resources. Create a dedicated online project portfolio so you can communicate, share ideas, ask for and give advice and feedback outside class. You will need to consider the editing privileges and privacy settings for your project space, and ensure all team members have equal access. Explore these tools and settings with others, and check you understand the options available to you.

Activity 2: Investigating your problem – what's at stake?

a) Work with a partner from your team. Which of the following are appropriate sources of information that you can access for your team project? Why or why are they not appropriate sources?
- official publications, e.g. white papers or reports from government, company or charitable organisations or non-governmental organisations (NGOs), where available
- presentations
- books
- journals (peer-reviewed)
- news reports and press releases (audio-visual, digital or print)
- social media posts
- interviews
- magazine articles
- books (contain bibliographies or lists of references that may be useful).

You must begin with some detective work. First, you need to identify the potential of your sources to inform the investigation of the team's problem with *database searches* using *keywords* and phrases. Choosing the correct keywords for the local problem your team selected, and the perspectives you are researching, will be crucial. You will identify several sources of potentially useful information to evaluate. Try keywords as # on social media used by local academics and authors. As you work, keep local and global relevance in mind. Aim to get an overall impression of the information to decide if it is worth evaluation.

b) Work with your team to decide on keywords, for example: [cultural AND heritage] and economic aspects.
c) Select up to eight sources to evaluate. How might each source effectively inform research of the problem from the perspective you are investigating?

You are responsible for managing and maintaining individual records of your work as it progresses. An illustration of this is the detailed information you need to record about precise *dates* of original publication, for any updates and when a source was accessed. The purpose of this record maintenance is so that you can investigate and reflect any changes that new information makes necessary. It is also needed for referencing your presentation accurately.

Key advice

Start by thinking about the title or a question you are researching, for example: *How does **facial recognition** technology affect our **privacy**?* The key terms are in **bold**. Brainstorm a list of alternative words with your team. These could be synonyms or narrower or broader ideas. So, for this question, you could use these alternatives: *facial feature recognition, remote biometric identification, data privacy, personal data, data protection*. You can try conducting searches using these words, and try a range of search engines and browsers. Remember, you can combine key terms with AND and OR.

Activity 3: How to evaluate sources to research

a) A student evaluated the following source for global relevance to the problem featured in Unit 8.2, concerning the loss of cultural heritage as a result of new buildings being developed on sites of importance, artefacts being taken for sale on the open market, and so on. Work together as a team to explore and understand the purpose of each section in the form below. Do you think the source is suitable? Why/why not?

Name of website/book	The Journal Digital Culture (online only)
Title of article/book	Examining the socio-economic impact of cultural heritage on local communities
URL	http://digicult.it/article/-socio-economic-impact-of--cultural-heritage-on-local-communities/
Publisher of website/book	The Da Vinci Foundation
Author of article	Napolitana, L.
Date of publication and last update	?? not stated
Date accessed	19/04/23
Type of website/book: A platform exploring the impact of applied sciences and digital technologies on contemporary culture. Funded by different EU government arts grants.	
Evaluation of this source: • fact ↔ opinion • objective ↔ persuasive • level of bias • assumptions • up to date? • reliable?	• Fact and opinion – arguments are supported by evidence and linked to primary sources. • Objective (qualitative) research based on case studies, surveys, interviews and observation through secondary data sources. • The research was funded by the city council the author lives in – so maybe biased? • New arrivals to a city will be interested in the cultural heritage. • ? No dates on the article so it's hard to tell (could contact author on social media to find out?) • ? No because undated, but linked primary sources, reports, etc. are useful.
Summary of main points: • Redefines the concept of 'active protection' (2005 Faro protocol) for tangible and intangible cultural assets. • Analyses social and environmental sustainability with reference to EU commission reports (2023). • ….	

b) Use the same format as the form above to assess the suitability of the sources you have found. You do not need to summarise the main points at this stage – evaluating the suitability of your source will determine if this is necessary. You can also apply RAVEN or CRAAP as discussed in Unit 3.2.

Metacognition – your hidden superpowers unmasked

Have you presented your research perspective? When you have further developed your ideas, you may be ready to organise them into content for your presentation. You may not feel fully prepared yet, but this can be viewed as a positive. To illustrate this, thinking about what you *don't yet know* will inform your research both profoundly and productively. The gaps in your knowledge, research or understanding are revealed by reflecting on how best to approach your next task, and self-monitoring (e.g. *Do I really understand this text? Have I tried to find competing points of view? Who can I ask for help?*). As you grow aware of and reflect on your own thinking and learning processes, your metacognitive powers develop.

Metacognition, put simply, is what you know and do about your learning.

Thinking about problems in different ways to seek solutions from different angles with others is a creative act. In fact, divergent thinking and creativity in problem-solving are what distinguishes human brains from AI (Artificial Intelligence) and are highly valued by employers. Imagine the superpowers that your team of diverse thinkers can bring to the process of problem-solving your local issue from a global perspective.

Final task: What steps are needed to organise your preparation?

a) Copy and complete this checklist individually to clarify your next steps. Interview another team member and discuss your progress. Which tasks have been completed so far? Which tasks are covered in previous units/this unit?

Task/objective	Deadline?	In progress? Complete?	Improvement needed?	Further action needed?
Identify, evaluate and select a variety of sources to research your local problem from a global perspective.	20 October	20 October ✓	Yes. Insufficient variety and two are not academic enough (24.10)	Find 2–4 more sources and start with .org (and .edu or .ac) NB not Wikipedia
Read and analyse texts (media and print-based) closely to identify any ideas of relevance.				
Make detailed notes to synthesise and summarise main points, possible arguments and evidence.				
Decide on and organise arguments. Select appropriate supporting evidence from your research and investigate further if needed.				
Decide on possible solutions to your problem, discuss and compare the distinct perspectives.				
Present a summary of individual perspectives on the team problem with arguments and solutions for peer feedback and review.				
Draft text of presentation slides.				
Draft presentation cue cards.				

b) Work with your team. Share your progress. Identify any problems and help you require to complete the next actions you need to take individually (and as a team). For example: *Bertha and Charlie kept work records/reflective logs up to date —> set deadline to check and alerts to remind everyone in the team (sync our calendars!)*

Quick task

Discuss: Which superpowers can the members of your team bring to the project? (For example: *word-wizard, memory-keeper, argument-picker, tech-queen...*)

Reflective plenary

Work together. Discuss the questions below *as a team*.
- How suitable and varied are the sources you evaluated? Justify your decisions.
- How easy/difficult was it to find sources to support the perspectives chosen?
- Does anyone think the problem, or their perspective, needs revising? Why? How?
- Were any knowledge or skills gaps revealed by this unit? Who can help? How?
- What are your next steps as a team/an individual? (For example, read – or view, or listen – to texts, analyse the arguments/evidence and make notes synthesising and summarising the main points.)

8.4 Organising your argument

In this unit you will:
- identify the main points of your arguments and consider their strengths, weaknesses and supporting evidence
- organise your main points and arguments into content for your presentation slides.

Critical Path

You will need to:
- communicate the strengths and weaknesses of arguments from all perspectives
- evaluate how varied the team solutions are.

Deconstruction	Reconstruction	Reflection	Communication	Collaboration
✓	✓	✓	✓	✓

To fulfil the team project brief, it is necessary to identify the team's progression through the tasks required when creating a successful presentation. You will remember that team members need to present *distinct solutions* for the local problem you identified together. Since you are each exploring a unique global perspective, proposed ways of solving the problem *should be substantially different*. *Avoiding overlap* is just one of the reasons why it is important for teams to *meet, discuss, record* and *reflect on* their progress. Other reasons to check in with your team include *keeping each other on track,* and *sharing ideas, knowledge or skills*. More significantly, people learn better when they communicate their arguments and develop, refine and review ideas with others.

Starting point

Reflect and discuss with your team whether you are meeting the project brief so far.

Read the introduction above again and answer these questions about your team:
- In what ways are our solutions different?
- What types of records are we keeping?
- How do our reflective logs differ?
- How well are we keeping ourselves/each other on track?
- Which ideas, knowledge or skills have we shared so far?
- How true is the final sentence of the introduction?

Activity 1: Organising ideas to tell the story of your presentation

a) **Read the advice below.**

It is useful to begin organising your arguments into a coherent narrative, or story. One way of doing this is to think about what you will say in each section of a presentation. More importantly, if you can't yet decide, then you have identified what you need to think about and research further. Further research may include a combination of activities: reading, viewing, listening or discussing your findings, queries and thoughts with others. Look at the sections a student, Jen, is using as the outline for her presentation story.

Greeting/welcome ➔ Introducing local problem/the **rationale** for my perspective ➔ Outline of presentation structure ➔ First section (the state of play; hosting international sporting events and corruption) ➔ Analysing and evaluating the main point(s) ➔ Communicating arguments, clarifying with supporting evidence ➔ Giving examples ➔ Second section ➔ (repeat)

b) Identify which sections you can say something about in relation to your problem/solution, and those that are less clear.
c) One way you can test your readiness to present is to try out these alternative ways of getting your 'story' across. Work with a partner. Adapt or use the presentation structure above to complete one of the following tasks:
   - **Micro-blog** your presentation story in 140 characters (set up a #).
   - **Walk and talk** – tell your presentation story on the move and record a draft version.
   - **Record the highlights** of your presentation story as a trailer (audio or video).
   - **Sketch-note or storyboard** your presentation story.
d) Work with a partner from another team to outline your presentation. Take it in turns to be each other's 'non-specialist audience' and clarify any points that are unclear.

> **Key advice**
>
> Organising your arguments and ideas into a narrative for your presentation and reflecting on the processes involved should reveal insights into your own strengths and areas for development. Don't forget to keep records (e.g. voice notes) to inform your reflective journal or log.

> **Quick task**
>
> Discuss: Which stage(s) of the team development process have you been through? Which stage(s) are you at now? Check back with the diagram on page 129.

Building your presentation

You are ready to start thinking about how to present your ideas. The language you need to structure the oral (spoken) content of your presentation is focused on in Unit 8.5 and the visual content in Unit 8.6. The focus of this section is on the texts for your slides. Use these success criteria to evaluate how effectively you communicate your ideas on presentation slides:
- **Legibility:** Can you read the words from the back of the room? Is the font easy to read? Is there too much text?
- **Clear expression:** Is the language accurate? Is it appropriate for the audience?
- **Layout:** Is the text aligned and positioned consistently on each slide? Is there any room to add visual information? Are headings and subsections clear?

> **Key terms**
>
> **rationale:** a reason for doing something (e.g. why you chose your particular global perspective in relation to the local problem, and how it complements those of others)
>
> **micro-blog:** a very short blog, usually comprising 140–280 characters, designed to allow users to share small pieces of content

Activity 2: How effective is the content of these presentation slides?

a) Work with a partner. How effectively are the messages communicated? Use the success criteria to evaluate these slides.

The problem = Food instability

'The economic and social condition caused by the state of having limited or uncertain access to adequate food' [2019, Ministry of Agriculture]

1 in 4 children are living in food poverty

4.2 million kids die because they are malnourished every year

>830 million people don't have enough to eat

THIS EXISTS ALL OVER THE WORLD AND IMPACTS ALL COMMUNITY IN THE US IN EVERY SINGLE STATE

Why does social inequality hurt a society?

It can impact negatively on:

- the freedom to travel, assemble and speak freely
- the right to vote
- rights over property
- access to health-care services, education, adequate housing, jobs, banking services, holidays, etc. etc.
- linked with gendered, racial and economic inequality
- childhood inequality can lead to adult poverty & academic underachievement

---

HOW PARTICIPATING IN SPORTS REDUCES INEQUALITY IN OUR RURAL COMMUNITIES

- WINNING IN WORLD EVENTS PROVIDES ASPIRATIONAL MOTIVATION FOR LOCAL AREAS
- HOWEVER, THE CHANCES OF BLACK AND MINORITY ETHNIC BACKGROUND BECOMING CHAMPIONS IS ALMOST NON-EXISTENT. WHY IS THIS?

Universal access to electricity?

Over a billion people are estimated to be living without electricity globally, and hundreds of millions of people can access only limited, expensive or unreliable power.

Most of those with limited or no power access live in poor and remote areas of south Asia and sub-saharan Africa.

However, 1 in 9 families in the UK are in fuel poverty, unable to heat their homes adequately. 14 million Americans live in fuel poverty too. 23.5% of people in the EU are in the same boat, as we will see in these graphs.

---

b) Decide where edits are necessary and rewrite the slides together. Remember to consider the success criteria:

- legibility
- clear expression
- layout.

c) Work with your team. Compare your improved versions of the slides. Which section of the presentation structure might the slides come from?

Activity 3: How effective is the referencing of these presentation slides?

a) Look at these examples of slides that reference sources used in student presentations. Do they meet the brief your teacher gave for sources/referencing? Why, or why not?
b) Fix the references so they meet the requirements for your referencing system.

References of cited works/images

Scott, W. (2018) The new rules for business and PR; using social media productively. New York: John Wiley and Sons.

Digicultural Annual Report (2020) Retrieved from https://www.wdp.com/investors/annual-report-2020 21.4.2020

Digital Image. Web. Civil unrest locations, Black Lives Matter. U.S. State Dept. Retrieved from https://www.aljazeera.com/indepth/interactive/2020/06/mapping-citiesprotests/200319.html 17.4.20

Sources

○ 'Escape from A Modern day Sweatshop; How the Slaves of Today become activists'. OK! magazine N.p., .n.d. Last accessed 09.05.2020

○ 'Ethical fashion; sweatshops still exist everywhere' Good World magazine N.p., .n.d. Last accessed 03.03.2020 https://good.net.uk

○ Finkelstein, J. (2012) '7 Good reasons sweatshops persist' N.p. Last accessed Apr. 20.2020 www.doublelepundit.com

Activity 4: What do you know? The dos and don'ts of writing your slides

a) Work together to decide if the statements below are dos or don'ts. Discuss and clarify the answers with other groups/teachers.

do	don't

Use eight + bullet points on a slide. → (Why not?)

Use complete sentences on slides.

← Cite sources. (How?)

Use different layouts on each slide.

Use lots of quotations.

Use a large font size.

Check spelling and grammar.

Write each section title.

Summarise each argument.

Use a maximum of ten slides.

Final task: Drafting your slides

Look back at the presentation outline in Activity 1, and the 'research story' you prepared. Draft the written content of each slide, choosing a template from the presentation software you are considering or designing your own.

Reflective plenary

Work with your team. Review and feed back on the strengths and weaknesses of the content you created, and the presentation template design. Identify and discuss what you have learned from this drafting process.

8.5 Using language to present effectively

In this unit you will:
- create an effective presentation script
- explore and use 'signpost' language.

Critical Path
You will need to:
- communicate your arguments clearly, effectively and persuasively.

Deconstruction	Reconstruction	Reflection	Communication	Collaboration
		✓	✓	

The language you use to introduce ideas in an oral **presentation** should help your listeners follow and navigate through the arguments you make. Understanding how to involve your audience by using clear verbal signals and selecting appropriate language will make your presentation effective.

Good afternoon! So today I'm going to talk about how to keep your audience's attention. No 'Death by PowerPoint!' from me!

Starting point

'Death by PowerPoint' describes the boredom an audience might experience during a presentation. A dull presentation often contains too many slides with many bullet points and poor graphics, which the presenter reads aloud verbatim, often losing eye contact with the audience.

a) Work with a partner. Discuss how to avoid 'Death by PowerPoint'.
b) What tips would you give for a better presentation?

Effective speaking is a million-dollar skill, a pathway to success in all areas of your life.

Ty Boyd

Activity 1: What is required in this presentation?

a) **Focus group:** What *don't* you know? Discuss and correct these tips from a student blog. Work together to identify any knowledge gaps to research.

> **Top tips**
> a The aim of the presentation is to express arguments in spoken form.
> b The presentation gives the team's perspectives on a global problem.
> c The presentation must be recorded in front of a live audience.
> d The presentation must use video.
> e The presentation should last up to seven minutes.
> f The 'listening audience' for the presentation includes teachers and examiners.
> g References are cited orally during the presentation, and on accompanying slides.
> h Technology isn't obligatory; posters, paper, photos and books can be used.
> i All presentation software may be used, but each team should use the same format.

Key term

presentation: a talk for an audience to give information, ideas and evidence for arguments that make a case or tell a story about something from a unique perspective

b) **Peer review:** Work with a different group to evaluate the accuracy of your research. Each group member should present a (different) 'take away' presentation tip to the class in one sentence.

Activity 2: How clearly is the message communicated?

The four extracts below are from different presentations given in class to rehearse and prepare for this part of the course. If you want to understand how to communicate effectively, you first need to consider how clearly messages are conveyed.

a) Read these extracts from a Team Project presentation. Are there any examples of 'Death by PowerPoint'? Identify these and discuss why.

A I'm happy to have this chance to speak with you all and I wish everyone welcome. I hope you are having a good day and I'd like to say big thank you for coming to watch me present my solution to our Team Project. I mean I am going to tell you about the research I did to try and find ways of solving the problem we have been looking at, but from another angle, from the perspective of activism at school and climate change strikes.

B This afternoon I will show you how we can address the impact of 'fast fashion' on the environment from the perspective of sustainability. As we have heard, the economics of fast fashion drive the fashion industry on a global level. Mo presented his solutions to the industry's exploitation of migrant workers. Earlier, Gayani discussed the ethics of fast fashion. Now I'll divide this talk into four sections, first of all I'll…

C So moving on to the issue of animal rights, I will begin by outlining the legal situations worldwide… eight different ones as you can see on this world map. I believe that we should adopt a new civil code, so quoting here from the Global Animal Law Association's website 'giving a new status to animals'. You can read their definition of this – nothing more boring than a presenter turning round and reading the exact same words on the slide out loud, right?

D Hey everyone. Thanks so much for being here today, I'm going to have a short chat about why fish are so important for a sustainable future. I think it's a good idea to start with the fact that scientists know about 32 000 species of fish. But! These guys are discovering more than 2000 previously unknown types each year. Generally speaking, there are two distinct and separate types…

b) Use these questions and example answers to analyse the language used in A–D.
 - Is the language appropriate for non-specialist audiences (i.e. classmates/teachers/examiners)? For example, D is too informal (*Hey*; *But!*; *guys*; *short chat*).
 - Is the message clear? For example, A is too wordy – it will make audiences fall asleep before the presentation begins!
 - Could it be easier to understand? Improved how?
 - D sounds unprepared: *I think it's a good idea to start with…*

c) Work with a partner to improve and rewrite A–D.
d) Work in groups. Compare your edits. Which expressions or strategies could you use in your presentations? Note any issues, knowledge or language gaps to research.

How is presentation language constructed?

Each presentation is unique. However, language that helps the audience to follow a presentation and connect arguments is referred to as 'signposting' language.

A student called Anika is working on the language for her presentation, using the grid in Activity 3 to help her structure the different sections. If you want to construct an effective presentation, this is a process you will need to work through.

Activity 3: Signposting language

a) Read these extracts from Anika's notes and identify the expressions that help signal or signpost the arguments and sections of her presentation.

Outline of sections	Anika's notes
Greeting/welcome Introducing topic and rationale	Good afternoon everyone. My name's Anika, and today I'm going to make a case for banning the use of private cars in our city centre from an environmental perspective.
Outline of presentation structure	This presentation is divided into three parts: I'll begin by introducing an analysis of the current problem, go on to analyse the impact on air quality, and finally I will present possible solutions.
Introducing the first section	First of all then, I'd like to start by showing you some of the data so that you can better understand the big picture.
Analysing and evaluating the main point(s)	So why is this important? Well, there are three reasons. The first is the fact that our city is currently breaking the law by exceeding the legal limits set for nitrous dioxide. The second reason is…
Communicating arguments, clarifying with supporting evidence	So, according to the World Health Organization's calculations, around 15 000 lives a year are lost due to poor air quality. Let's consider the economic cost of this public health problem; Greenpeace estimates this to be 6.4 billion dollars over the last five years.
Giving examples	To illustrate the reduction in air pollution that could be made by banning diesel engines, 99.4% of our city would comply with international legal limits of NO_2.
Completing a section	I have argued that more sustainable alternatives to travelling in private cars exist, and we have examined these in detail.
Introducing the different sections of your presentation	The next issue I'd like to focus on is how to solve the problem of transporting people through our city sustainably.
Summarising	So, to summarise the points discussed, we need to think about how many *people* we can move through our city, *not* how many *cars*. We can do this, as you have seen, by…
Closing Coming to conclusions	Finally, I'd like to conclude by asking you to close your eyes and imagine our city in 2040. Will it look like this? Or this?

Activity 4: What other examples of signposting language may be used?

a) There are many different ways of signalling your intentions as you present. Here are some more examples that Anika has decided to use to show her ability to use a *variety* and a *range* of language. Identify what these 'signposts' indicate. In which section(s) of Anika's presentation could they fit?

To sum up the main points…
Finally, let me summarise the arguments/points I have made…

Then I'll…
After that I'll go on to… (and)
Next, I'll…

We have seen/learned that/how/why…
I've shown how/why/the way(s) that…

In other words…
So, what I'm saying here is…
So, on one hand… while on the other…

Finally, I'll…

Moving on, let's turn to… (e.g. the question, issue of…)
I'd like to explain/expand on/discuss/demonstrate/elaborate on/look

Therefore/in conclusion/to conclude…
So, I'll conclude by… (-ing)

Let's consider how/why/the fact that…
Looking at… in more detail, we can see that…
This can be explained by…
X is significant/crucial/the key to…
Taking an alternative perspective/view…

Activity 5: Using signposting language to create a powerful script

Now it is your turn to construct and signpost the outline of your presentation. Create and use your own grid with signposting language from Anika's examples. By completing the steps below, you will be ready to practise giving your presentation.

a) Decide how many sections you need in your presentation.
b) Decide how long the sections should be.
c) Write a title (or heading) for each section.
d) Write your main points and arguments in each section of your grid.
e) Write a script for your presentation using appropriate signposting language.
f) Rehearse, record and time yourself speaking.

Final task: Practising the presentation

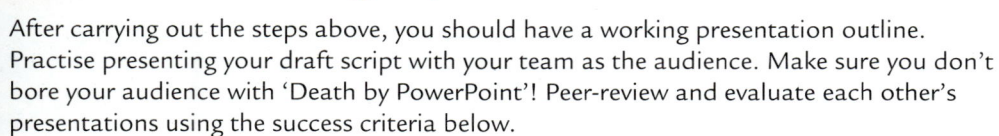

After carrying out the steps above, you should have a working presentation outline. Practise presenting your draft script with your team as the audience. Make sure you don't bore your audience with 'Death by PowerPoint'! Peer-review and evaluate each other's presentations using the success criteria below.

Success criteria
Check that the presentations:

- provide a solution for the problem researched
- give a distinct perspective
- are no more than ten minutes long
- use signposting language and a logical structure
- make arguments and points clearly.

Reflective plenary

What have you learned about communicating your message effectively in a presentation?

Make a list in your reflective journal or Workbook. For example: *Signposting language helps presenters to keep the audience's attention because they know where the presentation is going. I've learned expressions to introduce each section of a presentation – different ways of saying the same thing add variety to my language.*

8.6 Supporting your presentation visually

In this unit you will:
- consider how to communicate information visually in order to engage an audience
- create infographic support for your slides.

Critical Path

You will need to:
- communicate the strengths and weaknesses of infographic information.

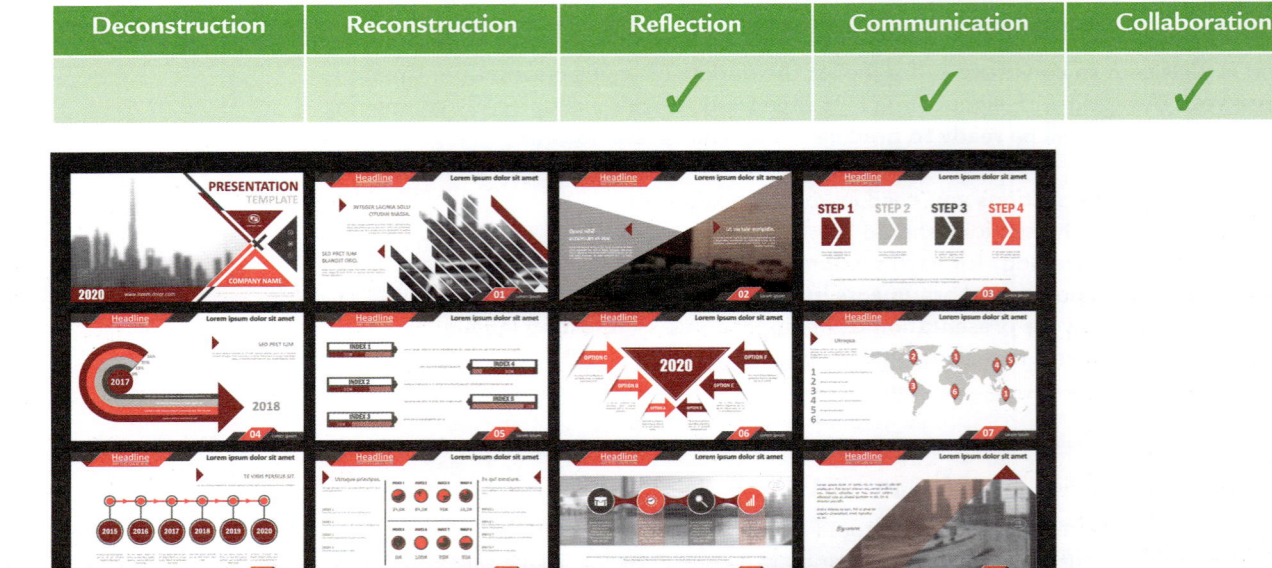

Deconstruction	Reconstruction	Reflection	Communication	Collaboration
		✓	✓	✓

Have you heard the saying 'a picture can paint a thousand words'? To complete your presentation, you need to consider how to make it visually appealing, and ensure that colours and visual information support your content. Presentation software might help by providing suggested templates and colour schemes. In this unit, you will explore some important guiding principles.

Activity 1: What image types will enhance your presentation?

a) Look at these notes a student team is considering for visual elements of slides. How familiar are you with these? What else can you add?

Image/media type	Potential elements to research
typeface	check accessible fonts
layout, shapes (e.g. arrows)	check what the software allows (or import?)
background, font colour	decide! everyone will use different ones!
graphs, charts, statistical data	from original sources (take a screenshot? check how to reference!)
infographics	check best digital file types (GIF, TIFF, JPEG, PNG, EPS?)

photographs (cropped?)	Creative Commons or open source image banks (check attribution) or use our own?
icons (?)	ditto
drawings and cartoons	unless professional, inappropriate (? check)
animations	?
transitions	? maybe too 'old school' and unnecessary?
audio	check microphone for narrating slides (who selected this option/live presentation?) sound check – quiet recording space?
video	will any of us use film/video? maybe very short, less than 30 seconds? (what would PURPOSE be? Team to feed back and help)

b) Work together to decide which of these different visual and audio elements you would each like to use on your slides. Arrange a skills swap session to help each other.

What design principles will help to achieve a visually pleasing presentation?

Presenters play the most crucial role of conveying information in accessible and inclusive ways for their listening and viewing audiences, whether presentations are live, or they are narrating slides to be viewed by audiences in different locations at different times.

A slide deck should engage the attention of audiences and communicate the content of a presentation (summarise main points, arguments, supporting evidence, solutions, etc.). However, the visual information should guide and support points made orally or in writing, and never clash with or compete with an audience's attention.

Presentation design experts believe there should be a sense of equilibrium or balance in the 'visual weight' of a slide, so you should consider how many elements to include, i.e. size, colour, number of objects (words and images). It is important to think about where to place these on the slide, so they are equally weighted on both sides of a horizontal or vertical axis, or around a central point. You can balance by judicious use of colour, space and shapes.

A **visual hierarchy** is also important to emphasise and lead the eye, so look at the position of the objects on a slide in terms of focal points, size, style, borders and frames, and negative space. The way we perceive colour varies, but darker ones are 'heavier' to the eye, so arrange colours across the slide from dark to light. The contrast between background colours and text or images is important for audiences to be able to 'read' and interpret these correctly. Certain combinations to avoid are brown/black, red/green, red/blue and purple/blue.

🔑 Key term

visual hierarchy: the arrangement of elements on a page so users can understand the information

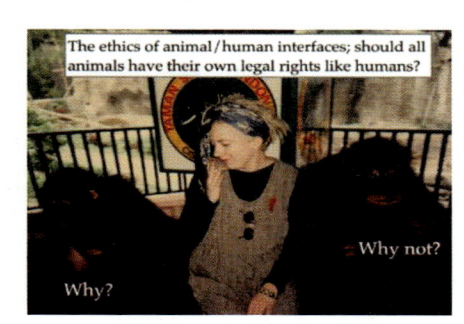

Activity 2: Evaluating the 'readability' of slides

a) Look at the four slides on page 147. In what ways are or aren't the slides easy to read? Are they balanced, visually appealing and engaging for an audience? Why, or why not? What needs to be improved?
b) Work with a partner to compare your evaluations. How far do you agree?

Activity 3: Assessing the visual elements needed for 'slide-appeal'

a) Look at these examples of presentation slides with a partner. Identify the text layout and design features that need editing and decide what edits are needed.
b) What images or other visual elements would you add to your revised text? Find useful examples.

What is my solution?

- innovative local desalination plants
    - provides work
    - reduces reliance on international aid
  1. Use reverse osmosis & solar power

Some nations get up to 45% domestic H_2O

  2. Use human waste and sewage to make water, e.g. NEWater plants

Singapore invented in 1972, completed in 2000 – by-products are usable electricity and ash

---

HUMAN GENETIC MODIFICATION

Arguments against proposed law

- Designer Babies
- Gender Imbalance
- Longer-term unforeseeable consequences
- Ethical regulation
- Religious opposition
- Creating 'enslaved' workers

Final task: Selecting visual elements for your slides

After working through and discussing the activities in this unit, you should have a clearer idea of good design for presentation slides. Now work on your slides for optimal visual appeal and audience engagement. Peer-review and evaluate each other's completed presentation slides using the criteria below.

Check if your presentation slides:
- are clear and easy to read
- have a layout and design that is pleasing/is balanced
- have visual information that adds (rather than detracts) from the message
- use background colour, fonts and other elements
- communicate clearly and engagingly.

Reflective plenary

What have you learned about designing harmonious presentation slides? Make a list in your reflective journal or Workbook. For example: *The colour-wheel we studied in Art and Design is so helpful for considering contrasts.*

8.7 Practice and evaluation

In this unit you will:
- practise your presentation with a live audience
- evaluate and receive peer assessments for improvement.

Critical Path

You will need to:
- communicate your reflective analysis of your own and others' presentations.

Deconstruction	Reconstruction	Reflection	Communication	Collaboration
		✓	✓	✓

Starting point: Audit: Are you ready to present?

Work with a partner. Interview each other by asking and answering these questions to discover how ready you are to present:
- Have you decided to read your script and narrate slides, or to present 'live'?
- If you are presenting live, what prompts/cue cards have you prepared?
- Will you use any objects or hold a demonstration to engage the audience?
- Have you rehearsed and recorded your presentation? Which areas for improvement did you/others identify?

Final task

You are now going to make your presentations. Follow the guidelines below and on the following page.
- Speak clearly so that the audience can hear you, and use language appropriate for your non-specialist audience.
- Engage your audience with eye contact, a relaxed and appropriate posture and a central position in the room. Don't turn your back on your 'listening audience'. Make sure your face shows that you are focused and enthusiastic about communicating your research and solution(s). Use clear and appropriate gestures where needed – for example, to refer to your slides.

Take it in turns to present your distinct and contrasting perspectives on the local problem your team identified. As you listen to the others in your team, and watch the presentations, make notes under these criteria headings to inform your feedback when giving peer evaluations.

Presentation slides

- Is the information communicated clearly and legibly?
- Is the slide layout and design pleasing? Is it balanced?
- Is there engaging visual information? Have you made good use of colour, fonts and other elements?

Giving your presentation

- Are the arguments and points communicated clearly throughout each section (i.e. volume sufficient? language? logical structure?)
- Are you creating an engaging 'presence' throughout (facial expression, eye contact, gestures, body language, position)?
- Is there a solution provided for the problem researched?
- Is there a distinct perspective given – clearly different from that of other team members?
- How is the timing – is it more than seven/less than ten minutes?

Presentation self-evaluation

Make notes using the guidance above after giving your presentation to evaluate your own performance and slides. This will help you to benefit fully from this rehearsal.

Team feedback and peer assessment

Take it in turns to start by assessing your own presentations, using the notes you made to evaluate your slides and performance. Then listen to the members of your team give their feedback, using the notes they made to assess how successfully your presentation met the criteria above.

- If a presenter identifies an area for their own improvement, this does not need to be repeated by others. Instead, suggest ways of achieving this successfully.
- Be kind and thoughtful, but honest. Your team may not always agree, so don't forget to ask your teacher's opinion.

Reflective plenary

Identify a *minimum of three areas for improvement* after discussing your presentation with your team, your teacher and classmates. You could start: *The most significant areas for improvement are…*

Write an entry for your reflective log identifying what you need to do change or improve, why this is necessary and how you can make this happen, i.e. what strategies/skills you could try.

For example: *My voice isn't always easy to hear at the back of the room, so I need to increase my volume. I am going to practise projecting my voice with Cigdem standing at the back of the room – she can indicate when she can't hear me. I may decide to record my presentation and narrate my slides as a voiceover instead of giving a live presentation (although it is a good life skill to go 'live'!).*

Chapter 9

Reflecting on the Team Project: the Reflective Paper

Reflection is an important stage of the Critical Path, and becoming a reflective learner is central to the Cambridge International AS & A Level Global Perspectives and Research syllabus. This chapter will develop your understanding of reflection by looking at reflective learning models. You will explore how reflection is applied to your Team Project, and you will focus on how to approach the Reflective Paper that charts your response to the experience of the Team Project.

9.1 Reflection and reflective models
9.2 Reflecting on collaboration
9.3 Writing the Reflective Paper

9.1 Reflection and reflective models

In this unit you will:
- develop your understanding of what reflection involves using reflective learning models.

Critical Path

You will need to:
- understand the principles of reflection and how they are applied through models.

Deconstruction	Reconstruction	Reflection	Communication	Collaboration
		✓		

In this unit, you will be looking further into what constitutes reflection and, in particular, how reflective learning models can support the process of reflection. In Unit 9.2, you will then apply your learning to the Team Project and the Reflective Paper.

Starting point

Read this quotation by the author Paulo Coelho and work with a partner to discuss the questions below.

'When you repeat a mistake, it is not a mistake anymore: it is a decision.'

a) How true is this quote from your own experience or observation of others?
b) How does the quotation relate to your understanding of reflection?

What is reflection?

In Chapter 4, you learned what reflection is and how it supports learning and skills development. Reflection is defined as a 'critical awareness of the learner's personal standpoint and how that impacts on their response to different opinions and diverse ways of thinking'. It involves thinking deeply about content and making links between new and previous learning; it also involves the ability to reflect on which strategies and behaviours are helpful for learning, communication and collaboration.

Reflection is a skill that is beneficial for all areas of life, professional and personal. By becoming a reflective learner, you will develop a mind-set that will help you to constantly improve the way you approach and complete tasks in all areas of your life.

Reflection is central to the Critical Path and should be seen as an iterative learning process which needs to be practised. An iterative process means doing something again and again, each time with modifications to improve performance. By reflecting on a project, you will be able to analyse and evaluate what went well and which things could be improved. When you are using the Critical Path, you should always be asking yourself questions, for example: *What do I think now? Why is this information useful? Does my plan need adapting? What is the impact of that perspective on my personal opinion?* This type of self-questioning, to better understand yourself, your learning and your experiences, is central to reflection.

Activity 1: Learning from experience

Think back to a task you completed for the first time. This could be anything, from organising a party, to writing an essay, to playing a new piece of music.

a) How did the completed task match what you hoped to achieve?
b) What would you do differently next time around?

Discuss your answers in small groups.

What are reflective learning models?

Reflection is a thinking skill that is designed to help you learn and improve in all areas of life, so you need to learn *how* to reflect. This is where reflective learning models come in. Reflective learning models all share the same basic aim, which is to learn from past experiences in order to inform the present and the future.

Probably the most well-known reflective model is Gibbs' reflective cycle. This has six stages and can be visualised like this:

Gibbs' reflective cycle

Description → Feeling → Evaluation → Analysis → Conclusion → Action plan → (Description)

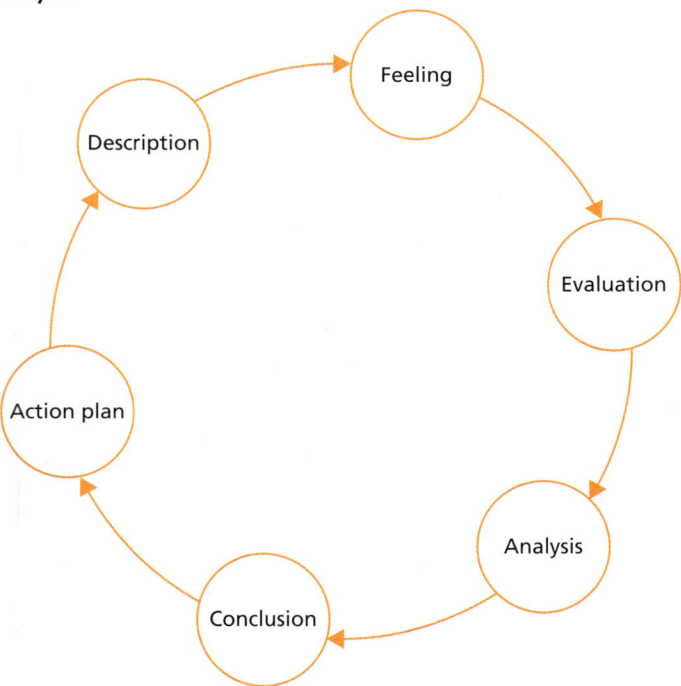

As the model takes the form of a cycle you will see that the process, once completed, begins again with learning applied to a new improved version of the task, or to a task with similarities.

The first stage of this reflective cycle is **Description** and aims to give a full picture of what happened. If you want to describe a situation or events in detail, you need to ask yourself some key questions, such as: *What happened? What did I do? Who was there? Where was I and why was I there?* Record your answers in detail.

The next stage focuses on **Feeling**. This stage of the cycle is about understanding how you feel. This is important because how you feel will ultimately impact on what you do. Here, you should ask yourself questions such as: *How did I feel during a situation? How do I feel about the situation now/afterwards? If others were involved, what were they thinking and feeling?*

Reflecting is often a personal experience and you should be mindful that your feelings may be private and that you should only share what you are comfortable to share. That said, in order to reflect successfully, you need to be honest with yourself, and your feelings may be mixed or complex.

The third stage is **Evaluation**. You will have come across this term throughout the course as it is an important part of both deconstruction and reconstruction. In the reflective cycle, evaluation requires you to be objective and honest when thinking about a particular situation and what happened. You need to ask yourself questions such as: *What went well? What didn't go well? What was good? What was bad? Was I a positive or negative force?*

The fourth stage is **Analysis** and this is another concept you will be familiar with. So far you have concentrated on *identifying* aspects of a situation and your feelings about them. At stage four, you should focus on your *analysis* of key details so that you can begin to learn from them. The focus here shifts from 'what' to 'why'. *Why did that go well?* or *Why did that go badly? Why did I perform in that way?* Then go further here and ask yourself: *What additional knowledge is needed to understand the situation?*

The fifth stage involves drawing **Conclusions** and follows logically from the previous stages of reflection. You will be able to look at the strengths and weaknesses of your original response and draw conclusions that will help you to form an action plan at the next stage. The questions you should ask yourself here might include: *What have I learned? What worked well and would I do again? What didn't work? What would make the experience more positive? Are there other things I could have done?*

The sixth and final stage is the **Action plan**. This is where you convert your conclusions into a clear action plan that details all the steps you will take next time you do a similar task.

And then the cycle begins again.

You will see Gibbs' reflective cycle applied to the Team Project in the Special focus sections of this chapter.

Besides Gibbs, there are other reflective models that you might choose to use, such as Bassot's integrated reflective cycle, which comprises four stages:

1. The Experience – describe the situation.
2. Reflect on Action – identify the positives and negatives and take account of your thoughts and feelings.
3. Theory – what have you learned that can be used in future situations?
4. Preparation – use your reflection to prepare for future situations.

Also, see the model described in Unit 4.3 Developing reflection.

Final task: Comparing reflective learning models

You will find more reflective learning models online.

a) Choose any two models to compare.
b) What are the similarities and differences between the models?
c) Is there a model you prefer? Why?

Reflective plenary

Work with a small group. How would you summarise the core purpose of reflective learning? Discuss your ideas and create an infographic poster to present to the class/ another group.

9.2 Reflecting on collaboration

In this unit you will:
- learn to apply reflective learning models to collaborative work in the Team Project.

Critical Path

You will need to:
- understand the principles of reflection
- reflect on collaboration, applying appropriate models.

Deconstruction	Reconstruction	Reflection	Communication	Collaboration
		✓		✓

How are reflective learning models used?

In Chapter 8, you focused in detail on the Team Project. Alongside your project, you will need to write a Reflective Paper to track your experience and learning, specifically looking at how effective your team collaboration was and also your individual learning journey.

Starting point

Reflective learning models tend to be cyclical – why is this? Discuss with a partner.

In this unit, you will be applying Gibbs' reflective model to your observations in your reflective log. In Unit 9.3, you will use these logged entries to feed into your observations in your Reflective Paper.

Special focus: Applying Gibbs' reflective model to the Team Project

The six stages of Gibbs' reflective model

Stage	Key advice
Stage 1: Description Our teacher assigned us groups to work in that were based on broad areas of interest. I was in a group of four people: Joseph, Aadesh, Laura and myself, Prisha. We were brought together because we have a shared interest in public health issues. We decided to set up a WhatsApp group and also two face-to-face meetings for the following weeks.	You should make notes at the time or soon after your meetings. Having an accurate description of what happened, what you did, who was there and why you were there will make further reflection easier and more complete. However, when writing your reflective paper, try to avoid too much description.

Stage	Key advice
Prisha's observation Even this relatively straightforward task took more time than expected. So we knew that actually finalising a problem to focus on, and then assigning perspectives for the four of us was not going to be easy.	
Stage 2: Feelings Having to work with new people was daunting. Initially, I was keen to agree with the majority and felt nervous about expressing an opinion. Aadesh was quite dominant at the start and I could tell that not everyone was comfortable with the group dynamic. We quickly agreed on our local problem of unsafe water supply, we live in Flint, Michigan and in 2016 a state of emergency was declared after high levels of lead were found in the water supply. At our second meeting we assigned perspectives. I was initially nervous about this as I thought we would argue as a group.	It is important to acknowledge your feelings honestly. There is no requirement for the rest of your group to see your reflective paper so there is no need to feel constrained. Part of being a reflective learner is to understand how your feelings impact what you do. Remember, your feelings and those of your team mates will develop and change over the course of the project.
Prisha's observation Using WhatsApp between face-to-face meetings reduced some of the tension. Joseph, Laura and I felt more comfortable in sharing thoughts (and some jokes) and it appeared that Aadesh became less dominant in online group chats.	
Stage 3: Evaluation As a group we wasted too much time; we didn't work efficiently. Although group work evolved and improved, it took too long to reach a positive group dynamic. From the start we were more like a group of individuals than a cohesive team. Aadesh was too dominant and Joseph was too willing to just go along with whatever was said, thinking this would make things easier. Laura and I took too long to assert ourselves. On the positive side, it was really useful to have scheduled meetings in advance, this gave us a sense of obligation and a clear timeline. The WhatsApp group helped us as individuals come together as a team. It provided an easy space to communicate and that seemed to break down some barriers.	What went well and what didn't go well are really important details for your reflective paper. This evaluative stage of the reflective cycle should be to the fore in your reflective paper.

Stage	Key advice
Prisha's observation As time went on, I felt my role in the team became more pronounced and I felt I was good at negotiating compromises between individuals that helped the project move forward.	
Stage 4: Analysis I think there were a couple of reasons why we wasted time initially. Firstly, we didn't have a plan or an agenda and so we didn't allocate time effectively. We spent ages just working out dates for future meetings and this meant we rushed through other more important things. Secondly, bringing a team of people together for the first time is difficult and it isn't easy to get things going. At the beginning I didn't know much about formal meetings but having done some research I can now see how having an agenda, taking minutes, allocating action steps and other elements of formal meetings are essential for them to be effective. I have also researched the concept of ice-breakers for new teams. This would have helped us understand each other's interests and personalities from the start. WhatsApp was effective as it allowed us to share thoughts in our own space and time.	In the evaluative stage you were able to identify what went well and what didn't. The analysis stage goes further and requires deeper reflection. The questions you ask of yourself and the team are not 'what' but 'why'. For example, at the evaluative stage Prisha identified that she was not assertive enough and at the analysis stage she is able to say why that was the case. She went further and gathered knowledge of techniques, such as ice-breakers, that would help overcome this problem in future situations.
Prisha's observation I think in future I would use technology more, I think particularly for my generation that using communication technologies comes more naturally and harnessing other software beyond WhatsApp could really improve teamwork. It was clear that using technology to communicate enabled more of us to express our opinion and that is really important because it prevents **groupthink**.	
Stage 5: Conclusions I think the main thing I learned was that planning meetings in advance is crucial for their success. Setting expectations and sharing relevant information in advance will give meetings both a focus and a framework. I now believe I have learned new skills in terms of collaboration that I will bring to new teamwork situations. Most important is having the confidence to challenge ideas but at the same give space for others to share their thoughts.	The conclusion stage is the culmination of previous sections. Having analysed why things went well or not and extended your knowledge base to take account of any gaps, you are now in a position to succinctly sum up what you have learned, what skills you need to develop and how things will be more positive next time.
Prisha's observation I think one of the most interesting things I learned about teamwork was just because you all agree on something, doesn't mean it's right. It is important to challenge the decisions the team agree on as this will prevent groupthink.	

🔑 Key term

groupthink: when individuals concur with the group decision, even when it may be a bad one, because they don't want to express opinions, suggest new ideas or seem different to everyone else

Stage	Key advice
Stage 6: Action Plan Next time I work collaboratively I will develop techniques to establish the strengths and weaknesses of the individual members. I would assign roles in the group with a facilitator who will allow everyone to speak and keep on task, a note-taker and a time-keeper, plus maybe someone who is a 'groupthink' challenger. This will enhance the fabric of the group and ensure that each member's potential contribution is appreciated. In essence, a group should be more than the sum of its parts. Developing a group dynamic will allow individuals to see the value of the team as greater than their own personal interests.	As you will know, the Critical Path is an iterative process; that is, a process that you repeat and each time you repeat the process you will improve your performance. Your action plan details the improvements you would make based on your learning from a previous experience. This is a key skill that this syllabus seeks to instil in learners.
Prisha's observation Applying Gibb's reflective learning cycle has really helped me to crystallise my thinking about group work and I look forward to having the opportunity to use this reflective learning next time I'm involved in a team project.	

Reflective plenary

Seeing Gibb's reflective learning model applied and reading Prisha's comments will have demonstrated the value of practising reflection.

What does Prisha understand about setting up a team project as a result of the process?

How would you characterise the benefits of applying a reflective learning cycle?

9.3 Writing the Reflective Paper

In this unit you will:
- learn how to structure and write the Reflective Paper.

Critical Path
You will need to:
- reconstruct reflections to form a coherent overview
- communicate your reflections in writing.

Deconstruction	Reconstruction	Reflection	Communication	Collaboration
	✓	✓	✓	

How do you communicate your reflections?

The aim of the Reflective Paper is to pull together and analyse your reflective thinking and learning on the Team Project. You will have a maximum of 800 words in which to reflect on the effectiveness of the team collaboration and on your individual learning. Your learning may be about the problem itself, your research skills and/or your presentation skills.

Starting point

Think again about a task that you completed for the first time. It could be the same task you thought about in Unit 3.1.

a) Take two minutes to tell your partner about the task and how you completed it. Record this.
b) Now listen and reflect on what you said in a). How frequently did you use the pronouns 'I' and 'me' in this personal account?
c) How much of what was said was descriptive or narrative? Did you include analytical comments?

How do I communicate my reflections?

You will need to pay attention to the following when writing up reflections:
- the balance between description and analysis/evaluation
- the tone of voice.

The first stage of Gibbs' model is **Description** – recounting what has been done. This can be useful in your research log for reference, but when communicating your reflections in an assignment, you must focus more on evaluation and analysis rather than descriptive narration. This means exploring how and why you took certain decisions, or what the effect of those decisions was. Description has a place, but the word limit for all of the assignments is strictly enforced so it is important not to waste too much time on simply telling the reader what happened.

How you communicate personal thoughts and feelings is usually very different to the way you write an essay or a report. Writing in the first person in academic assignments is not usually appropriate academic style. However, the Critical Path also involves communicating *personal reflections* and that is quite difficult without using the first person ('I' or 'we').

Activity 1: Focus on purpose and tone

Read the following example based on Ushi's chosen topic of immigration.

I initially believed illegal immigration was negative for the local economy, but the perspective put forward by UNIDOSUS challenged my original thinking. It was clear I had some knowledge gaps and so I began to do further research on some of the evidence put forward in that article.

Ushi's account includes some description of what he did ('I began to do further research') but it is also personal *and* analytical/evaluative.

a) Where does Ushi show he has analysed what he has done or thought?
b) Where does he show that he has evaluated his personal knowledge or perspective?

Ushi's reflective response has begun to consider the impact of other perspectives and is perfectly acceptable written in the first person. What will be important is the structure of your assignment, which will determine when and where you should write in the first person.

What sort of structure will be effective for your written reflection?

There are a number of ways you can approach the organisation of your writing, but the following will ensure you address the core elements of reflection.

Successful structure at a glance

Introduction to topic

Reflections on the effectiveness of teamwork

1. What didn't go well and why.
2. What did go well and why.
3. Intermediary conclusion with suggested areas for improvement.

Reflections on the learning journey

a) **Knowledge**
   1. What were my initial opinions and the impact of further research?
   2. What was the impact of other approaches within the team?
   3. Conclusion on learning journey recognising knowledge gaps.

b) **Skills**
   1. How effective was my approach to research? Consider both strengths and weaknesses.
   2. What would I do next time to improve the research process?
   3. Was the form/style of my presentation engaging and clearly articulated?
   4. Having watched my presentation back, what would I do differently if I had to do it again?
   5. Were my arguments logical and coherently expressed?
   6. In future, how would I better integrate my argument with the supporting visuals?

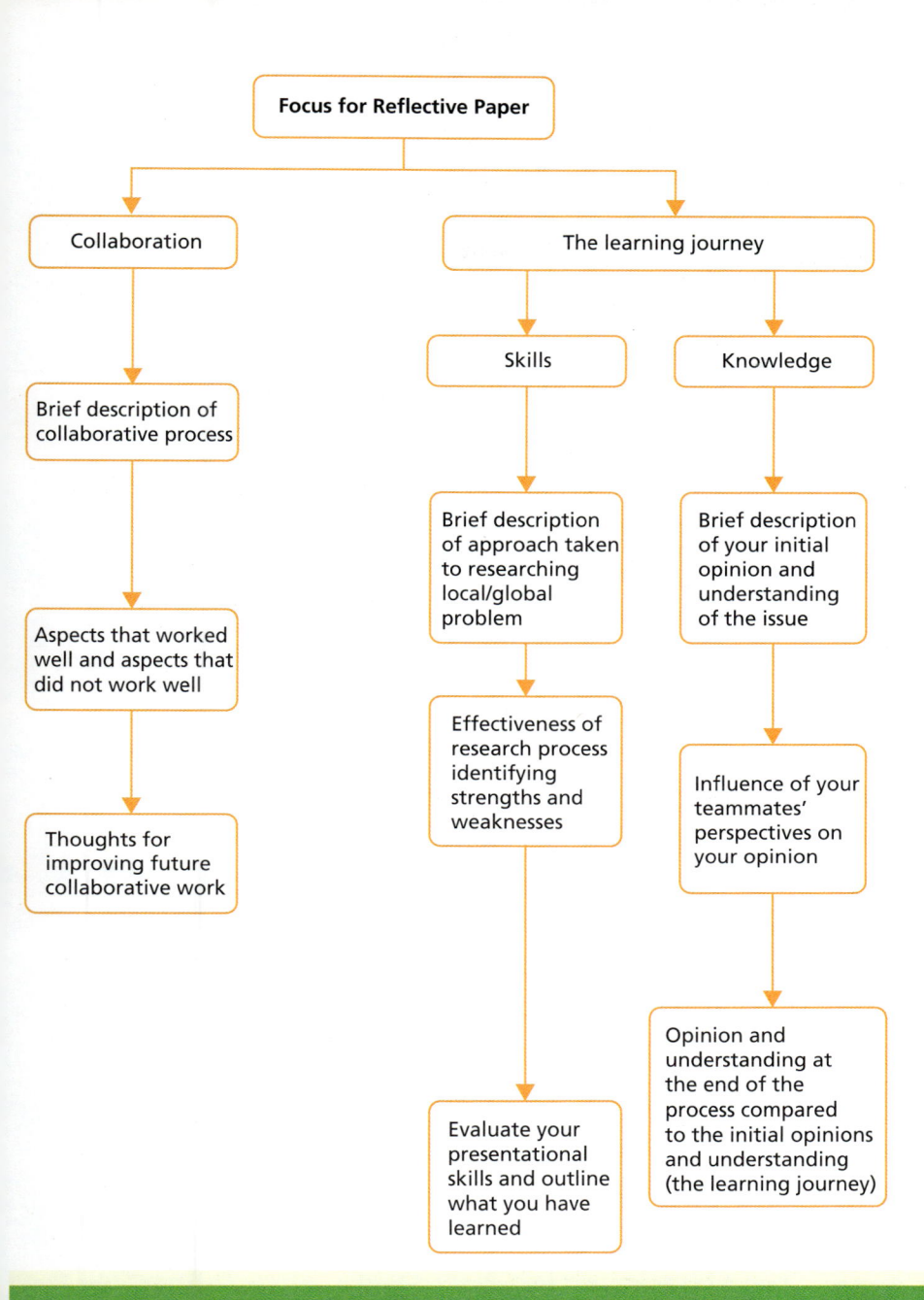

```
                    ┌─────────────────────┐
                    │ Focus for Reflective Paper │
                    └─────────────────────┘
                              │
              ┌───────────────┴───────────────┐
              ▼                               ▼
      ┌──────────────┐              ┌────────────────────┐
      │ Collaboration │              │ The learning journey │
      └──────────────┘              └────────────────────┘
              │                         │              │
              ▼                         ▼              ▼
      ┌──────────────┐          ┌──────────┐   ┌──────────┐
      │ Brief description │     │  Skills  │   │ Knowledge │
      │ of collaborative  │     └──────────┘   └──────────┘
      │ process           │          │              │
      └──────────────┘               ▼              ▼
              │               ┌──────────────┐ ┌──────────────┐
              ▼               │ Brief description │ │ Brief description │
      ┌──────────────┐        │ of approach taken │ │ of your initial   │
      │ Aspects that worked │  │ to researching    │ │ opinion and       │
      │ well and aspects that│ │ local/global      │ │ understanding     │
      │ did not work well   │  │ problem           │ │ of the issue      │
      └──────────────┘        └──────────────┘ └──────────────┘
              │                       │              │
              ▼                       ▼              ▼
      ┌──────────────┐        ┌──────────────┐ ┌──────────────┐
      │ Thoughts for  │        │ Effectiveness of │ │ Influence of your │
      │ improving future│      │ research process │ │ teammates'       │
      │ collaborative work│    │ identifying      │ │ perspectives on  │
      └──────────────┘        │ strengths and    │ │ your opinion     │
                              │ weaknesses       │ └──────────────┘
                              └──────────────┘          │
                                      │                  ▼
                                      ▼          ┌──────────────┐
                              ┌──────────────┐   │ Opinion and      │
                              │ Evaluate your  │   │ understanding at │
                              │ presentational │   │ the end of the   │
                              │ skills and outline│ │ process compared │
                              │ what you have  │   │ to the initial   │
                              │ learned        │   │ opinions and     │
                              └──────────────┘   │ understanding    │
                                                 │ (the learning    │
                                                 │ journey)         │
                                                 └──────────────┘
```

Special focus: Writing the Reflective Paper

Earlier in this chapter, you learned how to apply Gibbs' reflective learning model to the collaborative process through the experience of a student called Prisha. Using Prisha's and her teammate Joseph's papers, you will now focus on how to write the Reflective Paper.

As seen in the diagram above, there are essentially two areas for reflective focus:

1. evaluating the effectiveness of collaboration
2. reflecting upon the learning journey.

As these two areas are quite distinct from one another, it is advisable to structure your Reflective Paper accordingly and treat each area of reflection separately. You could use headings in your paper to help structure your response.

Activity 2: Comparing introductions

Read the following two introductions by Prisha and Joseph.

Prisha	Joseph
Introduction My team consisted of four people: Joseph, Aadesh, Laura and myself, Prisha. We were assigned to the team by our teacher because of our shared interest in public health issues. Our problem was access to clean water. This problem had a local dimension following the discovery of high levels of lead in our local water supply in Flint, Michigan. The problem also has global significance given that over 4000 people die every day as a consequence of not having access to clean water. (83)	**Introduction** First the teacher split us into groups then my team and I went to a small study room to try and choose a topic. We shared ideas and eventually decided on the topic of 'access to clean water'. We then arranged to meet later on that week. (51)

a) Which of the following teacher comments go with which approach?

Comment A: This beginning is essentially a descriptive narration of what happened. It lacks any evaluation, so the reflections do not address the effectiveness of teamwork.

Comment B: This student's introduction is clear and succinct, yet provides a context for why the group are working together, as well as details of the issue.

Now read these further extracts from the next stage of Prisha's and Joseph's paper.

Prisha

Reflection on collaboration

I was apprehensive about working with a team of people I didn't know very well. Our first task was to find a local issue that interested us all. We dived straight into this task and it quickly became clear that some voices were more dominant than others. On reflection the team would have benefited from establishing a process first which would have provided a much needed framework for deciding on our project's focus. (74)

Laura and I quickly realised that we were not operating as a team but as four individuals. To give our group some coherence, we did two things that proved effective. Firstly, we set up a WhatsApp group which provided a different space for group conversations and helped break down barriers between team members. Secondly, we scheduled future meetings in advance. This improved the group performance as it gave us a sense of obligation and a clear timeline to adhere to. (81)

> **Comment**
>
> Prisha's tone is evaluative. She is able to make a judgement about how effectively the team began the process and make a suggestion for improvement. She also uses headings to give the paper a structure.
>
> **Structure**
>
> Having started with weaknesses, Prisha has moved on to strengths. Having done this, she can now offer an intermediary conclusion on the effectiveness of teamwork before moving on to reflect upon her **learning journey**.

> **Key term**
>
> **learning journey:** a useful analogy for developing your skills of reflection; when tackling each element of the course there will be a point of departure or start and a point of arrival or end; when you reflect upon your learning journey you will be reflecting on what you have learned about the issue and about the process

Reflection on learning: Knowledge

My interest in access to clean water began after problems of contamination in my local area were given wide media coverage. Although I understood the importance of access to clean water, it was only through research that I began to understand the complexities of providing clean water to huge populations. Like many, I thought the failures in my local area were solely due to poor leadership, but research showed that the problems were multi-dimensional. (74)

> **Comment**
>
> Prisha begins by stating that her understanding of the issue at the outset of the team project lacks both breadth and depth. She also offers her opinion as to why there are problems with the clean water supply in Michigan. This is useful because Prisha will be able to contrast her understanding and opinion of the issue at the start of the process with her thoughts, having finished the project.
>
> **Structure**
>
> Prisha has continued using headings and has now clearly signalled that she has moved to reflections on her learning journey.

Joseph

Access to clean water is a basic necessity and it is really important that everyone is able to have a reliable supply. Contaminated water and poor sanitation are linked to transmission of diseases such as cholera, diarrhoea, dysentery, hepatitis A, typhoid and polio. This is why the World Health Organization see access to clean water as a Sustainable Development goal. (60)

> **Comment**
>
> What Joseph writes is both accurate and interesting, and although it is offering detail and explanation of the issue, it fails to reflect upon his learning journey. What might be appropriate for an essay on clean water access is not appropriate for a reflective paper.

Activity 3: Identifying success criteria

Read this further paragraph from Prisha.

My focus on clean water access was approached from using the theme of the environment. This was really useful for developing an understanding of the reasons how water supply is contaminated and how this could be prevented. Aadesh approached the issue using an economic theme and it was his findings that had the biggest impact on my understanding of the issue. I hadn't realised that wider economic structures were so important for understanding the difficulties of managing clean water supply, for example, whether water supply was provided by the state or the private sector. This really broadened my understanding and helped in finding a well-rounded solution. (106)

a) What evidence is there that Prisha has considered both her own thematic approach and someone else's?
b) How does the second part of the paragraph show that she is able to structure her ideas to show what she has learned?

In this next section Prisha is beginning to reflect on her approach to research.

Reflection on learning: Research skills

All of my research was done online using search engines. Initially I found the search results overwhelming; there were simply too many sources to choose from. I quickly realised being specific in typing the search term was really important. Finding local information was easier because using 'Michigan' as part of my search term naturally filtered down the results. The global search results were more difficult to organise and I found breaking this down in to a two-stage process really useful. First, I found information from large organisations such as the UN or the World Health Organization. These sources offered a good overview and also made reference to specific cases studies, such as one from Hintalo Wajerat in Ethiopia. I could then focus my research from the general to the specific and this really improved the quality of my research.

Comment

Although Prisha is less evaluative here, the description of her research process shows a real progression. By stating how she progressed from generalised searches to more specific searches, she demonstrates how her research skills improved on her learning journey.

Structure

Again, Prisha introduces her paragraph with clear reference to research. The paragraph is written with logical progression. She begins with the subject of research and then outlines the research problems she encountered. Following on from this, she details the approach taken to try and solve the problem and then concludes by stating how the two-stage approach was successful.

Reflection on learning: Presentation skills

Before giving my presentation, I watched some of my classmates do theirs. I felt many didn't integrate their talk with the PowerPoint; they seemed to just talk without interacting with the visuals and the audience seemed bored. Especially so when the presenter read from a script. With this in mind, I began my presentation with a prop (I appeared to drink filthy water from a glass). This both engaged the audience and perfectly encapsulated the importance of clean water. As a result, my confidence increased and I felt empowered to make direct eye-contact with the audience during my talk. I used my presentation slides to illustrate my arguments by explicitly highlighting features on screen to support my verbal argument. This worked so much better than simply repeating in words what was on the slides.

Comment

Prisha has analysed the presentations by some of her classmates and from there she has been able to assess why some presentations did not engage the audience. This is a really useful form of reflection that then informed her own presentation. There is understandably a tendency to be descriptive about her own presentation but Prisha still maintains an evaluative tone when concluding that her presentation was successful.

Structure

Prisha has indicated in the first few words of a new paragraph that she is now addressing what she has learned from the team project about giving presentations. Logical paragraphing with clear introductory sentences helps create a coherent structure.

Final task

Here are some extracts from a Reflective Paper on a different problem.

I'd never worked in a group before so I wasn't sure what to expect. Once we were all together my anxieties quickly died away as we all got on really well. All of us were interested in medical ethics and we were able to discuss the many associated issues. We had a good group dynamic and I felt we all worked well together.

I thought I had a good understanding of medical ethics before the project started but through initial research I quickly realised there were substantial gaps in my knowledge, particularly in our chosen area of gene therapy. Gene therapy is the process of replacing defective genes with healthy ones, adding new genes to help the body fight or treat disease.

I focused on the ethical theme and whether it was right to edit the genetic profile of unborn babies, whereas my teammate Jonjo focused on the technical theme. Jonjo's research taught me a lot about how the process of gene therapy is actually performed.

a) Read through the extract. Identify or highlight on a copy of the text:
   - where the student reflects on the learning journey for knowledge
   - where he/she reflects on the group dynamic.

   Which aspects of the learning journey are not covered here?
b) Now, identify which parts of the extract are *descriptive* and which parts are *evaluative*.
c) How would you improve these three paragraphs? Write a brief commentary suggesting what the student needs to do.

Reflective plenary

Now that you understand what the Reflective Paper involves and how it should be constructed, think about your own work. Are there particular aspects of the reflective process that concern you?

What do you think will be the most challenging aspect of writing the Reflective Paper?

How can you address these concerns or make sure your Reflective Paper is as good as it can be?

Chapter 10
The Cambridge Research Report

In this chapter, you will focus on understanding what you will learn through the Cambridge Research Report. You will identify your subject and research question, prepare and write a proposal, and begin your investigation.

You will draw on the skills of research and analysis you developed earlier in the course, but you will now have freedom from local or global requirements and can research a topic of your own choice.

This assignment may be challenging, but it will also be rewarding because you will be demonstrating the skills you have acquired throughout the course. You will need to set your analysis within a conceptual framework, follow a research methodology that is specific to your subject, and justify your motivation for selecting your question. You will also need to reflect as you research and develop your ideas and record your reflections in a research log.

10.1 Understanding the task
10.2 Writing the proposal
10.3 Research log
10.4 Identifying a topic
10.5 Primary research and the research process

10.1 Understanding the task

In this unit you will:
- explore and learn about what is expected of you in the Cambridge Research Report.

Critical Path
You will need to:
- review and evaluate the research and academic writing skills you have learned so far
- understand the task in terms of constructing a methodology and analysis of concept.

Deconstruction	Reconstruction	Reflection	Communication	Collaboration
✓	✓	✓		

The Cambridge Research Report is where you have complete independence of choice to pick your area of study. Free from topic and global constraints, it is your opportunity to research a subject of your own choice. It can be based on a specific interest or for a specific purpose, such as preparation for further study. It provides the opportunity for you to bring together your skills and apply them to your personal project.

The focus of this unit is understanding how you can build on the skills you have already learned, particularly from your work on the essay, to complete the Cambridge Research Report effectively. In addition, you will explore new elements, such as setting your own research area and justifying your choice; relating your research choice to appropriate concepts and evaluating your methodological approach.

Starting point

Work with a partner(s). List the skills that you think will be of benefit to the research report. These may be those you have acquired on this course, from other subjects or from other areas of your life. Share your ideas with another pair and identify the three most beneficial.

What is involved in the report?

In simple terms, the report requires you to research an issue and write a 5000-word report about it. There must be a debate around the issue and it must be able to withstand academic analysis. So, for example: *Is Adidas better than Nike?* or *Is popcorn the tastiest treat?* would not be appropriate research issues, even if one could argue a case for or against.

Your report will enable you to demonstrate a number of skills you have already developed from your work on the essay. For example:
- evaluation of perspectives on a chosen issue
- evaluation of a range of sources
- reflection on the impact of alternative perspectives on your argument
- reflection on your conclusions.

Your report will also enable you to demonstrate these *new aspects*:
- Selection and analysis of appropriate **concepts**, for example, feminism. This requires understanding the academic theories that underpin a subject and a demonstration of how your research sits within them.
- Use of discipline-appropriate **methodology** and evaluation of that methodology, for example, the methods commonly used in your subject area. This requires understanding that different methods are applicable to different subject areas and the sources available.
- A more enhanced justification of your research topic and analysis of the question you select, for example: *What is your motivation? How does it help you with further study or develop your knowledge?*
- Reflection on the progress you make while working on your research proposal in your research log; analysis of your research question in your research log.

> **Key terms**
>
> **concept:** an overarching idea or theoretical framework(s) for research
>
> **methodology:** the reasons why you chose the method(s) you use for your research and data collection, e.g. interviews, focus groups (qualitative) or surveys, experiments (quantitative)

Activity 1: Skills you will demonstrate in the Cambridge Research Report

a) Work with a partner(s). Reflect on the new skills you will have to demonstrate in the Cambridge Research Report. Discuss what you think they mean and how the skills you have acquired from planning and writing the essay will help you to develop them.

Special focus: Case study: Understanding new elements of the Cambridge Research Report

A class is about to embark on the Cambridge Research Report process. They are feeling confident as they have already learned to analyse and synthesise arguments and select and evaluate sources at AS Level. However, they have noted some important distinctions and additions. The students decide to review some of these elements and incorporate them into a poster.

The new elements fall into two types: subject appropriate and generic.

Subject appropriate	Generic
Select and analyse concepts	Justify my topic and question
Use appropriate methodology	Complete a research log

Initially, they decide to look at one discipline, social history, as an example. They want to identify and connect some associated concepts and methodologies. The class divides to research each aspect separately. Some students approach subject-specific tutors, while others consult the internet or course handbooks. They bring their ideas back to the class and build their poster for the wall.

Historical concepts
Social history
Marxist
Feminist
Political: Liberal, Conservative

Methodologies
made up of a selection from:
- Literature reviews: what has already been researched in your area of study
- Interviews: gathering data by asking people questions orally
- Surveys: gathering data by asking people questions in a written questionnaire

Primary sources
- Eyewitness accounts of events
- Newspapers, diaries, images, census information
- Fiction
- Oral testimonies: stories passed down through generations or interviews
- Polls and surveys

Sources

Secondary sources
- Academic literature, articles examining/interpreting moments or periods of history
- Documentaries
- Biographies

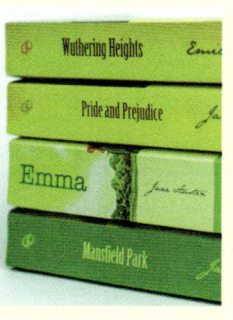

See Unit 2.3 for more information on primary and secondary sources.

Final task

a) Using your own discipline for study, list the associated research methods sources and concepts.

b) Design your own poster and present it to a partner/group/the class.

Reflective plenary

Work in groups. Look back at the skills you identified as the most beneficial for your research report. Consider new aspects covered in this unit and decide which are the most *important* skills for your success. Report these to another group.

10.2 Writing the proposal

In this unit you will:
- understand the purpose of the research proposal
- learn how to write a research proposal.

Critical Path
You will need to:
- deconstruct the debate, reflect on your limits and communicate effectively.

Deconstruction	Reconstruction	Reflection	Communication	Collaboration
✓		✓	✓	

The focus of this unit is to recognise that the proposal is where your research officially begins and to understand how to structure your research proposal. In it, you will see that the writing of the proposal is conducted with guidance from your teacher in the role of supervisor of your research.

Discussions about your proposal

As with every other part of the Cambridge Research Report, the focus here is on skills for life. In the future, you may need to write a research proposal for a university dissertation, a grant application or even for a workplace project. Therefore, learning to write a proposal has independent value beyond the research report.

A research proposal needs to give clear evidence of the value of the research. It must demonstrate that your research project is sustainable in terms of you being able to find enough material to complete it, and worthwhile in terms of its relevance, suitability for academic study, and so on.

You should not expect to write your research proposal in complete isolation, but in discussion with and with feedback from your classmates and teacher. You can expect your discussions to cover your motivation, the debate, the scope, sources and intellectual engagement.

> **Key advice**
>
> Collaboration is not assessed in the Cambridge Research Report, but you will need to communicate effectively with your teacher (for example, listen to guidance).

Motivation

Your teacher will ask you about what motivated you to choose your particular area to study. This is important as it must be an area that will hold your interest and, hopefully, be helpful in your future career path or studies. It is completely acceptable to choose an issue that you are interested in at a personal level, but you may wish to consider linking your interest to an area you will study in future, as this will be beneficial to your university application or personal statements. All of these considerations can be detailed as motivational aspects that have driven your research proposal.

Debate

Here, your teacher will be trying to ascertain that a debate actually exists and that you are not entering a closed topic. They will ask you about any literature review you have undertaken and the primary perspectives on both sides of the issue. They may ask you about your opinion with regard to the issue as it stands, whether you have a hypothesis and if so, why.

Scope

If the arguments and perspectives around the issue are wide, sustaining a 5000-word research report is not going to be a problem. What your teacher really needs to know here is that the area you have selected is not too wide for the word limit. They will explore with you the correct range for your report and the limitations that the word count may place upon it. You will list these limitations in your proposal and they can also form part of your report. In fact, they may even form part of your suggestions for further research or recommendations. You will need to demonstrate that you have thought this through and that you have narrowed your research accordingly. You may, for example, have refined your title to specify a particular country or even region – or if discussing education, you may have narrowed to a specific qualification.

Sources

You will be expected to list the sources that you have used for your preliminary research and the further sources that you will review. One of the most common barriers to research is access to credible sources. Therefore, your teacher will want you to demonstrate that these sources are readily available. For example, if the sources require payment or are not at your local library or online, you should reconsider. Similarly, if you are going to use primary source interviews, you will need to demonstrate that you have access to enough people and have thought about privacy or ethical issues.

Method and methodology

Your teacher will also want to make sure that whatever methodology you have chosen, it is relevant to the issue you have selected, that it is achievable in terms of access to sources and feasible in terms of timetable. You have a short period of time in which to complete your research, analyse, write and submit your report. This may be particularly pertinent to methodological approaches that include surveys, polls or experiments.

Ethical considerations

If your research report includes interviews, you have to consider the ethics of what you are doing and include a section in your proposal.

Your school or college may have an ethics procedure – universities definitely do. This usually requires sign off from an ethics committee. Once the procedures are signed off, you should not deviate from them in any way. Even if there is no ethics procedure, your school may well have guidance around safety or particular processes you need to follow. Make sure you check them out.

Where you choose to use interviews or other forms of face-to-face research, you should prioritise and demonstrate in your procedures that you have considered the following for the participant:
- safety
- dignity
- consent
- privacy (including confidentiality of data; data protection)
- anonymity.

You must also demonstrate that you will:
- avoid deception or exaggeration about aims and objectives
- be honest and transparent
- avoid bias and misleading information.

Your teacher will assist you in making sure that you cover the relevant aspects.

Intellectual engagement

This section of your proposal ensures the academic nature of your research. Your teacher will want to know how your research fits into or adds to your current or future programme of study and the academic debate in your chosen field. Your teacher will also need to understand the concepts you will be using and how they relate to your research.

Timetabling

Finally, your proposal should show that you have considered the deadline and put a schedule in place. Your teacher will ensure that you are aware of any internal deadlines set by the school or college and will discuss the feasibility of your schedule. It should be noted that with any proposal, this can only be an educated guess and you must be flexible. There will be **soft** and **hard deadlines** within this schedule.

> **Key terms**
>
> **soft deadline:** one that is movable
> **hard deadline:** one that cannot be missed

> **Activity 1: Planning questions**
>
> a) Consider the conversations you are likely to have with your teacher and list any questions or areas that are not clear. Raise these at your first supervisory session or within class.

What should be in your proposal?

The following set of headings can be used as a guide.

Question
For the Cambridge Research Report, this comes in the form of a research question. It is not a statement, but a frame for opposing perspectives.

Debate
This will include your motivation, an outline of the debate to be addressed, and the scope.

Key concepts
A brief outline of the concepts relevant to the question.

Methodology and sources
This will include examples of sources which you intend to use, an explanation of your methodology and any ethical considerations.

Limitations
Although this is not essential to the proposal, it is a good idea to briefly mention anything you are not going to include due to time, access or academic capacity. This is also a good place to return to when you are reflecting, as limitations may become apparent as your research progresses.

References
This is a list of the sources you have looked at and those that you intend to review in the course of your research. You should keep recording these as you progress through your research. Any source that you review, but do not cite within the proposal, should be listed in your bibliography.

> **Key advice**
>
> Your proposal should include:
> - the question you are researching (the title)
> - relevant key concepts related to the research
> - an outline of the debate you will explore
> - examples of sources you intend to use.

> **Key advice**
>
> Generally, only research that includes human or animal subjects requires ethical considerations.

How to structure your proposal

There are many templates that can be used for a research proposal. In fact, your college may have a preferred one. If this is the case, make sure that you use it in order to meet the expectations of your supervisor.

Below is an example of a research proposal template. You can write your proposal as a piece of free writing with headings, but a table is a good way to keep a record as it prevents you from overworking your proposal. A plan like this is clear to read and something you can easily add to.

NAME	
TEACHER	
REPORT TITLE	
INTRODUCTION	What is your motivation? What is the debate? What are the opposing arguments in the debate? What areas of the debate are you concentrating on?
KEY CONCEPTS	What are the key concepts that will inform or shed light on the debate?
METHODOLOGY	What methods are you using? Why are you using these methods? (This is the justification of methodology.)
SOURCES/REFERENCES	What sources have you located? List your sources. Include details of references so you can refer to them again.
LIMITATIONS	What areas of the debate are you excluding and why? Are you geographically narrowing the scope? Are there issues with accessing sources? Is time a factor?
SIGNATURE	
DATE	
SIGNED OFF	
POSITION	
DATE	

Key advice

Remember, this is your proposed research not the finished piece. Your report will be 5000 words but try to keep to around 500 words (excluding any ethical attachments) for your proposal, in order to be concise and focused.

Final task

Copy and complete the table above using the questions as a guide.

Reflective plenary

Compare your proposal with a partner within your group. You could choose someone who has selected a related issue even if their question is entirely different. Is there anything you have not sufficiently addressed? If so, revisit your proposal and refine it.

10.3 Research log

In this unit you will:
- learn what a research log is
- explore what to include and how to structure your log.

Critical Path

In your log you will record the research that will form the basis for:
- your *deconstruction* of concepts and arguments, as you analyse and evaluate perspectives
- your *reconstruction* of arguments, as you identify synthesis and fit perspectives together to support your own **hypothesis**/opinion
- your *reflection*, as you review how the differing perspectives affected the path your research took, informed your argument/changed your mind or supported your hypothesis
- your *communication*, as it underpins your academic writing and informs your teacher.

> **Key term**
>
> **hypothesis:** a supposition; a starting point for further study

Deconstruction	Reconstruction	Reflection	Communication	Collaboration
✓	✓	✓	✓	

The focus in this unit is on the construction of a research log that is suitable for your particular question. It will take you, step by step, through the importance of the research log, how it relates to the Critical Path and how to construct it.

Starting point

Think of an occasion when you have kept a record of what you have done – maybe you needed to record what you had eaten because of allergies or have kept a gratitude journal (a reflective journal recording things you are grateful for) or sleep diary. Was it an easy thing to do? What made it successful or unsuccessful?

What is the function of the research log?

The research log is an assessed part of your report that you submit as an appendix. Its purpose should be to help you plan, monitor and review your own progress and thinking.

What does a research log help me to do?

> It directs your research and structures your report.

> It helps your teacher to guide you.

> It supports your reflective learning.

> It is the basis for your formal reflection in your report.

Activity 1: Your research log

a) Match the following descriptions to the correct speech bubble above.

A   Your log is key in showing you have been reflective in your practice and flexible in your approach:
  - Have you asked pertinent questions throughout?
  - Have your path and opinion been informed by your questions?

B   Your log is the way in which you can track and review your progress and map your thought process throughout your research; this will inform your written reflection.

C   At 5000 words, the Cambridge Research Report will be quite possibly the largest project you will have ever undertaken and the log keeps the direction and scope of the research under control. You can review where you have been in terms of argument and evaluation at any time, and reassess where you are going.

D   Your log gives your teacher the opportunity to review your progress and raise questions. It guides them through your research and, in turn, allows them to guide you.

Key advice

In strong reports, there is a direct relationship between the report and the log. The log underpins the research and can also stand alone as evidence of your investigation and reflection.

The research log and the Critical Path

In essence, a research log is a record of your investigations. It contains:
- a record of all the *books you review* and *URLs you visit*
- a list and description of each research method you use (for example, interviews you conduct, surveys you undertake)
- a *reflective record* of your *research process* that informs every step of your report
- a record of the *perspective of a particular source*
- a reminder of *where the sources/perspectives lead you, how they inform your thinking* and *what questions they raise*
- the *questions you want to ask your teacher* and the *direction(s) you want to take*
- a record of *your teacher's advice and your responses to it*
- a log of how *ideas interconnect,* how *reliable arguments and perspectives are,* and how they have *influenced your opinion*.

All of these points are intrinsically tied to the Critical Path.

Activity 2: Connecting the log to the Critical Path

a) In this activity, you will show your understanding of how the research log reflects the Critical Path. Copy and complete the following table, adding the relevant bullet points above. The first one is completed for you. Some may be relevant to more than one column.

Deconstruction	Reconstruction	Reflection	Communication	Collaboration
A record of all the books you review				

What to include in your log

Your log is both an academic and personal reflective record. Its key function is to support and reflect the research you are doing, and show how this has developed over time.

While there is no set way to structure your log, the following are key items you should try to include:

- **Full details of sources reviewed:** In the log, you will record the full reference details of every source you review.

- **The key concepts and arguments in the area of your project:** These arguments will be the basis of your literature review (see Unit 10.4), which will précis the literature and viewpoints already present in your field of study. The only report that will not contain a literature review is one which has this as its complete methodology.

- **How the perspectives/sources compare:** The log can begin the synthesising process. It will highlight, in brief notes, the similarities and differences between perspectives, and through this, you will find support for your area of focus.

- **Questions identified for further research:** The commentary on concepts and arguments in your log will help you narrow your focus and identify questions for further exploration. Some of these areas may be 'dead-ends' while others will open avenues for discussion not thought of before.

- **Any changes in the direction of your research:** Your log may change the direction of your research and you should be open to this. This is critical for reflective practice and growth. Not every path that opens needs to be pursued, but in the log you should reflect upon why you did *not* research the area. It may form an area of recommendation for further research.

- **Questions raised by your teacher:** You should record your teacher's questions in your log to ensure that you do not forget their enquiries. Their feedback will have a specific purpose and should be investigated.

- **Your response to your teacher's questions:** Your response is an important part of both your further research and reflective practice and should be recorded in your log. It shows reflective awareness and metacognition (see page 135).

- **A review of your research methods and methodology:** Your research methods and methodology form the framework of your research and it is important to comment on why you chose them and how they suit your subject area. Once again, reflect and be flexible. Different projects will lend themselves to particular methodologies; strong reports will evaluate a range of methods and demonstrate how the methodology is appropriate.

Research methods

There are two approaches:
- Qualitative research investigates through words, opinions and reasons – an example would be a literature review.
- Quantitative research is based in numbers and includes statistical data and analysis – for example, polls and surveys (see Units 3.1 and 10.4).

> ### Activity 3: How to use your log
>
> a) Explain in your own words why you should make brief notes on the perspectives from your sources in your log. This can be written in your Workbook or your journal.

Finally, it is worth noting what *not* to include in your research log.

A research log is *not* a diary. It is *not* a record of your every movement and every thought. Therefore, do *not* include:
- the hours you spend online
- the times of day you log on to your computer
- the number of times you visit the library
- the number of classes that you attend.

Maybe *most importantly*, the log is *not* included in your 5000-word limit and so must *not* be used to provide extra information, paragraphs or explanations.

Special focus: Case study: Structuring your log

Two students, Casey and Jonah, are undertaking the Cambridge Research Report. Both need to fill in a research log, but there is no template. As it is a working document, both Casey and Jonah use different formats that reflect their individual needs, but they both follow advice to keep the format simple.

Research log examples

Casey's log
Look at Casey's table. How effective is it? Read it carefully and then work through the task that follows.

The context for Casey's question is the experience of people, mostly children, who were sent away from areas under threat of bombardment in the UK during the Second World War. They were referred to as 'evacuees' ('evacuated' means removed from a place of danger).

Key advice

Keep the format of the log simple. Highlight the sources and their details in a different colour to make the bibliography easy to compile.

Working title [6]		Did the evacuee experience build a more or less resilient community?
Date	Source	Comments/questions
16/11/2019 [1]	Rose Davis (2019), Interviewed by Casey Robbins, 04/11	Rose's view: Rose found her time spent as an evacuee had a positive impact on her life. She had various coping mechanisms for the situation. I am not getting the information I need in my interviews. Note: research/ask teacher about questioning techniques. Questions: Should I use a literature review to source interviews with evacuees instead of primary source interviewing? Why did I choose interviews over a literature review? How do I measure resilience? What kind of resilience am I looking at – community spirit or emotional resilience? If emotional, do I need to examine mental health records both pre- and post-war? Note: Change title to show the specific evacuee experience I am investigating.

Activity 4: Casey's table

a) How effective and reflective is Casey's table? Match the elements listed below to the features in the table.

  A date and full source reference
  B perspective of the interviewee
  C a reflective question on refining the method used
  D a reflective question on her choice of methodology
  E reflective questions that refine the question
  F evidence the title is not necessarily the final one

b) Overall, how reflective do you think the table is?

Jonah's log

In this contrasting example, Jonah chooses a free form – journal style. Jonah has chosen the concept of Universalism.

> Research log
> Concept: Universalism
> 15/12/19
>
> I searched online using the search terms 'Shakespeare' and 'Universalism'
>
> **First result:**
> https://www.theguardian.com/commentisfree/2012/may/21/shakespeare-universal-cultural-imperialism
>
> 'Shakespeare, Universal? No it's cultural imperialism', Emer O'Toole, date accessed 15/12/19

Source reliability: The article is over 7 years old which may indicate a lack of present-day credibility, but this subject is less time sensitive than most. It is published in a newspaper, but is an opinion piece with no supporting evidence.

Note: research Emer O'Toole's background, credentials, etc.

Perspective: In this piece the author does not see Shakespeare as universal, she suggests that his plays are re-appropriated for our time and not very comfortably. She feels that his plays gained a foothold all over the world because of colonialism and that the myth continues to this day.

Notes:
Investigate colonialism and Shakespeare's plays.
Look at the concept of colonialism as a possible additional concept to Universalism.
Ask teacher for advice on Shakespeare and Colonialism – articles or books.

Activity 5: How does Jonah's log compare to Casey's?

a) What evidence can you find of:
- the results of his search – with date of access
- full details of the sources
- a review of the reliability of the sources – this will help with source evaluation
- brief notes on the perspective of each source – this will help with analysis
- reminders of further investigation – this will help with framework and concepts
- reminder to ask teacher for advice
- flexibility in drafting a question?

In Jonah's log excerpt, we see less reflective practice than in Casey's, but in Jonah's log there is evaluation of sources and a noting of a perspective. Again, there is evidence of flexibility, as Jonah follows the concepts that his research is opening up and looks to investigate colonialism. The evaluation of sources is important to note, as it can be a key factor in the overall justification of an argument.

Reflective plenary

Work in small groups. Compare and evaluate the format/content/organisation of your research log and suggest improvements. Look back at the list of contents on pages 176–177 to guide your discussion.

Final task

Pick a topic for research. In your Workbook or journal, start your own research log. Choose a template that suits your style of working and discipline.

You should record:
- your initial ideas of the issue up for debate and any key concepts
- the methodology and research methods you are intending to use and why
- what questions you have for your teacher.

10.4 Identifying a topic

In this unit you will:
- explore a range of topics and select a suitable one
- learn about the notion of a 'concept' and apply it to your work.

Critical Path

You will need to:
- reflect on your choice of topic
- evaluate its potential by beginning to deconstruct the perspectives and review how they interconnect/can be reconstructed.

Deconstruction	Reconstruction	Reflection	Communication	Collaboration
✓	✓	✓		

The focus of this unit is to revise how you pick a topic and devise a question. It will also help you to gain an understanding of how the Cambridge Research Report simultaneously differs and builds upon the approach that you used for the Essay. In this section, you are introduced to the notion of 'concept' and how it enhances your research process and critical awareness.

Starting point

Think again about the subjects, lessons or modules you are studying that most interest you, or what you are planning to study at university. Are there any particular areas that you would like to develop further? Exchange ideas with a partner.

Exploring subjects

Choosing a subject for this report is a very similar process to choosing a topic for the Essay. However, for the purposes of the report, the emphasis has shifted. Unlike the Essay, the report *does not have to be global*. There is an important reason for this. The objective of the Cambridge Research Report is to allow you to research a subject that is of particular interest to you. You are encouraged to explore an area that you are already studying or that you wish to pursue at university. You will build your research skills in preparation for further study and your report – writing skills for entry into the workplace.

Profiles

Student A: Rueben

Profile: Interested in studying Sports Science at university.

> For the Cambridge Research Report, he investigates whether time out for injury, illness or suspension has a lasting negative effect on an athlete's career.
>
> The research sparked his interest in psychology.
>
> He is looking to pursue a career as a sports psychologist.

Student B: Trudie

Profile: Interested in studying Economics at university.

> For the Cambridge Research Report she decides to research micro-economics and whether taxation is the best solution for negative trends in areas such as health and welfare.
>
> She is aiming ultimately for a place on a management programme for a large management consulting firm.

Student C: Sean

Profile: Interested in Journalism.

> Is studying English, History and Cambridge Global Perspectives and Research A Levels.
>
> For the Cambridge Research Report, he researches whether digital media has negative effects on minors.
>
> He would like to get a journalism apprenticeship.

How can you make sure your research topic is achievable?

Remember that whatever topic you choose, it must be able to sustain research for a 5000-word report. To do this, it must not present you with too many hurdles to overcome.

To ensure that you can write 5000 words, you should *not*:

- **pick an obscure area/try to be too original:** You might find there will not be a lot of information on an obscure area, or you might find that original areas of study become too large or time-consuming.
- **pick a topic that is too general:** It may seem appealing to pick a general topic area in order to fill the word limit, but you might find that you cannot be focused, clear and analytical, and you will not have the time or words to do it justice.
- **pick a topic that you are overinvested in:** Objectivity is key to the research project. If you pick an issue that you are overinvested in or one that is particularly sensitive, it may be difficult to take an objective stance or give adequate consideration to both sides of the argument.

Activity 1: Consider research topics

a) Copy and complete the table below. Share and discuss your ideas with a partner.

Subject area and title	Too obscure/ general/invested	Why?
Is AI a threat to humanity?		
Should the Catholic Church change its position on contraception?		
Is the negative perception of indigenous Hawaiian names a barrier to employment?		
Should there be more investment in mental health?		
Should transgender athletes be allowed to compete with **cisgender** athletes?		
Does Latin aid study in private schools in Lancashire?		

*****Glossary**
cisgender: relating to someone whose gender identity is the same as the sex they were assigned at birth.

How can you devise an appropriate question?

'Yes/no' questions

In Unit 6.1 you learned a strong way to set your essay title, and many of the same principles apply here.

Select a question that frames contrasting perspectives. For the Essay, this was best achieved through the use of a 'yes/no' question or through the use of a modal verb such as 'can', 'would', 'should' or 'will'. For the report, these openers can work too, but at this level, when more than one perspective on each side of the argument can be explored, you may prefer to use a question that begins with 'To what extent' or 'How far'. This formulation will allow you to explore the subtleties in the contrasting perspectives that fit within overriding concepts. At this level, crude oppositional argument is discouraged.

Using a provisional question

It is important to remember that in the report, you are expected to show effective and consistent reflective practice – and this includes your choice of topic and title. This reflection is included in your log and within the report itself and, therefore, it is recommended that you consider your title as a draft or provisional title when you begin your research and exploration. For example, a draft question may begin as one you consider narrow in focus (e.g. 'Are educational subsidies effective?'), but as you explore, it would quickly become apparent that it is far too general to be covered in 5000 words, and would need adapting or replacing.

This could be covered in your research log as follows:

16 March 2020

Began research into the efficacy of educational subsidies. [1] Amount of research undertaken is vast and covers many different groups divided by race, gender, socio-economic backgrounds, country, state, city. [2]

I found one article that particularly interested me regarding subsidies for Black male Americans only being effective if the family earns over a particular income. [3] (Henry Guillum, below) This socio-economic framework caught my interest because it suggests the poorest Black males in America do not benefit from subsidies. [4] My feeling is that this may be to do with the education already within the family (yet to be researched). [5] In order to look into this in detail I will amend my question to 'Are educational subsidies effective for Black American males?'. [6]

Henry Guillum: 'The Certainties of Education', Round and About Publishing, 1992, suggests that educational subsidies are effective for Black male Afro-Americans, where income is above $30 000 per annum, Aniket publishing, 2015

[1] General subject area selected by the student.

[2] Identification that it is a fruitful area, but too general.

[3] Narrows down to an area of particular interest.

[4] Notes main point of argument.

[5] Beginnings of hypothesis.

[6] Redrafts question to a more manageable scope.

Activity 2: Issues

a) Think of a subject that you are studying and the areas within it that interest you. For three of those areas, select an issue that:
  - is of concern to you
  - will be useful to your further area of study.

b) Discuss these with a partner who is looking at a similar discipline. Evaluate whether the issues are feasible. You should ask the following questions:
  - Is there a significant body of research in the area already?
  - Is there a link to my future area of study/is it a research interest of a professor on my intended course?

- Have I researched it before?
- Is there any relevant expertise at my school or college I could use for support?

Why is concept important?

Another major difference between the Essay and the report is that in the latter, you need to both recognise and evaluate concepts.

The introduction of concepts drives your research process in two main ways:
- It influences how you research.
- It aids reflection on different perspectives and the development of your own perspective.

Concepts can be either the starting point for researching your subject, or they can be analysed as the framework within which your contrasting perspectives fall.

Special focus: Case study: Using concepts

Amayra is hoping to study Business at university. She is taking Politics, History and English at A Level. Her aunt is a consultant at a large management consulting firm but is one of only a few women who occupy a senior role within her department. Amayra and her aunt have had many discussions around the use of **positive discrimination** as a solution to this issue. Amayra has broached this topic in both her History and Politics classes, where she has also learned about the history of the **feminist movement** and how these concepts apply to world views.

Amayra has devised a draft question.

Does positive discrimination undermine or promote the position of women in the workplace?

She evaluates her issue and title by asking herself questions annotated below. She records her evaluation and reflection in her research log:

*Glossary
positive discrimination: favouring groups of people that have been discriminated against
feminist movement: a series of political campaigns relating to the progression of women's rights

---

10 July 2012

I have picked an area and devised a draft question:

Does positive discrimination undermine or promote the position of women in the workplace?

This is an area where there is a lot of research already conducted. It was not difficult to find, so not obscure [1] and not completely original, so I should have enough evidence to explore and fulfil the 5000-word report. A primary internet search revealed many sources, both newspaper and academic articles and books, so there is a solid and credible foundation from which to begin my investigation.

I intend to study Business at university, where one of the courses is 'Women in Business' and therefore, I see this as a pertinent topic which will help with my future studies and my university application. [2] I have not submitted work for this question before or content for the topic, [3] but I have addressed the topic from various angles in both History and Politics and there is expertise at my college in this area. [4]

---

[1] Is there a significant body of research in the area already, or is it too obscure?

[2] Is there a link to my future area of study/is it a research interest of a professor on my intended course?

[3] Have I already written about it before?

[4] Is there relevant expertise at my college?

I am emotionally invested, as I am a woman who is ambitious and have had many conversations with my aunt about this very subject. However, I think that this will work to my advantage and will not cloud my objectivity. [5] In fact, this personal connection could be of use for primary research into my topic.

[5] Am I emotionally invested in the subject?

The question as it stands may be too general. [6] I may need to focus on a specific business area, but I feel it encourages discussion and comparative contrasting perspectives. These will be enhanced by exploring feminist approaches to the issue.

[6] Is the topic too general?

Activity 3: Reflecting on the topic and question

We can see from Amayra's log above that most of the questions she asks herself have positive answers and there is an indication of reflection.

a) What does she reflect upon?
b) Has she identified any concepts that will be a primary focus for her research?
c) Is this topic/question likely to be one Amayra should pursue? Why, or why not?

Amayra begins her research by examining the concept of feminism in relation to positive discrimination. She finds that it is not straightforward and quickly identifies two contrasting perspectives within the same concept. Both function within the framework of feminism, which Amayra basically appreciates as women's rights to equality. However, what she finds is that one perspective is for positive discrimination and the other perspective is against it.

Jess Butcher believes that keeping a certain percentage of jobs open for women is a patriarchal assumption that renders women victims. She also posits that to get special treatment due to a label is divisive and could be even more oppressive to women. (Butcher, Jess, 29 May 2018, https://www.cityam.com/calls-positive-discrimination-patriarchal-and patronising/)

Karrie argues that affirmative action is about reversing historical oppression and that both men and women can be victims of a patriarchal society. She highlights the benefits that positive discrimination can bring, such as encouraging discussion and debate and different economically beneficial viewpoints, despite it being seen as unlawful by the European courts. (Sound Girls, https://soundgirls.org/reverse-sexism-positive-discrimination-affirmative-action/, accessed 16/8/20)

When you analyse the arguments, it becomes clear that you need to synthesise them around the notion of equality. Both agree with equality, but neither see it as a solution to the imbalance between men and women in the workplace.

Further investigation into this concept of equality within feminism brings Amayra to an **abstract** by Cristine Koggel (Koggel, C. Canadian Journal of Law & Jurisprudence, Vol 7 (1), 1994, pp.43-59), which highlights this very issue of two feminist concepts of equality that are based on different notions of self. Another concept has opened up, based on the idea of the value of fair competition as it informs the idea of the feminist self. This concept may provide the synthesis to allow Amayra to understand the differences between the two perspectives and reconstruct the argument.

What we can see here is that researching a topic via concept can provide a plethora of nuanced perspectives.

Key term

abstract: a brief summary which comes before a longer report, research piece or article, summing up its purpose and approach

Activity 4: Next steps

a) What do you think will be Amayra's next step? Does she need to do any further investigation or recording of information? If so, what?

Final task

Devise a draft question and identify any concepts that could inform your research.

Reflective plenary

Work with a partner(s). Share your question and explain the different concepts and how they might help you explore different perspectives. What have you learned from this process?

10.5 Primary research and the research process

In this unit you will:
- review your understanding of research and sources
- explore effective note-taking.

Critical Path

You will need to:
- reflect on how research is defined by the deconstruction and reconstruction process
- understand how differing source material can be evaluated.

Deconstruction	Reconstruction	Reflection	Communication	Collaboration
✓	✓	✓		

In this unit, you will focus on how to investigate a subject and build an academic and critical awareness of the research process for the Cambridge Research Report.

What is research?

In its most basic form, research is the gathering of information. This is a skill that you utilise on a day-to-day basis, for example, when you decide on the purchase of a piece of clothing or a mobile phone contract. For the Cambridge Research Report, it is the collation of perspectives in order to identify and answer a suitable question that addresses a particular academic issue.

Special focus: Mini case study: Everyday research

Remi has ambitions to be a professional gamer and wants to buy the best console to help him achieve this goal. His question is simply: 'Which console is best for me?' There are many options on the market and also many differing perspectives.

He gathers the following information:
- How many consoles are on the market? (internet search, physical shopping trips) **Understanding**
- How old are they? Is there a new version imminent? (internet search, market analysis) **Analysis**
- Do they have any unique features? (review advertisements/ask friends) **Analysis**
- How much do they cost? (advertisement review, comparison site search) **Understanding**
- What are their reputations? (review gaming magazines, look at blogs/vlogs, ask friends) **Credibility**
- What are my needs? **Understanding and Analysis**

He then weighs up the advantages and disadvantages of each, before making a decision on a console that best suits his needs, while being cost-effective and reliable. **Evaluation**

What we see here is that Remi follows a very similar process to the one outlined in the Critical Path. He **deconstructs** the market by making sure he **understands** what is on offer. He **analyses** the market and ensures that his data is **credible** before **reconstructing** the information, drawing it all together and **evaluating** which option is best for his purpose. Conducting research for the report is just an academic formalisation of a process that you are already familiar with.

Types of data/sources used in research

The data and sources you might access for research break down into four main groups:
- qualitative and quantitative
- primary and secondary.

These are not always mutually exclusive.

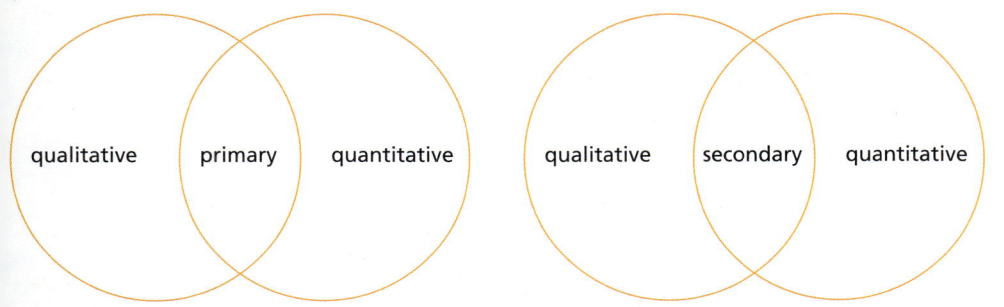

qualitative — primary — quantitative   qualitative — secondary — quantitative

As you will remember from earlier in this chapter, qualitative research is non-numerical and based on material such as notes and observations. It looks to understand reasons, motivations, opinions, and so on.

Quantitative research is about numbers. It is based on numerical data and statistics, and can be used on its own or in support of a qualitative standpoint.

One of the other key differences between qualitative and quantitative data is the way the evidence is collected. Quantitative evidence is structured and is conducted through, for example, surveys and polls. Qualitative research is unstructured and is conducted through unstructured interviews or the collection of opinions.

Primary research is research undertaken first-hand. It is unfiltered data, experience or opinion. Examples of primary research are interviews, surveys, artefacts, diaries, and so on. In the case study example, primary resources are the data regarding how many consoles there are, the age/release dates of the consoles and the cost. Another piece of primary data is Remi's information from friends.

Secondary research uses data that has already been collated and possibly analysed. It may already be subject to an opinion or perspective. A secondary source is often an article or a review. In Remi's example, the gaming magazines are a secondary source.

It is not always possible to identify whether a source is primary or secondary from its medium. Take, for example, a newspaper. It would be easy to identify this as simply a primary source. It is a document in which the news is reported. However, newspapers do not just report on events, they also contain opinion pieces. An opinion piece is a secondary source; a report on a protest is a primary source.

Your research for the report needs to examine alternate perspectives and can be based on either primary or secondary material, or a mixture of both. Remember, this is an academic report and therefore should be primarily based on an academic concept or on academic research.

There are differences to be found between the STEM subjects (Science, Technology, Engineering, Maths) and the Humanities.

Science and Maths projects are more likely to be based on primary research material. In this case, the evaluation is not of opinions, but on the quantitative methods used: *Were the methods appropriate? Were there more effective ways of collecting or analysing the data?* It is important to note that Maths and Science can also be addressed from a historical, social or philosophical aspect, which use secondary evidence. For example, if you are interested in the efficacy of vaccines, it can be productive to look at this issue through the lens of social or religious discourse. Rather than evaluating the data, you could evaluate these differing interpretations of the data.

Humanities subjects tend to use qualitative data and a mix of secondary and primary sources. The perspectives can be explored through the secondary material and supported by primary sources if required. Take the question 'Was Nelson Mandela a hero?' This would be a report based primarily on secondary research. However, it could be supported by primary interviews for a range of viewpoints from people who lived through and witnessed this period of history – the time of **Apartheid**.

*Glossary
Apartheid: a system of laws put in place by the mostly White government of South Africa between c.1948–93 in which people were segregated according to 'race', with Black people subject to prohibitions in terms of schooling, socialising, sport, and so on

> ### Activity 1: Primary and secondary sources for your subject
>
> a) Work with a partner. Identify and evaluate potential sources of primary and secondary material that could be used in your subject area. Make a list of these and share it with another pair, justifying your choices.

Research steps

There are three key steps to follow when you conduct any research.

Step 1: Choose a subject and devise a question

See Unit 10.4.

Step 2: Find information

Finding information can be overwhelming. Whether you are standing in a college library full of books or in front of your laptop, unsure of what phrase to type into the search engine, the task facing you may seem insurmountable. Not only do you have to search for the information, but you need to filter it for the credible and trustworthy; the pertinent and relevant.

The first myth to address is that you will know straight away what is credible or pertinent. There is of course some evaluation you can undertake to assess the credibility of a source. You can implement RAVEN or CRAAP, both useful tools which you encountered in earlier chapters. You can also assess whether you feel an article is relevant, but it may not be until you start to deconstruct the perspectives that you realise the real strength in the argument or its relevance to your question.

If you find that the source of the argument is not strong, this should not be considered a negative consequence or a waste of time. It is good to remember here that one of the key skills in the report is reflection. Reflection allows for these discoveries and shifts in opinion. If a piece of research unravels under scrutiny, you should make a record of that in your log and use it in your evaluation of the perspective. If an article is rendered less relevant, because your research takes a turn you did not expect, you should review why this is the case in your reflection – this is a skill in itself. (See also Unit 4.3.)

Now that you are ready to attack the research, here are some ways to do this.

Internet search

You will already have developed many strategies for internet research, but you may find the following helpful.

Search strategies	Examples
Queries are not case sensitive.	*Barack Obama* and *barack obama* produce the same results.
Results will typically include each word or punctuation mark included in the query. Some stop words or exceptions apply.	
Keep queries descriptive, but use as few terms as possible. Avoid natural language.	Use *colorado statehood* instead of *when did colorado first become a state*.
Google and other search engines automatically truncate search terms. To prevent this, use a + sign in front of each term.	A query on *child* retrieves results with 'children' and 'childcare'.
Use double quotations marks (" ") to search terms as an exact phrase.	A query on *"Barack Hussein Obama II"* will retrieve only those sites that refer to Obama by his full name. Sites that refer to him as simply 'Barack Obama' may be overlooked.
Use the 'site:' feature to limit your results to a specific website or class of websites.	The query *cloning site:online.wsj.com* will only retrieve articles about cloning from the online version of the *Wall Street Journal*. A query on *cloning site:.gov* will only retrieve results within the government domain.
To allow for several words to appear in your results, use the OR operator. The operator must all be in capital letters.	A query on *hotel OR lodging OR inn* will retrieve results with *any or all* of these terms.

School, college or local library

Your library may have a range of sources, both primary and secondary. It does not just hold books, academic journals and newspapers, but may also hold sources such as public records, diaries, ordinance survey maps, and so on.

The library is also a good place to go for advice. Many libraries run sessions on using the library effectively and librarians are often an underused resource.

Key advice

Familiarise yourself with your local library if you have one, or look for an online library with a lending site. Enrol yourself on a library session and consult your librarian about your project.

If you don't have access to a local or academic library, there are plenty of online resources – the internet is effectively one large library. And you can use search engines such as Google Scholar to access academic resources. You could also try Researchgate and other open sources.

Use specialist libraries for a more focused search. For example, the Wellcome Collection Library in London contains the 'largest collection of video and sound collections on medicine, health and welfare from the 20th century and beyond'. (https://londonist.com/2015/08/london-s-lesser-known-libraries https://wellcomelibrary.org)

Ask your teacher

All too often overlooked as a research source, your teacher is very important as they can advise and provide the first shortlisting process for you. Make appointments and respond to their advice. Working with your teacher in this way will be new to you, but it reflects the relationship you will have with lecturers at university and is a stepping-stone skill.

> ### Activity 2: Using libraries and other similar sources
>
> a) Work with a small group and research where you can access information for the Cambridge Research Report, such as your school or local library, then answer these questions:
>   - Do I have to join to use it?
>   - What type of information do they hold?
>
> b) Present your findings to the class.
>
> c) Make a note of any collections that may prove useful to you (or your classmates).

Step 3: Make notes

Effective note-making is the final piece in the research puzzle, and a skill you should continue to develop. You can also check back to note-making guidance in Unit 6.3. Some ways of taking notes are more time efficient and effective than others. Consider using these steps:

1) Scan
2) Reread and write
3) Revise

1) Scan

It is not necessary to make notes on an entire book or even an entire article. You need to identify the areas, if any, that are relevant to your research question. Read the index and locate any chapters that are of interest. Look through the relevant chapters, highlighting or recording key words, concepts or phrases.

2) Reread and write

Reread the text and summarise the author's main arguments, perspective and evidence, then add it to your research log. Make sure you capture the key words, concepts or phrases. You may find using your own personal shorthand useful, or you could use or incorporate some standard abbreviations.

Symbol/abbreviation	Meaning
&	and
+	in addition
>	greater than/more/better than
<	less fewer/smaller than
=	equal to
c.	approximately, around
i.e.	that is, that means
etc.	and so on
p.	page

> **Key advice**
>
> When you write your report, you will need to use precise, accurate, relevant terminology for your subject, so it is worth keeping a note of useful terms and definitions of their meanings as you make notes.

Symbol/abbreviation	Meaning
pp.	pages
para.	paragraph
≠	not the same as
δ	small change
Δ	large change
∴	therefore
∵	because
♂	male/man
♀	female/woman
→	leads to/produces
↓	causes decreasing/reducing
↑	increasing/upwards trend with
e.g.	for example
X	trans (Xfer – transfer; Xgender – transgender
C	century

You can try dropping all or some vowels:

Symbol/abbreviation	Meaning
cd	could
wd	would
educn	education

Or you can try shortening words:

Symbol/abbreviation	Meaning
info	information
govt	government
imp	important

3) Revise

Read over your notes, making sure they make sense. This is your opportunity to add your own comments, highlight any key differences and synthesise arguments and evidence. To identify the areas where you should focus, refer to your highlighted key words and phrases. This is also an opportunity to evaluate arguments. You may want to answer the following questions:
- What are the strengths and weaknesses here?
- Is the author convincing?
- Has the piece been **peer reviewed**?

Using technology

When making notes, technology can be helpful. Why not record your thoughts on your phone as voice notes and then transfer them into written form? Or use speech to text tools?

> **Key term**
>
> **peer review:** a review or evaluation of work by others who work in the same field

Key advice: Note-making mistakes

There are common note-taking pitfalls that you should avoid:
- **Highlighting:** Highlighters are a useful tool, but only if used judiciously. If every word is highlighted, there really is no point.
- **Linear copying:** When note-taking becomes copying word for word, there is no understanding conferred, no extension or evaluation, and it loses its meaning.
- **Not reviewing/making sense of your notes:** Always review your initial notes to make sure that they make sense. Do not be tempted to cut corners here. What seems logical and sensible when you have just read the original may not be in two weeks' time.

Activity 3: Using abbreviations and acronyms

a) Can you think of any abbreviations or acronyms that you could use to personalise the list in the tables on pages 190–191? Pick your favourite symbols and abbreviations and start incorporating them into your note-taking in class so that they become second nature.

Final task

a) Using the methods outlined in this section, find an article/book that is relevant to your area of study, and make notes.

b) In a group, peer review each other's work. Are the notes clear and comprehensive? Could they be improved?

Reflective plenary

Work with a small group to discuss and answer these questions:

What part of the research process are you really good at?
It may be finding material online, skim-reading, making connections…

What are your challenges?
It may be using the library, making notes…

What suggestions can you make to improve your skills?

Chapter 11
Writing the report

In this chapter, you will be using the research you have carried out to plan and write your Cambridge Research Report.

You will plan your project tasks, your time and the report itself. You will organise and develop your ideas using mind-mapping, and you will look at how to structure your report, for example, considering where to cover methodology and different perspectives, and how to conclude and make recommendations. As part of this, you will consider a range of student examples to develop your understanding of the most effective approaches to adopt in the different sections of your report.

Case studies and sample reports will also help you to understand how to write in an appropriate style for an academic report, adapting style and content for your particular subject area. Once you have completed the three units, you should be able to identify the most suitable approaches to take and how best to organise your material.

11.1 Planning for the Cambridge Research Report
11.2 Structuring the report
11.3 Writing the report

11.1 Planning for the Cambridge Research Report

In this unit you will:
- learn how to devise a plan from your proposal
- identify how to organise your ideas effectively.

Critical Path

You will need to:
- reflect on your proposal
- deconstruct and reconstruct arguments.

Deconstruction	Reconstruction	Reflection	Communication	Collaboration
✓	✓	✓	✓	

The focus in this unit is on planning, both for the overall project and for drafting and writing your report. The planning of the project includes scheduling, sifting through and ordering your research, and evaluating evidence and perspectives. The planning process for your writing includes mind-mapping and organising your research and ideas.

Starting point

Work with a partner(s). Think of any task you do regularly that you use a list for. What is the purpose of having that list? What does it help you to do? Discuss your ideas.

Planning your report

We can see that planning is important in everyday tasks, and being organised is also important for the Cambridge Research Report. Once you have written your proposal, you should prepare a project plan from which you will work. This will be useful for three reasons:
- to make sure that you keep to time
- to make sure that you keep on track
- to help you reflect on the progress of your studies.

Your project plan needs to include:
- a strategy – what you are going to research and the order in which you will attack it
- a timeline – when you will undertake each part and how long you will spend on it.

Activity 1: Making your 'to do' list

a) In pairs, copy the following activities, putting them in a logical order.

- ☐ Review and redraft
- ☐ Write introduction
- ☐ Write up body of report
- ☐ Research concept
- ☐ Research perspectives
- ☐ Reconstruct arguments

- [ ] Edit and proofread
- [ ] Construct writing plan
- [ ] Collate notes
- [ ] Reflect on progress
- [ ] Write abstract
- [ ] Write conclusion
- [ ] Write reflection

How to timetable

Make sure that you have a list of school deadlines so you can plan towards them using a timeline. You can use a table for this – see below.

Activity	Timeline	Complete [1]	Reflect [2]

[1] Tick this column when you have completed each stage.

[2] This forms part of the reflective process – the report is reviewed against your plan in terms of what went well, how and why you deviated from it.

Special focus: Project planning for the report

Balbinder has written both her proposal and her plan. She knows that her teacher wants her report written and submitted by the end of February so that she can spend the following term concentrating on her exams. She has been given dates already for the first and second draft, and has constructed her timetable accordingly. She submits the following plan:

Activity	Timeline	Complete	Reflect
Research concept	3 September–30 September		
Conduct interviews	3 September–30 September		
Research perspectives for	3 September–30 September		
Research perspectives against	3 September–30 September		
Meet teacher	30 September		
Collate research	1 October–15 October		
Synthesise research	15 October–31 October		
Create writing plan	1 November–14 November		
Meet teacher	14 November		
Draft	14 November–14 December		
Meet teacher	15 December		
Redraft	15 December–15 January		
Meet teacher	16 January		
Amendments	17 January–29 January		
Write abstract	1 February–7 February		
Write index	1–7 February		
Proofread	7–14 February		

Balbinder allocates an almost equal amount of time to both researching and writing up.

Regular appointments with teacher to keep on track.

All complete by 14 February, allowing two weeks' contingency time.

She receives the following response from her teacher.

> Thank you, Balbinder, for your plan which is generally well thought through. Before I accept it, I would like you to consider the school breaks and any breaks for yourself. Also, you have missed an important step at the beginning of your plan before your interviews – look at your research proposal to identify what is missing.

The fact that Balbinder allocates an almost equal amount of time to researching and writing up emphasises the fact that both of these parts of the project are of equal importance. You must not get lost in the research and find you do not have time to write up. These timescales will vary from student to student. You may be particularly efficient at writing, but less efficient at research and, therefore, your timetable will look different to this.

> **Quick task**
>
> Look at Balbinder's plan and identify the step she is missing.

Be aware that, as with all of your studies for the Cambridge International AS & A Level Global Perspectives and Research syllabus, it is just as important to be reflective and responsive as it is to plan. As you progress through the project, you should review against your plan and readjust timescales appropriately.

You will notice that Balbinder has included contingency time in her plan as she has scheduled her report to be finished two weeks before the deadline. This allows her time for mistakes, illness or unexpected events. You should never schedule to the deadline.

Finally, you can see that Balbinder has scheduled in an appointment with her teacher approximately once a month and after key stages. This makes sure she never has the opportunity to go too far down the wrong path. Balbinder's list of these meetings is by no means prescriptive and a personal schedule will be devised between you and your teacher.

Planning your writing

You can see that in the middle of the project plan, Balbinder has allocated two weeks for a task called 'create writing plan'. This is a very important stage – it is where you begin to deconstruct and reconstruct your arguments, evidence and ideas, as well as detailing the steps that you will follow when you write up your report. You can use a number of methods, but the two most popular are mind maps and spidergrams.

These two methods are often confused, but they can be defined as follows:
- **mind map:** 'a graphical representation of ideas or topics in a radial, non-linear manner... used to visualise, organise, and classify ideas' (1)
- **spidergram:** 'a drawing that shows a summary of facts or ideas, with the main subject in a central circle and the most important facts on lines drawn out from it' (2)

(1 and 2 from 'Comparison between Mind Map and Spidergrams', Chelsea Yang, 11/07/19 https://www.edrawsoft.com/author/chelsea/, accessed 2/8/2020)

Both of these methods start with a central concept – for the Cambridge Research Report, it will most likely be your question. Both include ideas connected to that central concept, but a spidergram tends to use more detail and include sentences, whereas a mind map generally uses one word that encapsulates an idea.

Spidergrams are quite rigid in nature, whereas mind maps tend to be more fluid as they allow for the use of curved lines. Mind maps also utilise colour, which can help you make links between ideas and perspectives and ensures that you do not miss any elements as you write your report.

Look at the following Cambridge Research Report tailored mind map addressing an environmental question. See how the colours help to show the overlap between ideas.

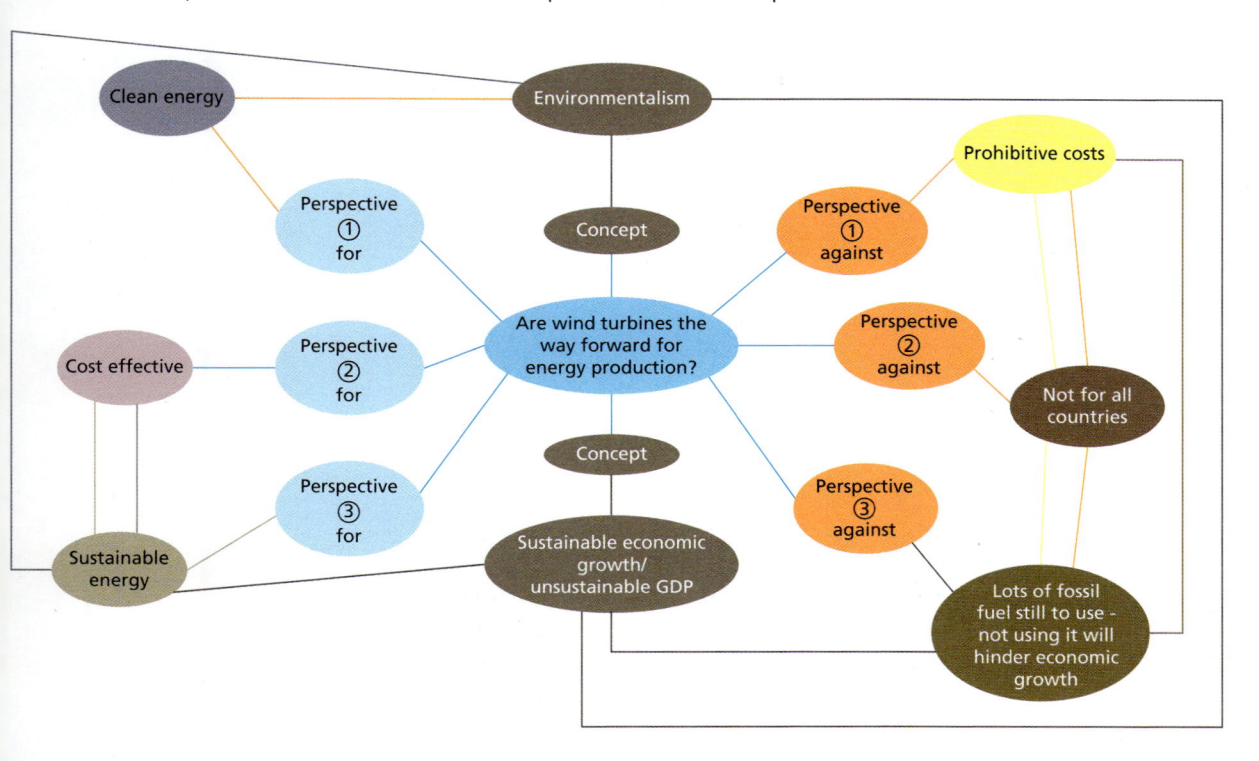

This where everything begins to come together. If you colour-code your perspectives, you can see the synthesis of ideas at a glance, which will help with your writing process.

The Diamond Plan

The Cambridge Research Report is a 5000-word report and can be broken down into three main sections: introduction, main body and conclusion. An introduction for any report should constitute around 10 per cent of your writing and the conclusion the same. For the Cambridge Research Report, this means approximately 500 words for the introduction, 500 words for the conclusion and 4000 words for the main body of the report.

As the main body will consist of 4000 words, you could divide it into the following subsections: three perspectives 'for' of 500 words each and three perspectives 'against' at 500 words each. This leaves 1000 words for the review and analysis of concepts and reflection, which can either be utilised throughout the report or in separate sections, depending on your writing style.

You can think of this visually as a diamond:

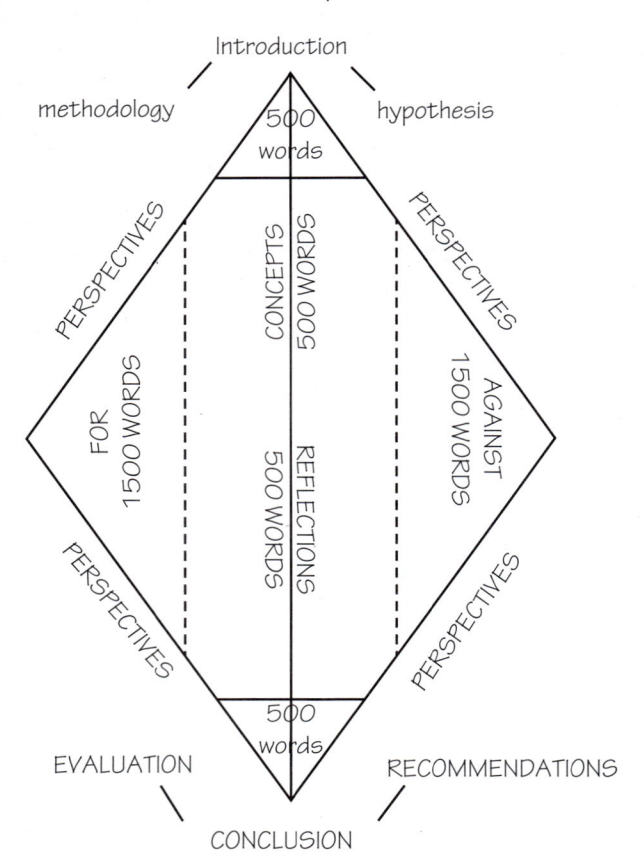

Diagram: A diamond-shaped structure showing the writing process:
- *Top: Introduction (500 words) — with methodology and hypothesis*
- *Upper middle: PERSPECTIVES*
- *Middle left: FOR 1500 WORDS*
- *Middle centre: CONCEPTS 500 WORDS / REFLECTIONS 500 WORDS*
- *Middle right: AGAINST 1500 WORDS*
- *Lower middle: PERSPECTIVES*
- *Bottom: Conclusion (500 words) — with EVALUATION and RECOMMENDATIONS*

> **Key advice**
>
> It is common for the conclusion to be rushed and too short. Keeping the diamond in mind will make sure that you give your conclusion the attention it deserves.

Final task

Look back to your proposal and draft your own plan to include a timetable and a mind map or spidergram. Work with a partner(s) to present, discuss and give feedback on each other's work.

Reflective plenary

Work in small groups to discuss these questions:
- Which aspect of project planning do you find the most challenging? Why?
- What is the most effective way for you to visualise the writing process? Why?

Share any helpful suggestions that occur to you.

11.2 Structuring the report

In this unit you will:
- identify the difference between the Essay and the report
- understand how to structure and what to include in the report.

Critical Path
You will need to:
- reflect on your choice of topic and deconstruct your methods
- reflect on the perspectives analysed, your methodology, question and plan.

Deconstruction	Reconstruction	Reflection	Communication	Collaboration
✓	✓	✓	✓	

The focus in this unit is on the structure of the Cambridge Research Report and how to produce a report that demonstrates all the skills that you learned throughout the research process.

Report vs Essay

Starting point

Think of a report that you have read – during your research process, for example. Discuss the following questions with a partner.
- Was it easy to read? Why or why not?
- What were the aspects that made it a report rather than an essay?
- Which elements of its structure helped make it clear to read?

The Cambridge Research Report is not a report in the traditional sense of the word. When it comes to structuring and writing the report, you need to clearly and precisely convey information, while demonstrating your understanding of perspectives and evaluating them. The Cambridge Research Report is a 'report format essay': it builds on what you have learned when completing the Essay but places it in a report format. This means that it is best to divide your work into sections with headings. This has two main benefits:
- It makes sure that you address the key requirements for the report.
- It makes the report easier to manage in terms of writing and also easier for the audience to read.

How to structure your report

There is no set template for the Cambridge Research Report, but because reports are used to convey specific information to a reader in the most accessible way, they generally include the following:

- Title page
- Abstract

- Table of contents
- Introduction
- Methodology
- Perspectives
- Conclusion
- Recommendations

It is important to recognise that when compared to the Essay, the Cambridge Research Report has some key additions in terms of content. This is reflected in the structure.

Your Essay included:
- an introduction (giving details of what you were going to do)
- a main body (an examination and evaluation of perspectives)
- a conclusion (stating what you had done, the outcomes and recommendations for further research).

The report follows this basic premise, but includes some other key elements.

Title page

This is a concise covering page that includes the title of the report, your name, the date and who the report is written for (in the workplace, this would be who it was commissioned by).

Abstract

This a summary of the report and should not be more than 250 words. This is where you tell the reader what the report analyses, the methodology you used, and the main conclusions. This is to aid the reader when they are deciding whether the report is of interest to them. As it is a summary of your findings and conclusion, you should write this last.

Table of contents

This is a list of what your report contains, and is not prescriptive. The sections are numbered in ascending order and with sub-sections, if necessary.

1.0 **Introduction**
2.0 **Methodology**
3.0 **Perspectives**
    3.1 Arguments for…
    3.2 Arguments against…
4.0 **Conclusion**
5.0 **Recommendations**
6.0 **Appendices**

Introduction

As in the Essay, your introduction explains what you are going to 'do' in your report. This is where you can state your hypothesis. In most reports, the hypothesis will take the form of the perspective that you find most convincing in answer to your question, once you have completed your preliminary literature review (see Units 10.1 and 10.3).

> **Key advice**
>
> You should read abstracts when you are doing your own research to help you shortlist articles that are of interest.

In simple terms, it is your personal opening viewpoint and will generally constitute just a sentence in your introduction. You should not feel constrained by your hypothesis – quite the opposite, in fact. As you research your hypothesis, you may find you disprove it and this can give you material for your reflection. For example, if you are writing a report on whether performance-enhancing drugs should be allowed in sport, your opening viewpoint may be that they should not, because it does not engender a level playing field and can be easily policed by drug testing. However, after further research, it may become apparent that there are many definitions of equality in terms of both performance and what constitutes an enhancing substance, and that monitoring the situation is complex, as science is generally one step ahead of testing. This may either change or modify your original hypothesis, which can be reflected in your conclusion. Of course, an exploration of different perspectives in your research may confirm your viewpoint and this should also be recorded and justified in your conclusion.

Another factor to include in your introduction is a justification of your research topic, question and concepts. This includes why you chose the topic and question, and how the concepts you have selected are applicable to your research. This may detail some of the following:
- the results of your literature review
- the reason the area is ideal for study
- the concepts that interested you and why they are pertinent.

These explanations can be both academic and personal in nature.

Methodology

This includes an explanation of how you planned and carried out your research. In this section, you should address the research methods that you used and how they combined to make a cohesive methodology. As seen in Chapter 10, different methods are relevant to different subject areas. In many cases, the report will be based on a literature review and a discussion of the arguments contained within it. There are many reasons for this – one being that a literature review of secondary sources around a topic is not only valid, but often the most efficient way of accessing perspectives for your project. However, if you are not using any other methods, it is worth justifying why you have chosen not to and, if applicable, citing them for any further studies.

Perspectives

This section is very similar to the Essay, apart from the division into subheadings. This is where you demonstrate the following:
- the arguments you have investigated
- the collation of these arguments into contrasting perspectives
- the evaluation of those perspectives
- the evaluation of sources
- the synthesis between them.

Conclusion

Your conclusion comes last and is where you pull all your arguments together. This again is an extension of your work in the Essay and can be where you do the majority of your reflection. This reflection can even be a separate section if you wish.

Your reflection should include:

- **an evaluation of your progress against your plan:** This will answer questions such as *Did everything go to schedule?* and is informed by your research log.
- **an analysis of how your research question developed over time:** This will include any changes that you made to your question – maybe it became more focused and nuanced, or changed direction.
- **an examination of how alternative perspectives affected your viewpoint:** This will look at how the alternative perspectives altered your opinion. Even if the perspectives confirmed your opinion, you must still show that you have considered alternatives and the reasons you maintain your viewpoint. For this section to work well, it is a good idea to set out your hypothesis at the beginning of the report, otherwise it is hard to measure the progress you have made during your research. It is much easier to reflect on your journey if you are clear where you started.
- **a critical evaluation of your methodology:** This looks at how well your chosen methodology worked for you. In this section you can add an overview of the impact of your research methods on your report and whether you would do anything differently.

Recommendations

These are very similar to your recommendations for further research in the Essay. This is where you identify areas that you possibly did not have time or space to address in your Report and note what they would add to the area of study.

Appendices

You may wish to use Appendices in your report. These always sit at the end, either before or after the references. Appendices contain any information that you have used and you think is useful to your report, but whose inclusion would break the flow of your argument. There are many types of information that get included in appendices, but as a general rule, this is the place for primary data that was either collected or sourced, and analysed and evaluated in your report.

Appendices are numbered or alphabetised in ascending order:

Appendix 1   Appendix A

Appendix 2   Appendix B

Appendix 3   Appendix C

Appendices should not contain any material that has not been used and evaluated in the report. They do not count as part of your 5000-word limit but should not be used to extend your argument.

Activity 1: Preparing for challenges

a) Consider the aspects of writing the Cambridge Research Report that you feel will present the biggest challenge to you. What will you do to address these challenges? Present your ideas to a small group. Work together to listen and offer any additional advice you can think of.

Special focus: Mini case studies

> Title page
> Abstract
> Table of contents
> **Introduction**
> Methodology
> Perspectives
> **Conclusion**
> Recommendations
> Appendices

Here, we look at an example of an abstract, introduction and conclusion in terms of *structure*.

It is the middle of 2020. Aurelia is a Biology student who wants to study Microbiology at university. She has an interest in epidemic control and, during the Covid-19 crisis, feels that investigating pandemics from an epidemiological standpoint would be a valuable study. To this end, she has answered the question: 'To what extent is herd immunity an effective way to control a pandemic?' (At this point, no vaccine had been identified.) She has researched this topic through the concepts of survival of the fittest (Darwin's theory of evolution), epidemiology and control theory. The following is an extract from her introduction.

1.0 Introduction

This report considers the efficacy of the policy of herd immunity as a way to control a pandemic. It examines the suggestions for the control of pandemics made by differing experts and undertaken by different countries both during Covid-19 in 2019–20 and the Spanish flu pandemic of 1918. Through the examination and analysis of varying government policies, both current and historical, and the commentary on both, this report evaluates the solutions proposed as they relate to herd immunity. [1] There are many studies that are of relevance in relation to the Spanish flu pandemic of 1918 that provide an historical context and a comparison to the current situation in regard to Covid-19, which in the absence of a vaccine at the time of writing all rely, to some extent, on a proposal around herd immunity. [2] To investigate this question, this report will consult the following three areas: evolutionary theory, epidemiological study and control theory. [3] All three of these concepts have value when addressing pandemics, particularly with reference to the question of herd immunity.

Survival of the fittest is a controversial approach and epidemiology is the mainstream approach that has a proven history in controlling epidemics, whereas control theory is an alternative concept based in engineering that some see as needed to evaluate practice in the face of the pandemic. [4] This report explores the hypothesis that, despite the controversial nature of survival theory, while we wait for a vaccine, herd immunity is the most effective way to address the Covid-19 situation. [5]

[1] What I am going to examine

[2] Results of the literature review

[3] Concepts

[4] Justification of concepts and why they are pertinent

[5] Hypothesis

Aurelia has completed her report and is writing her conclusion with her reflection within it. Below is an extract from her conclusion.

4.0 Conclusion

From the outset, I felt that herd immunity would have been the best way forward for the control of a pandemic, [1] and a survivalist concept was where my research began. Many articles, from Rush (2020) through to Kharti (2020), highlighted the benefits, under almost Darwinian principles [2], of building an immunity among a population while shielding the most vulnerable. They based their perspective on the data that the young and fit within the population were minimally affected and an indication that exposure could confer at least some immunity. This data indicated that either an easing or the limiting of any mass lockdown would be the most effective way of halting the virus. [3]

[1] Hypothesis
[2] Concept
[3] Summary

However, the comparison of measures taken during the Spanish flu when the states in America that took a more cautionary stance were not only less negatively impacted, but also first to recover from virus (Power, 2015 alongside a UK Government paper: 'Research into...2020') indicating that the trajectory of the virus would mean that the health services could not cope with the number of people hospitalised, made me reassess the herd principle. [4] It became clear that the answer was more nuanced. Every perspective [5] that was not reliant on a vaccine or treatment, and even those that were (Rose 2020, Huang, 2020), were reliant in some aspect on the building of herd immunity, but as the end goal not the overriding concept.

[4] Comparison and reflection
[5] Evaluation

The issue of whether herd immunity could be effective informed my original question and initially appeared non-negotiable. However, it became apparent that the key question to be answered was how quickly and safely herd immunity could be achieved, and I altered my title accordingly [6] [7]. This similarly redirected my research and plan, as it now contained the examination of additional concepts in the realms of epidemiology and engineering control theory (Stewart, van Heusden and Dumont, 2020). From the outset, my methodology had been based on an examination of secondary research through a literature review. This was effective as there was a wealth of up-to-date research being undertaken in this area, and there were also many reviews surrounding the only previous pandemic in modern history, Spanish flu. However, my research also altered to encompass some primary material in the form of diaries and letters written during the Spanish flu pandemic and also letters from National Health Service staff in the UK published in the *Recorder* ('We are too overstretched...', May 2020) and the *Post* ('To all who will listen', April 2020). These primary sources brought a social aspect to my research and had a significant impact on my argument [8]. The objectivity of Rush and Kharti was brought into question by these accounts, and the data and outcomes of social distancing and response theory (Timpson, 2020 and Robson, 2020) were persuasive both in terms of data and peer review. It appeared that fast and effective herd immunity came at a significant cost, which would be socially hard to bear and ethically hard to justify.

[6] Question development
[7] Alteration of research
[8] Critical evaluation of methodology

We can see that Aurelia has formulated her introduction and conclusion by using the structure highlighted above. There are other ways to go about this, but this is one method.

Abstract

Our global community faces a pandemic for only the second time in two centuries and it is critical that we understand the most effective way to manage this situation, both medically and socially. This is not only important for our current population, but for future generations also. Therefore, in the wake of the Covid-19 pandemic, this report analyses the hypothesis that herd immunity, as it is defined by evolutionary theory, is the best method to control pandemics. To do so, it looks at the efficacy of three main concepts: survival of the fittest, epidemiology and control theory. The methodology for this report is primarily a secondary literature review, supported by primary source research and analysis of letters and diaries from both the Spanish flu epidemic 1918 and the Covid-19 pandemic 2019–20. This report highlights that each concept relies to some extent on herd immunity and that the main driver for a solution must encompass ethical considerations and social responsibility. In addition, the report suggests that what may be required is an organic approach that incorporates different strategies to address the varying ways that the virus presents in different countries.

As a result, this report concludes that it would be beneficial to conduct further research once the Covid-19 pandemic has subsided. This research should compare the different approaches in relation to population size, circumstance and outcome.

(All references in this piece are fictionalised for the purpose of demonstration.)

Activity 2: Identifying features of an abstract

a) Review the description of an abstract on page 200 and identify the main points in the abstract above.

b) Work with a partner to compare and refine your answers.

Citation structure

You have learned about citations and the fact that it helps to use the correct citation method for your discipline. Check back over the citation procedure and formatting in Chapter 3 and review your own use of it.

Remember:
- Choose a citation method and use it consistently.
- If you use a system with endnotes or footnotes, similar to the appendices and the research log, do not use these notes to add to argument and analysis in the main body of the text.

A reader should be able to read your report without the footnotes and get a full understanding of your argument. For the Cambridge Research Report, the reader should only need to look at the footnotes or endnotes for the reference.

Activity 3: Citations

a) Look at the following in-text citations and identify them. Are they footnotes, endnotes, reference or parenthetical citations?

Example A

Jameson looks at the concept of drug use in sport and expresses concern that the prolific nature of the usage undermines any attempt to control it. (1)

1. Jameson, A. *Sports & Drug Use Control or Licence*, Bramstead Publishing, 2004, pp42-43

Example B

When looking at the cultural aspects within the community, it becomes clear that, as Stevens notes, a solution may only be found if a constant dialogue is maintained. (5)

Example C

Jackson posits that organised religion is declining and that a secular society is inevitable (Jackson, 2015, p.15).

Final task

Consider the factors you need to include in your introduction, conclusion and abstract. Examine the introduction, conclusion and abstract in the Special focus in this unit, and write a paragraph explaining the similarities and the differences between them and their specific function in the report.

Reflective plenary

Reflect on what you identified as your biggest challenges in Activity 1. Are they the same now? What have you learned that has helped the most and why?

11.3 Writing the report

In this unit you will:
- explore effective strategies for writing your Cambridge Research Report.

Critical Path

You will need to:
- deconstruct your sources and arguments
- synthesise and reconstruct perspectives
- reflect on impact
- communicate in an academic manner.

Deconstruction	Reconstruction	Reflection	Communication	Collaboration
✓	✓	✓	✓	

The focus of this unit is on exploring academic essay writing and finding your academic voice. Throughout this section, you will learn how to approach the writing of the Cambridge Research Report, what language to use and how to troubleshoot if you reach an impasse.

Academic writing key: dos and don'ts

Do

✓ **Be clear:** Being clear should not be confused with being non-academic or simplistic. Therefore, you should use key words and terms, but not presume knowledge for your non-specialist audience.

✓ **Be concise:** A key rule would be 'do not use 20 words if 10 will do'. This is a job for redrafting.

✓ **Use precise, accurate, relevant terminology:** Your language should be appropriate to your discipline and include key terms.

✓ **Use signposting language:** You should use signposting language in order to make your evaluation structured and clear. Examples include: 'alternatively', 'furthermore', 'in comparison', 'in addition', 'similarly'. See Chapter 8 for more examples.

Special focus: Mini case study: Aati

Aati is analysing a source that he used for his Cambridge Research Report in the area of economics. It is one that deals with negative externalities. He writes the following:

> Fisher writes persuasively about the use of the sugar tax to remedy the **negative externality** of obesity that is caused by purchasing products high in sugar. [1] [2] He recognises that this may not work, as consumers may still continue to buy the product despite any potential price rise. [3] However, [4] he counters this [5] with the proposition that this tax needs to be instigated alongside a clear message from the government on healthy eating.

[1] Explains a technical term specific to his discipline.

[2] Supports statement by referencing.

[3] Provides evidence to support the claim of the argument being persuasive.

[4] [5] Signposting words and phrases signal student's evaluation of the argument.

*Glossary
negative externality: a cost that is suffered by a third party as a consequence of an economic transaction

(All references in this piece are fictionalised for the purpose of demonstration.)

Activity 1: Identifying terms

a) Annotate a copy of the abstract on pages 204–205, highlighting the evaluative and specialist terms used and any supporting statements.

Don't

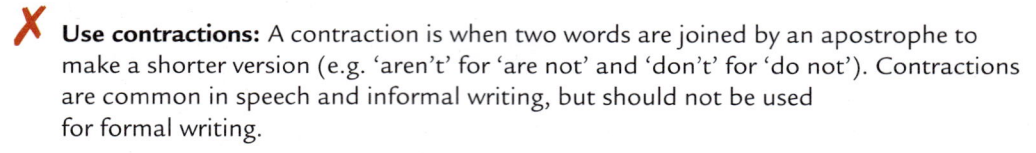

✗ **Make unsupported assertions:** Make sure that your statements or inferences are supported and evidenced.

✗ **Use contractions:** A contraction is when two words are joined by an apostrophe to make a shorter version (e.g. 'aren't' for 'are not' and 'don't' for 'do not'). Contractions are common in speech and informal writing, but should not be used for formal writing.

✗ **Be colloquial:** Colloquial language is the language of everyday speech and can contain idioms. For example, when examining how test subjects performed in a certain task you would not say, 'the task was a piece of cake'.

✗ **Be informal:** You should not be conversational. This is at odds with your research log – in your log, for example, you could say: *Today I looked at Joseph Glim's article 'The Inferno Effect' – it is a really good piece of persuasive writing. His point about the cyclone is similar to Thomas's.* In your report you may write: *Joseph Glim makes a persuasive point about cyclones in 'The Inferno Effect', which is supported by Nicholas Thomas in his…*

✗ **Be dismissive:** Sometimes you will disagree with a perspective and this is absolutely acceptable – in fact, it is productive academic practice. However, you must not be *dismissive*. It is important that you acknowledge valid points in any perspective, and you should justify why you find another perspective more compelling. Do not include an argument that is worthless and dismiss it in your writing – this has little value.

✗ **Use unnecessarily complex or misplaced vocabulary:** It can be very tempting to overuse a thesaurus, but this can make your sentences unclear. This does not mean you should not use synonyms, but you should make sure that you are using them in the correct context.

Look at this worked example of the last point in the list above.

Boxler's writing style is extremely persuasive. He is particularly persuasive when he...

It sounds awkward to use the word 'persuasive' twice in quick succession and you could use a synonym here.

A quick search in a thesaurus presents these top ten synonyms:

alluring, cogent, compelling, conclusive, convincing, credible, eloquent, energetic, forceful, impressive

Although these words are all synonyms, you must be careful to contextualise them. Even the first on the list, which should be the closest meaning, would not work in context here:

*Boxler's writing style is extremely persuasive. He is particularly **alluring** when he...*

However, the word 'compelling' does work in context:

*Boxler's writing style is extremely persuasive. He is particularly **compelling** when he...*

If you are not familiar with a synonym, look for it in another piece of writing to test its suitability.

Academic vocabulary

This section looks at different types of academic language and phrases that you may adopt in different parts of your report. You will see another method of producing an introduction, but this time using academic language to guide you.

Introduction

In your introduction, you will set out what you intend to do. Therefore, the key words that are likely to appear in your report will reflect the skills you need to demonstrate. These key words are listed in the word bank opposite.

> **Word bank**
>
> analysis
> implications
> contrasting
>   perspectives
> critical insight/
>   comparison
> justification
>   (judgements and
>   sources; choice of
>   topic)
> wide range of sources
> evaluate concepts
>   methodology
> identifies methods
> reflects (impact
>   of perspectives)
>   (nature and
>   limitation of
>   conclusion)

Special focus: Mini case study: Amayra

Amayra, the student from Unit 10.4, is about to start writing the introduction for her report: 'Does positive discrimination undermine or promote the position of women in the workplace?' She uses appropriate objectives for the report as listed in the word bank on page 209. This is useful, as it confirms that she has covered the skills that she needs to demonstrate.

Amayra writes the following extract for her introduction.

> This report deals with the **topic** of positive discrimination in the workplace as it relates to gender. It **analyses contrasting perspectives** both in support of and in opposition to the use of positive discrimination for the promotion of women to executive level positions. It relies on this analysis to **justify** the use of positive discrimination to redress the inequality that is present in the promotion of women to positions of power and responsibility across continents, but with particular reference to the western hemisphere and first world economies and business. To explore this phenomenon, this report examines the **concepts** of liberal and Marxist feminism and their perception of the equalities argument. In doing so, it **evaluates** the role of history in the shaping of these **concepts** and **critically** examines how they still influence the **topic** of the inequitable status of women in the workplace today. This report concludes with a **reflection** on the **impact** of these perspectives on the hypothesis that there is no alternative to breaking the 'glass ceiling' for women in a patriarchally informed hierarchical system, and recognises the **limitations** of the imposition of such a system on both men and women in the workplace.

In order to address this question, the report uses the following methodology:
- interviews
- literature review
- statistical analysis.

For her own reference, Amayra places the words that she has used from her target objectives in bold. She will 'unbold' them before the submission of her report. It is important to note that her introduction does not use all of the vocabulary listed. There is no need to state them all at the outset, as long as they are demonstrated in your report. Amayra's introduction does, however, utilise key words from the word bank to frame the report. As a result – and remember, her introduction is likely to have been written last – Amayra can be confident that she will have met most, if not all, of the criteria in the report's **exposition** of her topic.

> **Key term**
>
> **exposition:** the explanation of an idea

There is, of course, other academic terminology within Amayra's introduction. She also uses the following words and phrases that could be termed 'academic'.

Signpost phrases that help set out Amayra's path through the material:
- in support of this
- in opposition to
- with particular reference to
- to explore this further.

Precise and accurate vocabulary that clarifies thinking:
- examines
- perception of
- hypothesis
- patriarchally informed
- imposition of.

Main body

In the main body of the report, you will be analysing and synthesising perspectives, arguments and evidence. It is not possible to do this without the use of signpost words and phrases, which help evaluate arguments and encourage comparison.

The following are examples of comparative language:
- On the other hand…
- A contrasting perspective…
- This is supported by…
- Even so…
- Yet, we can also see…
- However, … explains that…

The same is true of the language of analysis:
- By way of explanation…
- To further explain…
- This is detailed in…
- This reveals that…
- At this point…

Activity 2: Writing in an appropriate style

a) Rewrite the following in a formal academic style, incorporating signposting.

> In this report I'll look at the whether you should be made have you're kids immunised against illness. It is obvious that this is an important thing to do as no-one want their kids to get ill. Some people think that having an injection that gives their child a dose of the illness will harm their children but this is just nonsense. To help me investigate this subject I read a few articles on immunisation and interviewed my family on what they thought about it. The articles I read were generally for it and I could not easily find articles against it. There was one piece of research that spoke about human rights, but what about the human rights of those who do not want to catch the disease?

b) Compare your new paragraph with a partner and discuss the errors you found.

Subject-specific lexicon

We have seen that one of the 'dos' at the beginning of this section is that you should use subject-appropriate academic language. (As you are writing for a non-specialist reader, you may wish to include a glossary.) The language related to your discipline will have specific definitions, and using this language will make your report more precise and critically accessible. This is important as, in order to discuss ideas within a subject, academics have to ensure they are discussing the same thing. A subject-specialist **lexicon** is a way to guarantee this.

> **Key term**
>
> **lexicon:** the vocabulary specific to a branch of knowledge

Let's take an example from the world of assessment, where reliability is a key principle. The general definition of the word 'reliability' is:

People or things that are reliable can be trusted to work well or to behave in the way that you want them to. Information that is reliable or that is from a reliable source is very likely to be correct.

Source: www.collinsdictionary.com

However, the definition of reliability for assessment, as defined by the Cambridge Approach, is:

Reliability relates to the stability of the assessment, for example, whether on different occasions or using different markers the same outcomes are rated in the same way.

From cambridgeassessment.org.uk

What you can see here is that the definition of reliability in assessment is much more specific than the general definition. A reliable assessment under the terms of the general definition is one that can be trusted, whereas in the more specific definition, it relates to the comparison of more than one year group or 'sitting' of that assessment – there is an element of time and situation involved.

Activity 3: Using appropriate terminology

a) Consider the discipline that your Cambridge Research Report will fall under. Research the academic lexicon for your discipline. For example, what might 'reliability' mean when applied to an international vaccine trial by a group of university research centres?

b) Record specific terminology that you feel may be useful and make sure you understand it. Contextualise these words and phrases by using each one in a sentence and writing it down.

Types of academic writing

There are several main types of academic writing: **descriptive/narrative**, **analytic**, **persuasive**, **critical/discursive**.

All four of these types of writing have their place in the report but there are some common pitfalls to be aware of:
- Do not make your writing just a narrative. The use of a question for a title that engenders two sides of a debate will help with this, and you will need to compare and contrast, and synthesise your arguments.
- Do not forget to explore how arguments inform your own perspective.

Your report must not simply describe different perspectives and then state which one you agree with, without looking at why you agree and analysing how your position builds.

Key terms

descriptive/narrative: describing/narrating another viewpoint (in the report, these are perspectives)

analytic: arguments and perspectives

persuasive: your own viewpoint tied to reflection

critical/discursive: comparing and evaluating viewpoints

Avoid making your writing mechanical

When using subheadings, there is a risk of writing becoming a 'tick box' exercise. Writing in this manner fulfils marking criteria, but does not produce a fully coherent piece.

Let us look for a moment at the use of RAVEN or CRAAP. These methods for evaluating sources are, as you saw in Chapter 3, useful tools and can add structure to your work, but when used prescriptively they can make your writing lack fluency. For example, you should be wary of splitting your source analysis into sections based on a subheading for each perspective: **C**urrency, **R**elevance, **A**uthority, **A**ccuracy, **P**urpose. This structure is too rigid, not always relevant, and difficult to read. This is because it may not be essential or pertinent to address every RAVEN or CRAAP point and there may be overlap between the areas. This point is further illustrated by the following example that utilises RAVEN:

> This author has an excellent reputation, they are a professor at University of Washington [1]. They have the ability to observe as they will have access to many reliable sources at the university library. [2] They have a vested interest in promoting reliable research and debate into their area of specialism. [3] They are an expert in their field and speak regularly at symposiums on the topic. [4] They are neutral as there is no evidence of bias in the work. [5]

There is repetition in this example and it also has no support or evaluation; no framing or context.

A more useful example is as follows:

> The author is a professor at the University of Washington with a long history of research into this field of study, which he drew upon throughout the article and which gave weight to his perspective. This was particularly evident where…
>
> He regularly speaks at symposiums and some of the work he cited had only recently been presented, which gave insight into some cutting-edge thinking. Although this was not extensively peer reviewed, the links and development to previous ideas regarding… helped me to consolidate my argument that…
>
> It cannot be denied that this author, with his evident specialism, may have a bias towards this particular school of thought, but when he considered, examined and deconstructed opposing opinions he showed an objectivity that was persuasive. This was particularly evident where… and reflects my own opinion that…

[1] Just because they are a professor does not automatically make their work credible or reliable – this point needs more scaffolding. You can infer something from status, but at this level, you need to add more.

[2] This is, again, far too general – any student would have access to the same facilities. Again it has some value, but it is limited. What research have they undertaken, has it been primary, are they from a particular region that gives them authentic insight, etc.?

[3] There is overlap here, linked back to the role of professor. Other questions to ask here are about motivation. Are they on any particular boards as advisors; does anything affect their objectivity?

[4] This needs validating. How does a regular attendance confer expertise? Are they invited key-note speakers or just prolific? What is the status of their peer reviews?

[5] This is a standalone comment of little value without support.

Activity 4: Improving fluency and relevance

a) Compare the first and second examples. Identify and comment on each of the improvements in terms of both content and language.

Use of tenses

There are three basic tenses used for academic writing:

Present simple is the default tense, for example:
- *this study looks at/examines/investigates*
- *Gerray's perpective is/suggests/posits.*

Past simple is used for describing how something was investigated. This is very good for source evaluation, for example:
- *Gerray interviewed many pensioners from varying walks of life and income streams.*

Present perfect is used to summarise a body of work or in the case of the report, the arguments that form a particular perspective, for example:
- *These academics have found that…*

Final task

a) Using the mind map/spidergram you created in Unit 11.1, and the writing guidance in Units 11.2 and 11.3, write an introduction to an essay that reflects what you have learned.
b) Work with a partner to evaluate and suggest improvements, and identify any ideas that are unclear to you.

Reflective plenary

Consider which of these aspects of writing will be the most difficult for you. What can you do to make these more achievable?

Glossary

ability to see: how close the source is to the evidence and whether the author has first-hand knowledge or relevant expertise

abstract: a brief summary which comes before a longer report, research piece or article, summing up its purpose and approach

analysis: a way of examining something complex in close detail, by breaking down the whole into smaller parts so it can be more clearly understood

analytic: arguments and perspectives

argument: one or more reasons given to persuade readers or listeners to support or oppose an idea or viewpoint, and lead to a conclusion

assertion: an unsupported claim; the purpose of research is to find evidence and reasons to substantiate a claim

assumption: an unstated reason that is accepted to be true without proof

audit: a dispassionate review of your strengths and weaknesses

authority: the right someone has to influence an issue based on their level of understanding and expertise

bias: an inclination or prejudice for or against an argument, opinion, person or group

bibliography: a list at the end of a piece of work detailing all the sources used

causation: the act of causing or producing an effect or a result (e.g. photosynthesis produces oxygen)

citation: the method used within a text to indicate the use of someone else's work; it can either be numerical or alphabetical

claim: a statement that may or may not be true – it is debatable

concept: an overarching idea or theoretical framework(s) for research

conclusion: a judgement reached by reasoning, based on preceding argument and evidence

content editing: checking and improving on the content, structure and clarity of your work

context: the things that influence an issue or event, including geographical location and environment (where), the people cultures and languages involved (who) and timing (when)

controversial: likely to invoke strong opposition

correlation: the relationship or connection that exists between two or more things

corroborate: to support a statement with evidence

counter-argument: an argument made to challenge another argument

credibility: how believable a claim is

critical/discursive: comparing and evaluating viewpoints

currency: how recent information is and whether it is still relevant

debate: a discussion or reasoned argument that reflects different, usually contrasting perspectives on an issue

demographics: data relating to a population or groups within a population such as age, wealth, what people spend their money on

descriptive/narrative: describing/narrating another viewpoint

discursive essay: a structured, balanced, written debate made up of arguments exploring various perspectives on a particular topic that weighs up the perspectives and comes to a conclusion

e-learning: learning that occurs via electronic media, typically on the internet, digitally delivering all or part of a course of study

empirical: derived from or relating to experiment and observation rather than theory

evaluation: identifying strengths and weaknesses in order to make a judgement

evidence: facts, research, data or testimony that is used to support reasoning, arguments or perspectives

exposition: the explanation of an idea

facilitator: a person on a team whose role is to help everyone on a team work together better by 'facilitating' or making it easier to understand and achieve common goals and objectives

footnotes: brief details of sources collated in numerical order at the bottom of a page

generalisation: a broad universal statement based on only one or a few facts

gist: the overall focus or meaning of a text

global relevance: when an issue of local or national importance affects people and societies internationally

graphic organiser: a knowledge map, chart or diagram showing relationships between concepts, facts or ideas that can help you to organise your thinking and make it visual

groupthink: when individuals concur with the group decision, even when it may be a bad one, because they don't want to express opinions, suggest new ideas or seem different to everyone else

hard deadline: one that cannot be missed

hypothesis: a supposition; a starting point for further study

inferential gap: the gap between the knowledge of a person trying to explain an idea and the knowledge of the person trying to understand it

informed opinion: the opinion of someone who is an acknowledged expert in their field

issue: a specific, defined area within a topic, often with global relevance, that is suitable as a subject for deeper research; people may hold different points of view about an issue

learning journey: a useful analogy for developing your skills of reflection

learning strategies: the techniques used to maximise your ability to learn, understand and use information, and to develop new skills and competences

lexicon: the vocabulary specific to a branch of knowledge

methodology: the reasons why you chose the method(s) you use for your research and data collection e.g. interviews, focus groups (qualitative) or surveys, experiments (quantitative)

micro-blog: a very short blog, usually comprising 140-280 characters, designed to allow users to share small pieces of content

mode of address: the way an author communicates with the audience

objective: describes judgements that are made without personal beliefs or preconceived ideas influencing the process

paragraph: a block of text used to explore one idea, usually containing a topic sentence and supporting sentences, concluding with a transition to the next idea/paragraph

paragraph heading: a one word/phrase summary of the content of a specific paragraph; useful in drafting to help highlight sequencing

peer review: a review or evaluation of work by others who work in the same field

personal opinion: an individual's own thoughts or feelings about an issue; often used in journalism, it can be useful for gauging public opinion, but it is likely to be subjective

perspective: a coherent world view which is a response to an issue. A perspective is made up of argument, evidence, assumptions and may be influenced by a particular context.

persuasive: your own viewpoint tied to reflection

plagiarism: passing off the words, work or ideas of others as if they are your own – i.e. without acknowledgement

point of view: the opinion you have about something – the way you consider or see an issue

policy: a course of action taken by an individual or organisation, but usually intended to mean a planned strategy or approach

presentation: a talk for an audience to give information, ideas and evidence for arguments that make a case or tell a story about something from a unique perspective

proofreading: checking your work for more technical concerns, such as to correct errors of grammar and spelling and to confirm the accuracy of referencing

provenance: the place of origin or history of something

rationale: a reason for doing something

reason: an explanation of why something is true or happens

rebuttal: a statement that contradicts what has been said, pointing out the ways it is not true

redundancy: using too many words to express a simple idea, such as 'it is often the case that' rather than 'often'

referencing: an overall term referring to the acknowledgement of others' work in an essay or other research assignment

reliability: how trustworthy or reliable something is

rhetorical device: language deliberately designed to convey a specific message or meaning, to persuade an audience and evoke particular emotions

rhetorical question: a question asked for the purpose of making a statement; a question that does not expect an answer

skills audit: an assessment of your own skills (e.g. research, knowledge management, organisation) to help you identify your competences and areas in need of development

stakeholder: someone involved in or affected by an issue

soft deadline: one that is movable

subjective: describes judgements that are influenced by or based on personal beliefs or feelings

synthesis: the combination of multiple sources and ideas from research to create perspectives

theme: an approach to a topic or issue – for example, technology or ethics; a thematic approach can help you to identify a perspective and focus your research (you will find the seven themes listed in the Cambridge International AS & A Level Global Perspectives and Research syllabus in Unit 1.2)

topics: broad areas of interest that have global significance; they provide the context for more defined research from which issues will arise (you will find a list of global topics in Unit 1.2; they are defined in the Cambridge International AS & A Level Global Perspectives and Research syllabus)

topic sentence: the sentence that contains the key idea in a paragraph, usually (but not always) the first sentence

transition words: words that act as signposts, clarifying the direction of debate; transition words can be additive, sequential, contrasting/shifting direction or causal/explanatory

uncited: describes information or evidence an author uses without saying where it comes from

vested interest: a personal reason for getting involved in an issue, usually because it offers financial or some other type of gain

visual hierarchy: the arrangement of elements on a page so users can understand the information

Index

abbreviations 190–191
ability to see 41, 43, 51, 215
abstracts 184, 215
    Cambridge Research Report 199, 200, 204–205
academic journals and reports 46
academic vocabulary 209–212
academic writing 207–214
    fluency and relevance 213
    key dos and don'ts 207–209
    style 58–62
    tenses 214
    types of 212
access to clean water 156, 162–164
accuracy 51
action plan 153, 154, 157–158
active listening 14
addiction to painkillers 40
analogy 27
analysis 11–12, 186–187, 215
    arguments 21–29
    Gibbs' reflective model 153, 154, 155, 157, 159
    language of 211
analytic academic writing 212
animal testing 58–61, 64, 123
annotations 54–55
Apartheid 188
appendices 202
Ardern, Jacinda 27
arguments 31, 37, 176, 215
    analysis of 21–29
    assessing strength of 23–24
    common problems with 24
    evaluating arguments from two sources 86–93
    identifying strengths and weaknesses in 25
    organising the argument for the team project presentation 138–41
    structuring 89, 90–91
    summing up how convincing an argument is 89, 91–92
assertions 22, 208, 215

assessment 212
Associated Press 42
assumptions 31, 215
audience 27–28
audio sources 46–47
audit 2, 215
    self-audit 2–4
    skills audit 3–4, 69
auditory learners 2
author references 65
authority 50, 51, 215

Bassot's integrated reflective cycle 154
Beckett, Samuel 73
bias 23, 42, 51, 215
bibliography 63, 65, 115, 123, 124, 215
body of an essay 89, 90–91, 115, 118–19
    perspectives 115, 118
    reflection 115, 118, 119
    synthesis 115, 118

cacophony 108
Cambridge Research Report 166–214
    planning for 194–198
    research log 174–179
    research process 186–192
    structuring 199–206
    topic identification 180–185
    understanding the task 167–169
    writing the proposal 170–173
    writing the report 207–214
causation 24, 25, 215
challenging perspectives, engaging with 36
cholera 54–56
citations 63, 65, 123, 205–206, 215
    see also referencing
claims 21–22, 23–24, 215
clarity 139–140, 207

coding information 113
coherence 31, 215
collaboration 11, 13, 14
    reflecting on 155–158
    reflecting on effectiveness of 160, 161, 162–163
    teamworking *see* teamworking
colloquial language 208
colours 147
communication 11, 13
    audience and rhetoric 27–28
    clarity of 143
    non-verbal 13, 149
    of reflections 159–160
comparative language 211
concepts 168, 172, 176
    importance in research 183–185
conciseness 207
conclusions 215
    arguments 21, 22, 23–24
    Cambridge Research Report 200, 201–202, 204
    essays 89, 92–93, 115, 119–20
    Gibbs' reflective model 153, 154, 157
    interim conclusions 89, 91–92
content editing 121, 124, 215
context 31, 215
contingency time 195, 196
contractions 208
contrasting perspectives 34–35, 182, 184
control theory 203–205
controversy 97, 116, 215
conversational writing 208
correlation 24, 25, 215
corroboration 12, 43–44, 215
cosmetic research 58–61, 64, 123
Costa Rica 16–17
counter-argument 25–26, 90, 92, 215
coursework essay 94–125
    format 121–122
    organisation of ideas 111–113
    research for 106–109
    structuring 115–120

time management 103–105
topic selection 95–102
weighting for parts of 104
writing 121–125
Covid-19 pandemic 203–205
CRAAP test 50–51, 55, 107, 188, 213
credibility 40–41, 43, 50, 186–187, 188, 215
critical/discursive academic writing 212
Critical Path 5, 6, 11–14
approach to topics, themes and issues 15–19
research log and 175–176
stages 11–14
see also collaboration; communication; deconstruction; reconstruction; reflection
crucible 5
cultural heritage, loss of 131, 134–135
culture 9, 10, 33
currency 51, 107, 215

data, types of 187–188
deadlines 172, 215, 216
debate 68, 96–97, 170, 172, 215
deconstruction 11–12, 15–19, 187
definitions 116, 117
demographics 96, 215
description 153, 155–156, 159
descriptive/narrative academic writing 212
design principles 147–148
developmental stages of teams 128–129
diamond plan 197–198
different perspectives 34–35
direct quotation 57
direction of research 176
discursive/critical academic writing 212
discursive essays 114, 215
dismissiveness 209
domain name suffixes 48

e-learning 35, 215
economics 9, 10, 18–19, 33
ecotourism 16–19

editing 121, 124–125
education 34–35
empirical (evidence) 10, 215
energy 36, 44
environment 9, 10, 18–19, 33
plastic pollution *see* plastic pollution
epidemiology 203–205
essays
coursework essay *see* coursework essay
discursive 114, 215
structure 89–93, 115–120, 200
ethics 9, 10, 18
considerations in the research proposal 171–172
evaluation 12, 187, 215
arguments and perspectives from two sources 86–93
evidence 40–44, 55, 83–85
Gibbs' reflective model 153, 154, 156
of the presentation 150
sources 50–53, 107, 134–135, 188–189
everyday research 186–187
evidence 23, 31, 37–44, 46, 112–113, 215
evaluating 40–44, 55, 83–85
finding 54–55
identifying strengths and weaknesses 25, 83–85
incorporating into writing 56–57
primary 37, 39, 169, 187–188
secondary 37, 39, 169, 187–188
types of 37–40
uncited (unsourced) 41, 50, 216
writing about evidence from an unseen source 83–85
see also sources
expertise 39, 50, 51, 215
exploitation 28–29
exposition 210, 215
expression 125

facilitator 129, 215
facts 38, 39

Fairtrade 28–29
feedback, team 150
feelings 153–154, 156, 159
feminist movement 183–184, 210
fluency 213
focused attention 133–134
footnotes 63, 65, 205, 215
fossil fuels 36
further research 115, 119–120

gender equality 32
generalisations 24, 25, 215
geologic strata 84, 87
Gibbs' reflective cycle 153–154
application to the Team Project 155–158
gist 79, 84, 215
global education 34–35
global reach 54, 55, 112
global relevance 127, 131–132, 215
global thinking 1–5
global topics 6–7, 9
graphic organiser 68–69
group perspectives 4–5
groupthink 157, 158, 215

Harare 55–56
hard deadlines 172, 215
highlighting 192
history 7
social 168–169
human rights 34, 35
herd immunity 203–205
Humanities subjects 188
hypotheses 174, 200–201, 215

ideas
organising 111–113, 138–139
writing up 56
image types 146–147
implicit information 81–82
independent working 67–69
inferential gap 24, 215
influenza vaccines 52
informed opinions 39, 50, 51, 215
intellectual engagement 172
interests, exploring your own 96
interim conclusions 89, 91–92

internet searching 47, 48–49, 106–107, 134, 164, 189
interviews 171
introduction
    Cambridge Research Report 200–201, 203–204, 209–211
    essays 89, 90, 115, 116–118
issues 7–8, 9, 18–19, 167, 215
    identifying 80–82, 182–183
iterative learning process 152

jumping to conclusions 3

Kennedy, J.F. 81–82
key points, identifying 80–82
key words in questions 77
keyword-based searching 106–107, 134
kinaesthetic learners 3
knowledge 160, 161, 163–164

language
    academic vocabulary 209–212
    presentation 139, 142–145, 149
    signposting 123, 143–145, 207, 210–211
layout of slides 139–140
learners, types of 2–3
learning journey 160, 161, 163–165, 216
learning strategies 67–68, 216
legibility 139–140
lexicon 211–212, 216
libraries 189, 190
limitations
    coursework essay 115, 116, 117–118, 119–120
    of research 172
linear copying 192
literature review 176, 186–192
local problems 127–128
    identifying a suitable local problem 131–132
logic 23–24

meaningfulness of evidence 42–43
metacognition 135–136, 176
methodology 168, 169, 171, 172, 173, 176, 200, 201, 216

micro-blog 139, 216
migration and work 9
mind maps 112, 113, 196–197
mode of address 27, 216
motivation 116–117, 170
Mozambique bridge project 25
multimedia sources 47

narrative/descriptive academic writing 212
negative externality 208
neutrality 51
non-verbal communication 13, 149
note-making 54–56, 108, 190–192
    common mistakes 192
    evaluating arguments and perspectives from two sources 86–89
nuclear power 44
numeric references 63, 65

Obama, Michelle 73
objective judgements 22, 216
objectivity 181
ocean soundscape 108
online searching 47, 48–49, 106–107, 134, 164, 189
online sources, reliability of 51
opening sentence 116
opinions 38
    informed 39, 50, 51, 215
    personal 39, 116, 117, 216
opioid painkillers 40
organisation
    argument for the presentation 138–141
    ideas 111–113, 138–139
    preparing for the presentation 133–134, 136

painkillers, addiction to 40
pall 79
paragraph headings 122, 216
paragraphs 59, 216
    structuring 90–91, 122–123
paraphrasing 57
past simple tense 214
peacekeeping 26
PEE (point, evidence, explanation) structure 59, 61
peer assessment 150

peer review 191
personal opinions 39, 116, 117, 216
perspectives 18, 19, 30–36, 37, 127–128, 216
    alternative 32, 112
    Cambridge Research Report 176, 200, 201
    contrasting 34–35, 182, 184
    coursework essay 115, 118
    elements of a perspective 31–33
    engaging with challenging perspectives 36
    evaluating perspectives from two sources 86–93
persuasive academic writing 212
PEW 88
plagiarism 63, 216
planning
    Cambridge Research Report 194–198
    coursework essay 103–105
    writing plan 196–198
plastic pollution 46–47, 50, 52–57
    coursework essay 99–101, 106–109, 112–113, 115–120
points of view 8, 19, 30, 216
    see also perspectives
policy 96, 216
politics 9, 10, 18–19
positive discrimination 183–184, 210
practising a presentation 145, 149
present perfect tense 214
present simple tense 214
presentation 13, 133–150, 216
    delivering 150
    evaluating 150
    language 139, 142–145, 149
    organising the argument 138–141
    practising 145, 149
    preparation for 133–137
    visual content 139, 146–148
presentation skills 161, 164–165
presentation slides 139–141, 146–148, 149
primary evidence/sources 37, 39, 169, 187–188

project plan 194
proofreading 121, 124, 125, 216
proposal, research 170–173
provenance 4, 41–42, 43, 50, 216
provisional questions 182
purpose 51

qualitative evidence 38, 39, 216
qualitative research 177, 187
quantitative evidence 37, 39, 43, 187, 216
quantitative research 177, 187
questions
    coursework essay 97–102
    for further research 176
    key words in 77
    provisional 182
    raised by the teacher 176
    research question 172, 182–183, 188
    rhetorical 26, 27, 216
    that encourage effective research 98
    wording 99
    yes/no 97–98, 182
quotations 57, 90, 91

rationale 139, 216
RAVEN test 50–51, 55, 107, 188, 213
reading
    pointers 77
    skills 77
    unseen sources 77–79
reading/writing learners 2
reasons 21–22, 23–24, 216
rebuttal 26, 216
recommendations 200, 202
reconstruction 11, 12–13, 15–19, 187
record maintenance 134
recording sources 48, 64–65, 108–109, 134
redundancy 58, 60, 216
referencing 56–57, 63–65, 172, 216
    presentation slides 140–141
    see also citations
reflection 11, 13, 152–153
    Cambridge Research Report 188–189, 200–201
    on collaboration 155–158

coursework essay 115, 118, 119
    developing 73–75
reflective learning 2–3
    models 153–154
reflective log 73–75, 132
Reflective Paper 151, 159–165
    communicating reflections 159–160
    structure 160–161
    writing 161–165
relevance 43, 51, 188–189
    academic writing 207, 213
    global 127, 131–132, 215
reliability 48, 50, 51–53, 212, 216
repetition 27
representativeness of evidence 43
rereading and writing notes 190–191
research direction 176
research log 108–109, 174–179
    structuring 177–179
    what to include 176–177
research methods 171, 176–177
research process 186–192
    note-making 190–192
    steps in 188–192
    types of data/sources 187–188
research proposal 170–173
    template 173
research question 172, 188
    devising 182–183
research report see Cambridge Research Report
research skills 161, 164
reviewing notes 191, 192
rhetorical devices 26, 27–28, 216
rhetorical questions 26, 27, 216
rising sea levels 31–32, 33
rule of three 27

scanning 80, 107, 190
science 9, 10, 18
scope of research 171
scrutiny 4–5
sea level rise 31–32, 33
secondary evidence/sources 37, 39, 169, 187–188
seismographic activity 84, 87
selective evidence 42

self-audit 2–4
sentences 59–60
sewage pollution 54–56
Shakespeare, William 61–62, 178–179
signal words 57
signalling features 123
signposting language 143–145, 207, 210–11
Singapore 16
skills 160, 161, 164–165
skills audit 3–4, 69
skimming 80, 107
slides, presentation 139–141, 146–148, 149
SMART planning 105
social history 168–169
soft deadlines 172, 216
sources 45–65, 134
    academic style 58–62
    Cambridge Research Report 168–169, 171, 172, 176, 188–190
    evaluating arguments and perspectives from two sources 86–93
    evaluation 50–53, 107, 134–135, 188–189
    identifying 46–49, 188–190
    identifying key points and issues 80–82
    primary 37, 39, 169, 187–188
    reading unseen sources 77–79
    recording 48, 64–65, 108–109, 134
    referencing see referencing
    researching for the coursework essay 106–109
    secondary 37, 39, 169, 187–188
    types used in research 187–188
    unseen see unseen sources
    using 54–57
space colonisation 88
space travel 78–79, 81–92
Spanish flu 203–205
spidergrams (spider diagrams) 112, 113, 196–197
stakeholders 131, 216
Statement of Originality 109
STEM subjects 188

strengths and weaknesses of evidence 25, 83–85
structuring
　Cambridge Research Report 199–206
　essays 89–93, 115–120, 200
　paragraphs 90–91, 122–123
　Reflective Paper 160–161
　research log 177–179
　research proposal 173
style 125
　academic 58–62, 211
subject-specific lexicon 211–212
subjective judgements 22, 216
sugar tax 41
suitability of problems to research 131–132
summarising 15–17, 57
summing up 89, 92–93
survival of the fittest 203–205
symbols/abbreviations 190–191
synonyms 209
synthesis 12, 55–56, 115, 118, 216

table of contents 200
teachers, as sources 51, 190
team feedback 150
Team Project 126–150
　application of Gibbs' reflective model to 155–158
　delivering the presentation 150
　evaluation 150
　language used in presentation 139, 142–45, 149
　organising the argument 138–141
　practising the presentation 145, 149
　preparation for the presentation 133–137
　selection of problems to research 131–32
　steps to follow 128

　visual content of presentation 139, 146–148
　see also Reflective Paper
team roles 129–130
teamworking 14, 70–72
　developmental stages 128–129
　reflections on effectiveness of 160, 161, 162–163
　see also collaboration; Team Project
technology 9, 10
　in note-making 191
tenses 214
textual clues 77
themes 8–10, 18–19, 95, 216
　and broadening perspectives 33
time management 103–105
timetabling 172, 195–196
title page 199, 200
tone 159, 160
topic sentences 59, 61, 122, 216
topics 6–7, 9, 17–19, 216
　common topic in unseen sources 77
　identifying a topic for the Cambridge Research Report 180–185
　selection for coursework essay 95–102
topography 84, 87
tourism 16–19
transition words 59, 60, 123, 216

uncited (unsourced) evidence 41, 50, 216
understanding 186–187
United Nations 34
　peacekeeping 26
unsafe water supply 156, 162–164
unseen sources
　identifying key points and issues 80–82

reading 77–79
writing about evidence from 83–85
urbanisation 7–8
using sources 54–57

vaccines 52, 188
VARK 2–3
verbs 58, 59, 60
vested interest 41, 42, 43, 48, 50, 51, 216
visual learners 2
visual content of presentations 139, 146–148
vocabulary 58, 59, 209
　academic 209–212

water supply, unsafe 156, 162–164
weaknesses of evidence 25, 83–85
Wikipedia 52–53
word bank 209, 210
word count 121–122
writing
　about evidence from an unseen source 83–85
　academic 207–214
　Cambridge Research Report 207–214
　coursework essay 121–125
　evaluating arguments and perspectives from two sources 89–93
　reading/writing learners 2
　Reflective Paper 161–165
　research proposal 170–173
　writing up ideas 56
writing plan 196–198

'yes/no' questions 97–98, 182

Zimbabwe 54–55, 61, 118, 119

Acknowledgements

The publishers would like to thank Dean Roberts for reviewing a sample of the Student's Book and Teacher's Guide in development.

The publishers gratefully acknowledge the permission granted to reproduce the copyright material in this book. Every effort has been made to trace copyright holders and to obtain their permission for the use of copyright material. The publishers will gladly receive any information enabling them to rectify any error or omission at the first opportunity.

An extract on p.16 from "Singapore eco-tourism plan sparks squawks of protest" by Sam Reeves, AFP, 09/01/2019, http://doc.afp.com/1BL4Z5, copyright © Agence France-Presse, 2019. Reproduced by permission of the publisher; An extract on pp.16-17 from "Below the Surface: The Impacts of Ecotourism in Costa Rica" by Sujata Narayan, http://www.umich.edu/~csfound/545/1998/narayans/chap07.htm. Reproduced by kind permission of the author; Extracts on pp.25, 26 from "Rebuilding a bridge over Mozambique's troubled waters" by Rakesh Tripathi and Rafael Saute, 23/04/2020, https://blogs.worldbank.org/nasikiliza/rebuilding-bridge-over-mozambiques-troubled-waters; and "Most people think peacekeeping doesn't work. They're wrong" by Barbara F. Walter, 02/05/2018: https://blogs.worldbank.org/dev4peace/most-people-think-peacekeeping-doesn-t-work-they-re-wrong, © World Bank. Licence: Creative Commons Attribution (CC BY 3.0 IGO); An extract on p.36 from "Energy Means Food and Time" by Alex Epstein, National Review, 10/10/2019. Reproduced with permission of National Review; Extracts on pp.53, 117 from "Effects of plastic on oceans", https://en.wikipedia.org/wiki/Plastic_pollution#Effects_of_plastic_on_oceans; and "Plastic Pollution", https://en.wikipedia.org/wiki/Plastic_pollution, Wikipedia Foundation Inc., © Creative Commons licence Attribution-ShareAlike 3.0 Unported; An extract on p.55 from "'Medieval' Cholera Outbreak exposes huge challenges in Zimbabwe" by Jason Burke, The Guardian, 20/09/2018, copyright © Guardian News & Media Ltd 2020; An extract on p.57 from "Science-Based Solutions to Plastic Pollution" by Britta Denise Hardesty, One Earth, Elsevier, Vol 2 (1), 24/01/2020, pp.5-7, copyright © Elsevier, 2020. Reproduced by permission; An extract on p.64 from 'Animal Testing on Cosmetics', http://www.aboutanimaltesting.co.uk/animal-testing-cosmetics.html. Reproduced by permission of www.AboutAnimalTesting.co.uk - informed discussion on animal welfare in animal testing; An extract on p.65 adapted from 'Global Warming', https://www.britannica.com/science/global-warming, copyright © 2020. Reproduced by courtesy of Encyclopædia Britannica, Inc. and used with permission; Extracts on pp.78, 79, 84, 87 from "Do we really need to send humans into space?" by Donald Goldsmith and Martin Rees, Scientific American, 06/03/2020, copyright © 2020 Scientific American, a division of Springer Nature America, Inc. All rights reserved; An extract on p.108 from "Cacophony of human noise is hurting all marine life, scientists warn" by Damian Carrington, The Guardian, 04/02/2021, copyright © Guardian News & Media Ltd 2021; A diagram on p.129 adapted from Tuckman's developmental sequence in small groups; Extracts on p.196 from "Comparison between Mind Map and Spidergrams" Edraw Content Team, 11/07/2019, https://www.edrawsoft.com/mind-map-and-spidergram.html, accessed 2/8/2020. Reproduced with permission; and Definition on p.212 'Definition of Reliability' from the Collins Dictionary, www.collinsdictionary.com. Reproduced by permission of HarperCollins Publishers.

Image acknowledgements

The publishers wish to thank the following for permission to reproduce photographs. Every effort has been made to trace copyright holders and to obtain their permission for the use of copyright materials. The publishers will gladly receive any information enabling them to rectify any error or omission at the first opportunity.

(t = top, c = centre, b = bottom, r = right, l = left)

p1 REDPIXEL.PL/Shutterstock, p7 Pit Stock/Shutterstock, p15 Atosan/Shutterstock, p20 Osugi/Shutterstock, p22 Drop of Light/Shutterstock, p24 desdemona72/Shutterstock, p27 Creative Photo Corner/Shutterstock, p34 jakkaje879/Shutterstock, p37t GiuseppeCrimeni/Shutterstock, p37b Hadrian/Shutterstock, p38t Delices/Shutterstock, p38b Thaiview/Shutterstock, p45 Romolo Tavani/Shutterstock, p46 Siyanight/Shutterstock, p50 Nenad Nedomacki/Shutterstock, p52 Ananchai Phuengchap/Shutterstock, p54 leungchopan/Shutterstock, p66 goodluz/Shutterstock, p67 kagera/Shutterstock, p70 Oguz Aral/Shutterstock, p71t Prostock-studio/Shutterstock, p71c F8 studio/Shutterstock, p71b aslysun/Shutterstock, p72 Daniel M Ernst/Shutterstock, p73 K2 images/Shutterstock, p76 Dima Zel/Shutterstock, p78 Dima Zel/Shutterstock, p81 thatsmymop/Shutterstock, p83 FrameStockFootages/Shutterstock, p87 Stephane Masclaux/Shutterstock, p94 Ink Drop/Shutterstock, p97 Josep Suria/Shutterstock, p99 Nika Raw/Shutterstock, p103 Ollyy/Shutterstock, p108 Rich Carey/Shutterstock, p110 Lamai Prasitsuwan/Shutterstock, p122 Syda Productions/Shutterstock, p126 Siyanight/Shutterstock, p129 Cartoon Resource/Shutterstock, p134 Rawpixel.com/Shutterstock, p138 IhorZigor/Shutterstock, p142 ProStockStudio/Shutterstock, p146 Cannon Dm/Shutterstock, p147 Slides ©Lucy Norris, p149 Rawpixel.com/Shutterstock, p151 garetsworkshop/Shutterstock, p155 Linda Parton/Shutterstock, p156 Indypendenz/Shutterstock, p166 goodluz/Shutterstock, p169l rblfmr/Shutterstock, p169c VikiVector/Shutterstock, p169r Akhmad Dody Firmansyah/Shutterstock, p170 fizkes/Shutterstock, p174 Tom Wang/Shutterstock, p180t DavidPinoPhotography/Shutterstock, p180b Fanya/Shutterstock, p181t GaudiLab/Shutterstock, p181b kuzmaphoto/Shutterstock, p186 Kite_rin/Shutterstock, p193 dekazigzag/Shutterstock, p194 Kit8.net/Shutterstock, p207 qoppi/Shutterstock.